Misunderstanding Stories

Misunderstanding Stories

Toward A Postcolonial Pastoral Theology

Melinda A. McGarrah Sharp

PICKWICK *Publications* · Eugene, Oregon

Pickwick Publications
An Imprint of Wipf and Stock Publishers
199 W. 8th Ave., Suite 3
Eugene, OR 97401
www.wipfandstock.com

ISBN 13: 978-1-4982-5967-5

Cataloging-in-Publication data:

McGarrah Sharp, Melinda A.

   Misunderstanding stories : toward a postcolonial pastoral theology / Melinda A. McGarrah Sharp.

   xiv + 216 p. 23 cm—Includes bibliographical references and index.

   ISBN: 978-1-4982-5967-5

   1. Pastoral theology. 2. Intercultural communication—Case studies. 3. Peace Corps (U.S.)—Case studies. 4. Suriname—Social life and customs. I. Title.

BV4011 M43 2013

Manufactured in the USA

To Lucy Claire, James Henry, and Tommy

and

gi den Saakiki Famii

mi be wani sikifi bun sani ma un abi leti fu leli mi moo bun

kon meke wi leli makandi fu meke a hii goontapu kon a fesi

May we continue to learn together

Contents

Illustrations

Acknowledgments

Something else—something else entirely holds me in thrall . . .
That you have a life—courteous, intelligent—
that I wonder about more than I wonder about my own.
That you have a soul—your own, no one else's—
that I wonder about more than I wonder about my own.
So that I find my soul clapping its hands for yours more than my own.[1]

FOONDOO SIGNIFIES AN EMBODIED experience of wonder, astonishment, amazement, particularly in relation to other people. *Fanowdu* signifies the shared obligation to respond to need, to restore harmony across our various modes of being.[2] Misunderstanding stories invite the response of wonder into the immediate need of disruption. Words in Sranan Tongo, the lingua franca of the Republic of Suriname and linguistically similar to the Saakiki we spoke in MoiKonde,[3] *foondoo* and *fanowdu* point to my goals in this book as well as the process of acknowledging my deep gratitude around this book. Misunderstanding stories that disrupt us can evoke wonder. In a crowded and rushed schedule, in between tasks, in an unexpected phone call on a New Year's morning, we experience disruption. Disruptive moments provoke us to contemplate the loss of a person, a state of being, a way of life, a particular vision of the future. In moments of crisis, experiencing a disruption on the level of human existence leads to places of deep vulnerability.[4] Sustaining presence in such moments is made possible by communal support.

---

1. Oliver, "What Is the Greatest Gift?," 76.
2. Personal conversation with Gloria Wekker, April 12, 2012.
3. *MoiKonde* (translated as "beautiful place") is a pseudonym for an Afro-Surinamese village where I lived for two years as a Peace Corps volunteer.
4. Lester, *Hope in Pastoral Care and Counseling*, 44, 51.

Acknowledgments

My experiences in Peace Corps service in the Republic of Suriname allowed me to focus on understanding postcolonial dynamics of the present day from shared experiences and relationships. I am especially grateful for SUR 8, and the entire village of MoiKonde with whom I lived in community—especially for the village children, leaders, and partners, named with pseudonyms in this book. Village elders bestowed blessings upon me, granting me permission to draw on my experience in MoiKonde in this project within the oral-culture tradition. For this, I am deeply grateful. I continue to embrace the name given to me, AbbaMai, and hope to live up to its multiple meanings.

I thank all who have provided intellectual, financial, and emotional support for this project. Volney Gay, the director of my dissertation, Bonnie Miller-McLemore, Mark Bliton, John Thatamanil, and Tracy Sharpley-Whiting for their advice, care, challenge, and support. I will always be thankful for each of these teachers who met me when I was finally ready to embrace academic writing as vocation. I can trace the intellectual development of this project through years of personally meaningful and intellectually rigorous academic relationships with Heather Warren, Cassandra Fraser, Peter Ochs, Kristen Leslie, Margaret Farley, and Letty Russell.

This project has benefitted from financial support from Phillips Theological Seminary, the Vanderbilt Graduate Department of Religion, the Vanderbilt Center for Ethics, and a 2009–2010 American Fellowship from the American Association of University Women. Vanderbilt University and Phillips Theological Seminary provided intellectual space for this project to flourish. I am grateful for the opportunity to present pieces of this project in public venues. These included the Society of Pastoral Theology, the Women's Writing Circle, the International Conference on Clinical Ethics Consultation, the American Academy of Religion, Phillips Theological Seminary, the Vanderbilt Global Feminisms Collaborative, the Vanderbilt Center for Biomedical Ethics and Society, Belmont United Methodist Church, and Boston Avenue United Methodist Church.

I am grateful for the mentoring and provocative conversations with both Emmanuel Lartey and the group of women pastoral theologians with whom I was graciously invited to work on the *Women Out of Order* multi-authored book project (2010). Additional creative space was forged in the classroom with engaged and thoughtful students. The Wabash Center for Teaching and Learning and the Association of Theological Schools provided space and support for pedagogical reflection around this project that has sparked informal networks of communal support.

Among the most meaningful conversations opening space for creative and critical thinking was in making multiple returns to the misunderstanding stories in this text. MoiKonde hosted me and bestowed blessing on this project and on our continued relationship years after I had moved back to the United States. Mr. Salomon Emanuels graciously traveled to the United States to support this project in earlier stages. Mr. Emanuels reminds me of the importance of sustainability in relationships that endure over a lifetime, and not only for a brief two-year service commitment. Dr. Gloria Wekker graciously partnered with me in the Netherlands to introduce me to some of the postcolonial dynamics that Afro-Surinamese face in relation to the former colonizing country. Dr. Wekker also read and critically engaged an earlier version of the manuscript. For her mentorship and critical attention, I am most grateful.

I thank K. C. Hanson, Jeremy Funk, and Wipf and Stock Publishers for editorial support. Behind the scenes, my deepest gratitude to Kalbryn McLean for participating in a dynamic, creative partnership that grew from the seemingly straightforward task of editorial support. Mary Ann Morris and Rhonda Chester-Quiroz devoted countless hours to research support. I am thankful for my family, writing partners, colleagues, Peace Corps family, and especially for Dean Pittman, M. Y. Perkins, Elizabeth Munz, Lisa Davison, the A-Team, Amanda Peltz, Kairos, Cornerstone, Missy Boyette, Heather Daley, Cindy Arnn, the Meieres, Elizabeth Baggett, Liz Zagatta-Allison, Kate Lassiter, Leanna Fuller, Karla Van Zee, Nichole R. Phillips, Eileen Campbell-Reed, Virginia Bartlett, Kyle Galbraith, David Lott, Carolyn Mareburger, my sister Elizabeth, my parents Nancy and Jim, and all the rest of the McGarrahs and Sharps.

For supporting writing as an embodied process, I am grateful to Dr. Evon Flesberg's hospitality and writing space at Querencia, Julie Clemons, Miss Shelley and the tap ladies, and my Wabash colleagues.

Tommy McGarrah Sharp, AbaaPai, continues to be my best friend and most enthusiastic supporter. While completing this project, we birthed into the world two amazing children who continue to inspire wonder with their wisdom and energy. This book is dedicated to them as part of a commitment to name injustice, to remember to play and create, and to work toward healing as familiar practices in our family life in relation to the mending of the world. Finally, my deepest gratitude to the poets, musicians, artists, mystics and visionaries who continue to support me by helping me glimpse a greater depth of possibility where "I find my soul clapping" with you.

Introduction

When my friend saw her eleven-year-old daughter playing on my porch instead of helping with the evening chores, she angrily reached for my broom. I grabbed the broomstick from her hand before she could strike her daughter with it. We were caught in an intercultural crisis.

With permission of village elders, I was identifying sacred markers and taboos to encourage a new group of American volunteers to respect sacred spaces and practices. The matriarchal spiritual leader, who was also my neighbor and friend, raised her staff and scolded me for being the white man violating her people once again. We were caught in an intercultural crisis.

During the three-mile walk home from an exhausting day of peanut harvesting, I asked some village children: What do you want to be when you grow up? They told me they thought they would be successful if they could leave their village, which is in a former Dutch colony, to live in the Netherlands and become fluent in Dutch culture and language. I asked if they would ever want to come to America. They told me that America is a frightening place where they would be forced into slavery and would never be free. We were caught in an intercultural crisis.

I left the village setting for a month to interview for doctoral work in pastoral theology. When my life partner and I returned to the village, we learned that four of our neighbors' children had been publicly beaten and exiled from relationship with us after breaking into our home while we were away. We were caught in an intercultural crisis.

Misunderstanding Stories

STORIES OF INTERCULTURAL MISUNDERSTANDING point to powerful moments in intercultural relationships—the summaries above are insufficient to get at their complexity—that have required and continue to require a long process of growing in relationship oriented toward mutual understanding. Stories are so important that these and others become examples along the way, with the last vignette spanning the whole book. My immersion in interpersonal misunderstanding through my experiences has afforded me insights into possibilities and challenges of intercultural understanding that I share throughout the book.

The experiences of intercultural misunderstanding reflected here have a particular history. By the time I completed divinity school, I had clarified a sense of call to theological education. I also experienced a call to gain some experience before pursuing doctoral studies. As calling experiences often go, the certainty of call did not come with much clarity about the details. I had developed a healthy hermeneutic of suspicion through my first studies of liberation theology and feminist ethics in divinity school. I had studied histories of dehumanization of women and formerly colonized persons through intentional and unintentional religious practices that claimed to heal or offer special access to salvation. I also had acquired a strong appreciation for the intergenerational diversity and accompanying variety of life experiences within the seminary setting. This had not been the case for most of my education before seminary, during which I had been about the same age, give or take a few years, as most of my classmates. I needed to exit the academy, so to speak, to gather some life experience that exceeded anything I had encountered previously in order to be a more holistic scholar of pastoral theology and ethics.

Since the groundbreaking writings of Anton Boisen raised connections between religious and psychological dimensions of his personal experiences of suffering, pastoral theologians have considered narratives of lived human experience to be authoritative sources in facilitating healing. This means that good pastoral care requires hearing and telling stories to learn the most just and healing ways to participate in the continual unfolding of the stories. Extending this wisdom to our current condition of postcolonialism, I realized I could not discern how to participate in justice and healing in a postcolonial context without learning about it "from below."[1] In other words, I had to live in a former colony to learn what I needed to know. This was a privilege for me and would not necessarily be required or possible for everyone. I felt called to learn about the world

1. Chambers, *Whose Reality Counts?*

from the ground up in order to understand my role in resisting and reifying dehumanization in it. Much later I would find postcolonial studies as a conversation partner also concerned with global legacies of dehumanization and ongoing violence.

Along with my spouse, I decided to apply for service to the United States Peace Corps as a way to learn about the world that seemed so intangible to me from my privileged but limited classroom and text-based studies. Even in the process of applying, the intercultural context was already not neutral. All of our cultural situatedness was already in play. For example, even filling out the application for service, which one might think of as neutral, brought to the surface all sorts of conflicting values when we were asked to state "a preferred country of service." In the midst of entering into an experience to partner with "the poor," we could recognize our empowered choice from a place of privilege. The opportunity to state a preference about where in the developing world to serve reveals the extent of our privilege in being able to choose to serve the developing world and even the area of the developing world in which we most envisioned ourselves. Yet it also exposed the severe limits of our prior knowledge. How would we account for a preference among choices that were equally unknown to us? We did not state a preference, as we had no basis to account for such a choice.

We volunteered for the secular organization of the Peace Corps because of a hermeneutic of suspicion based in learning of the depth of Christian complicity in colonialism. While no organization is without its challenges, the Peace Corps's fundamental assumption is that Americans do not know or understand individuated persons and communities in other countries without a sustained engagement living in the same conditions as persons and communities indigenous to the host country. Further, only such sustained engagement in other countries can cultivate the kind of intercultural understanding and friendship that lead to peace in the world. One distinguishing feature of learning about and seriously engaging the whole idea of hermeneutics within theological education is that one opens oneself up to and must then live in the ambiguous contours of big questions. For me and my life partner, Christian missions became a question in which to live rather than a set of assumptions to take for granted. Although this book is not primarily about Christian missions, the intercultural understanding essential for justice in the world is certainly applicable to short- and long-term, local and global, Christian missions. There is no question regarding the historical resistance, complicity, and bystander practices of Christians in relation to global violence. The contemporary culture of fear heightens the already pressing opportunity to bring this historical knowledge to bear on moral discernment. The conversation with my young friends raised the question: What is a truthful and faithful response to worries about contemporary America being a place of limited opportunity for immigrants?

As much as is possible ahead of an immersion experience, the details of our Peace Corps service were almost finalized in the fall of 2001. In September, we were waiting for an assignment of our country and context of service. In the span of a few hours, September 11, 2001 opened questions of peace and justice around cultural understanding and misunderstanding as the world seemed to come together and apart all at the same time. In the midst of this, we were preparing to represent the United States government abroad for the purposes of peace and international friendship.

The complexity of questions about world relations only deepened as our actual Peace Corps experience unfolded. For example, as we were looking at the cover of a government-provided copy of *Newsweek* magazine with children in the rural village where we were living several months later, a child pointed to the cover and asked what the difference between a smart bomb and any other kind of bomb was. What is the difference? How would you respond? How might we understand this question theologically? Further, how does one respond in another language in wartime in a conversation between a theologically educated Peace Corps volunteer and an inquisitive child? Living in community in the ambiguity of big questions involves moments of shared vulnerability and learning required for understanding. The ebbs and flows of mundane life often disrupt these moments when our general state of misunderstanding becomes more acute, threatening to cloud out and cover over shared questions.

This book argues that misunderstanding and understanding are not so much achievements as they are moments in lifelong processes. Both moments of misunderstanding and rarer moments of understanding must be acknowledged. Understanding across differences is more challenging than misunderstanding because the former involves a willingness to recognize one's own complicity in the latter. Understanding requires investing in processes of hearing, voicing, and approaching narrative with a hermeneutic of suspicion guided by the value of intercultural understanding as a good and a goal worthy of sustained effort.

(MIS)UNDERSTANDING AND STORIES

Misunderstandings and histories of violence affect mutual understanding across diverse relationships—including within families, in local communities, in faith communities, within countries, and indeed in the twenty-first-century world of increased globalization.[2] Why is understanding such a difficult process? Is understanding even possible, considering our growing diversity and the violence that endures in our relationships and the world? This book explores two central and related concepts for pastoral theology: understanding and stories.

Understanding is a goal and a good for pastoral theology as a field thoroughly relational in practices of care, theologies, and methods of inquiry. By *understanding*, I mean both clarity of thought and an intentional understanding of persons' experiences. Therefore, recognizing and addressing misunderstandings are crucial. Practices of care hinge on careful attention to suffering through listening and mirroring within the context of interpersonal relationships. The character and consistency of relationships are themselves part of healing as a goal of good pastoral care. Pastoral theologies are also relational in the field's consistent commitment to draw on human experiences as an authoritative source for theology in combination with sacred texts, theological scholarship, psychological insights, sociological and anthropological contextual awareness, and the contribution of other cognate disciplines.[3] The field of pastoral theology is deeply relational in methods of inquiry because interdisciplinary conversations structure vocabularies, practices, and theories by which we correlate different discourses for the sake of constructing theologies accountable to experiences of suffering we learn about and which call forth participation.

Understanding also forms assumptions about the many contexts in which pastoral theologians work. As practical theologians, we are accountable to three publics: the church, the academy, and the public sector.[4] Each of these publics is vastly diverse and difficult to define succinctly. To communicate within and across these contexts is a complex relational endeavor. The understanding required for cross-contextual fluency and meaningful translation often eludes us, especially in a world that can reward narrow expertise and make segmented pockets of experience seem normative. In

2. In phenomenological terms, the horizon of possibilities of understanding is already populated with histories of violence.

3. See Doehring, *The Practice of Pastoral Care*, for a good description of authoritative sources for the work of pastoral theology in a postmodern world.

4. Tracy, *The Analogical Imagination*.

an increasingly complex world, leaders in faith communities participate in an increasingly complex network of multiple publics or spheres. Pastoral theologians also participate in multiple spheres. For example, I teach in a seminary, present my research at academic conferences and in academic publications, give workshops and lead Sunday school classes in local faith communities, attend and participate in a church, and occasionally work as a consultant in hospital clinical ethics. In every sphere of this vocation, more information and more conflicts and more striving for certainty operate in a context of less certainty. How can we become fluent in any one sphere of accountability, much less in several identifiable spheres?

Theological education, which is the primary vocation of many pastoral theologians, has classically been about the work of "faith seeking understanding."[5] Dan Aleshire, Association of Theological Schools executive director, describes the theological education that happens in seminaries through reading texts, discussing vital issues, writing, and teaching as "soul-shaping learning."[6] Theological education provokes self-understanding required for the ongoing formation of a pastoral identity. Understanding oneself in relation to other people, other places, religious traditions, and global issues is soul-shaping work that dislodges prior misunderstandings and opens pathways for deeper understandings. Leaders in faith communities also translate this kind of transformational learning into churches, nonprofits, hospitals, hospices, military chaplaincy, and the many other contexts where vocations of ministry find expression.

I am a United Methodist. Understanding is important to me in my efforts to correlate the four dimensions of John Wesley's quadrilateral, where Scripture, tradition, reason, and experience all contribute to meeting the world's needs by spreading my gifts and graces across the networks of relationships in which I live and work and have my being. Theologically, what is good and right contributes to *tikkun olam*, the Jewish expression for the mending of the brokenness in the world. Participating in this kind of justice-oriented work demands being willing to assess whether and to what extent one's participation is in fact contributing to mending with intercultural fluency. This requires a willingness to engage processes of mutual understanding. So why is this so difficult? As a pastoral theologian, my scholarship contributes to a field in which understanding personal experience is key to possibilities of healing; therefore, it is crucial to attend to processes of dehumanization operating in local and global contexts

5. Aleshire, *Earthen Vessels*, 15.

6. Ibid., 29.

(which are of course inseparable). Further, I must attend to the more difficult task of probing ways in which I participate in dehumanization by both deliberate and unintentional misunderstandings. This is a demanding and ongoing task of responsible ministry in culturally complex contexts.

Understanding within complexly layered relational life contributes to health and healing; misunderstanding exacerbates suffering and deepens fissures in relationships. As pastoral theologians have begun our work advancing the intercultural paradigm of pastoral practice and theology,[7] we know that recognizing cultural and intercultural aspects of identities makes understanding more challenging and misunderstandings more prevalent. The problem is that intercultural misunderstandings and histories of violence provide the context for occasional moments of mutual intercultural understanding. Language and ethical categories get complicated here. If mutual understanding is a good, then participating toward this good includes carefully examining what impedes this good from being realized. All of us live within legacies of past and present unfolding histories of violence. I contend that most of us live in continual states of misunderstanding ourselves and others to a far greater extent than we live in the midst of mutual understanding.

Understanding and misunderstanding turn on patterns of communication within relationships. Stories embody patterns of communication on which understanding and misunderstanding depend. From the beginning of its modern history, if not from the beginning of human effort to participate in the mysterious work of the care of souls, pastoral theology has recognized the importance of narratives. We communicate with each other through stories of lived human experience. We privilege stories in our theologies, study stories through verbatims and case studies, and affirm that our stories as caregivers, theologians, and leaders in faith communities matter deeply. We join other theologians in considering our shared biblical stories to be an important resource and guide in understanding. A hallmark of all stories, from personal experience to the biblical narrative, is the ways in which stories must be told and retold, heard and heard again, interpreted and reinterpreted over time.

Processes of misunderstanding and understanding happen through stories—the stories we tell, retell, and cannot, choose not, or otherwise do not tell, as well as through the stories we hear, have heard before, and cannot, choose not, or otherwise do not hear. In postmodernity, at our best

---

7. See Ramsay, *Pastoral Care and Counseling*; Lartey, *In Living Color*; and Lartey, *Pastoral Theology in an Intercultural World*.

we participate in *encouraging* and *liberating* stories that have yet to be told while at the same time *resisting* whatever prevents the telling and hearing of stories. Postmodernity has helped us realize that narratives of discrete individuals are inseparable from the communal narratives that provide texture and background to personal narratives. Pastoral theology as a field tends to use the words *self*, *person*, and *individual* to try to understand and recognize the crucial role of personal experience in constructive theology. In this book I employ the traditional language and add terms like *individuated experience* to indicate that my experience that feels bounded in my person affects and is affected at all times by contexts and stories that also exceed my person.

Stories help make sense of an increasingly diverse world of more information, more conflicts, and more desire for certainty in a context of uncertainty, ambiguity, and intercultural complexity. Narrative methods have made important contributions across fields of study from narrative medicine to narrative theology to narrative counseling.[8] Telling and hearing more stories in more ways becomes important to pastoral theology and care that attends suffering and participates in healing.

RISKS OF SPEAKING, WRITING, OR VOICING IN POSTCOLONIAL CONTEXTS

The stories of intercultural misunderstandings that form the ethnographic context of this book are postcolonial stories. What is theological about studying, writing, and reading about postcolonialism? Pastoral theology is a theological discipline whose task is to attend to suffering and to participate in healing. Postcolonialism as a condition of contemporary reality is a recognition of the inherent suffering that continues as a legacy of historical colonialism. Misunderstanding across cultural differences is almost inevitable because of the colonial assumptions so deeply embedded in individuated persons and communities. Postcolonial narratives are important resources for constructive pastoral theology because they expose the depth of complicity that challenges the *empowerment, liberation,* and *resistance* that the field of pastoral theology has claimed as the guiding paradigms of care in a postmodern world. Simply, pastoral practices that attend suffering and participate in healing are more theologically responsible when they recognize the legacy of colonialism active in our lives,

8. For example, see Montello, "Narrative Matters"; Zaner, *Conversations on the Edge*; Neuger, *Counseling Women*; Lester, *Hope in Pastoral Care and Counseling.*

relationships, and the whole world. The only way to do this is by becoming open to postcolonial questions, best grasped through postcolonial stories.

Postcolonial theories also compel academics to consider new ways of studying, reading, and writing.[9] Responsible academic practices must include grappling with how to live in the tension between wanting to recognize and not wanting to recognize complicities. Iris Marion Young suggests practicing resistance in a context of oppressive structural hierarchies by focusing on embodiment and actual bodies.[10] In *The Body in Pain: The Making and Unmaking of the World*, Elaine Scarry provides a complex view of the phenomenon of embodied pain. Pain destroys bodies and embodied expression of pain experiences through language. The way we tell and hear and read and write stories contributes to making ourselves and other individuated persons visible or invisible.[11] New questions inform studying, reading, and writing: who is seen and who is rendered invisible in what I read, how I write, and my methods of study?

What's at stake? Pastoral theologians have embraced models of care as *empowerment*, *liberation*, and *resistance* because these activities help to make pain visible, and other people visible to each other so that our many embodied wounds, and our wounded relationships and world, can experience healing. Scarry argues that the survival of the world depends on continual re-creating in response to continual destruction of bodies. The world is at risk of ultimate destruction; therefore, attempts must be made to counter this destruction. Scarry assumes that *language can be shared*. Recognizing that *I* cause pain without feeling it as such by objectifying it, Scarry implies a shared question of experience that we could phrase as, how can *I* be? Her ethical insights follow from this existential exploration, and attempt to address a second implied question, how can *I* be wrong?[12] As one theological educator recently asked, to what extent do we "embrace the challenge of really not knowing" that requires courage and humility?[13] Pastoral theology's embrace of *empowerment*, *liberation*, and *resistance* as goals of pastoral care needs to be wide enough to question how you and I participate in *disempowerment*, *imprisonment*, and *dehumanization*. Postcolonial questions help pastoral theologians better attend suffering and better participate in healing by the constant reminder that I have

9. Good et al., "Postcolonial Disorders," 4.

10. Young, "Lived Body versus Gender," 3–18.

11. Scarry, *The Body in Pain*, 22.

12. Gay, "Syllabus on Methods."

13. Yoder, "Two Associate Professors Reflect on Their Journeys."

something(s) to learn. In other words, we need to ask within the goals and methods of care: "how can I be wrong?" and "how am I contributing to harm?" when I think I am participating in healing.

The language of provisional understanding is more adequate than the idea that I can and do ever reach some sort of perfect understanding of myself or others. This requires making oneself vulnerable to misunderstanding, as the best intentions can be not only wrong but also harmful toward myself and my neighbor. Pastoral theology has come a long way toward a more liberative perspective; however, I am trying to ground this perspective in a foundation with room for questions and misunderstanding. A robust appeal to self-reflective experience recognizes that all of us can be wrong even at the very beginning where misunderstandings originate. Therefore, we must engage in a narrative process that makes room for misunderstanding stories.

This book explores postcolonial stories of intercultural misunderstanding in order to equip pastoral theologians with tools for asking and living in the ambiguous big questions that lead to renewed possibilities for understanding. Engaging the narrative process and particular narratives—both the postcolonial stories I tell and the stories evoked for you in reading this text—includes asking questions about being and being in community. This book argues that being engaged in a process of understanding includes misunderstanding stories.

AUDIENCES AND SOURCES

I write this book as a new model of a postcolonial story that also contains other postcolonial stories within it. As the subtitle suggests, this book advances the intercultural paradigm within the field of pastoral theology by arguing that as a field, we need to move toward a postcolonial pastoral theology. While indeed moving, the field has not reached a shared postcolonial understanding. This book contributes to the intercultural paradigm precisely by inviting conversations within and beyond the field of pastoral theology toward a deeper consideration of postcolonialism. A truly postcolonial project cannot be single authored because of the conversational model postcolonialism requires (i.e., I have to ask you how I can be wrong and then listen to your response and *vice versa*). However, single-authored books have always helped fields of study open new questions and deepen intellectual commitments. Individuated experiences shared through individuated stories contribute to understanding and misunderstanding of personal, communal, and global needs and resources.

I hope that leaders in faith communities and seminary students will read this book to help understand the complexity of pastoral care and theology in a postcolonial context. It is enough of a lifelong challenge to give an account of oneself, much less an account of one's participation or role in intercultural relationships. Therefore, consider each chapter as an invitation for you to examine your own experiences of misunderstanding and understanding. For example, chapter 1 presents a model and example of the kind of ethnographic work that enhances contextual understanding. Consider this chapter inspiration for your own investment in ethnographic work in your present and future communities. In chapters 2 through 5, consider my analysis of unique intercultural experiences as an invitation for you to cultivate and critically reflect on your unique intercultural experiences. Chapter 6 serves not only as a conclusion to the book, but also as a summary of the book's unique contributions to the field of pastoral theology.

Stories from my intercultural experiences hold a central place in the book. I supplement the standard methodological conversation in pastoral theology between theology and psychology with insights from postcolonial theories. Each chapter embodies strategic interdisciplinary partnerships that nuance dynamics of misunderstandings for the purposes of opening and participating in possibilities for more mutual understanding. Pastoral theology is a field of study open to conversation partners to help understand the suffering of the human condition and what it means to participate in the healing work of empowering, liberating, and resisting, which supplement and build on previously theorized pastoral functions of healing, guiding, sustaining, reconciling, and nurturing individuated persons and communities. The vocation implied by these pastoral tasks requires the depth of understanding described in this book.

A GUIDE TO ENGAGING THIS BOOK

The book offers an accessible, relevant, and complex way of considering understanding as a process. Like all stories, the stories of intercultural misunderstanding that frame and appear in narrative fragments throughout the book occurred in a particular context and point in time. Therefore, chapter 1 explains the anthropological concept of ethnography and provides a mini-ethnography of Suriname, South America, the host country of my Peace Corps service and site of inspiration for this study. The rest of the book outlines the difficult process of understanding that, in the best cases, is ignited and deeply engaged by individuated persons and communities when discrete and challenging experiences of intercultural misunderstanding occur. The project of engaging understanding as a process around the particular set of complex intercultural stories mentioned in this book is a lifelong process of participating in truthful telling, retelling, hearing, and rehearing stories from as many voices as possible. Chapters 2 through 5 employ and critically engage an anthropological framework that moves from breach to crisis to redress to reconciliation for understanding the movements or tensions that intercultural relationships negotiate.

Chapter 2 (Breach) gives a more elaborate description of one challenging story of intercultural misunderstanding mentioned above. The first step in engaging a process of understanding is to recognize the sharp lapses in communication that often surround misunderstandings. I draw on anthropological and political theorists to claim that pastoral theology needs a more complex conception of culture(s) to evaluate the complicated intercultural contexts in which our many forms of communication are located. Intercultural caregiving practices are enhanced when we envision cultures as constantly changing, internally diverse, internally contested, and ambiguous yet powerful contributors to interpersonal and intercommunal misunderstandings. I adapt a model of cultural conflict from anthropologist Victor Turner as a way of framing narrative structures around postcolonial stories that originate in a lapse in understanding and require a carefully storied communal response.

Chapter 3 (Crisis) describes crises of identity that accompany intercultural misunderstandings. I partner a classical understanding of identity crisis with a postcolonial claim that colonialism has institutionalized identity crisis in dehumanizing ways. Postcolonial theories reorient how participants in care attend to suffering by helping us realize some of the ways in which we participate in violence in even well-meaning and thoughtful attempts to engage the thickly intercultural nature of the contemporary church and world. Such recognition opens significant spaces for both lament and creative potential for renewed understanding.

Chapter 4 (Redress as Movement toward Resolution) describes the kind of shared vulnerability required to ask and live in the high-stakes ambiguous questions that intercultural misunderstandings provoke. Psychological theorists have long claimed a connection between (wounded) desire and domination that has fueled interpersonal and communal violence; systematic and pastoral theologians often draw on these psychological theories to help construct appropriate responses and practices. This chapter partners theological and psychological perspectives to understand and disrupt historical moments of deep misunderstanding as well as our own participation in and, in some cases, desire for misunderstanding that gets in the way of the vulnerability required for asking and living in challenging questions that identity crises evoke. I argue that shared vulnerability is a condition of opening up possibilities of recognition.

Chapter 5 (Conditions for Reconciliation) describes ways in which my intercultural misunderstanding in MoiKonde became open to new possibilities of understanding through a process of intercultural empathy. Empathy in this sense is a process of deeper recognition. I partner a traditional understanding of empathy with a postcolonial claim that the violence of colonialism makes intercultural empathy incredibly difficult. Serious consideration of intercultural relationships can redefine empathy. Here is another reason that we need to engage postcolonial theories. Concrete experiences of intercultural crisis call for theories of empathy that recognize the many intercultural misunderstandings and histories of violence that provide the context for occasional moments of intercultural understanding.

Chapter 6 concludes with implications of taking misunderstanding stories seriously as the most prevalent and most often masked narrative context of the attentive and participatory work of pastoral theology and care. Intercultural understanding is a process that deepens pastoral theological theories of mutuality by widening our sense of possibilities regarding occasions in which we can better participate in interpersonal and intercultural justice which affirms God's love and regard for all human beings. A deep pastoral theological engagement with postcolonialism involves nurturing practices of living communally and interculturally in the midst of complex tensions and difficult questions. I propose that pastoral theologians continue to nurture practices that will hold together an optimistic hope for a realized mutuality while expressing a realistic grief that reminds us of the sheer difficulty of experiencing mutual intercultural understanding. Pastoral theologians know something about holding together hoping and grieving, celebration and lamentation, human fulfillment and human brokenness in a way that draws diverse participants together in a community that strives toward healing and wholeness while taking care not to minimize real challenges and differences in our midst.

1

A Framework for
Understanding Intercultural
Misunderstandings

I INTERVENED IN MY home when a mother began to strike her daughter with my broom. In another experience, I arranged for a group of new Peace Corps volunteers to learn about cultural taboos in MoiKonde, inadvertently breaking a cultural taboo in the process. In another, I returned to my village home after a trip and learned that four young girls had not only stolen from me but had also been publicly beaten in my absence for their crime. Months earlier, in a conversation with some of these same young girls, I had come to realize some of the difficulties of engaging histories of slavery and colonialism across cultures. These brief stories merely hint at intercultural misunderstandings. In this chapter, I propose a framework for understanding intercultural misunderstandings and their dynamic nature.

Anthropologist Victor Turner's structural anthropology of ritual suggests a broad framework for understanding intercultural relationships. Turner claims that a disruption in so-called normal social relations proceeds from breach to crisis to redress to reconciliation. Turner provides a vocabulary for understanding challenges of intercultural relationships as a series of crises and efforts to repair. In a postcolonial context, conflict around identities and values can strain interpersonal and communal relationships, contributing to intercultural crises. Resolving these difficulties involves participation in intercultural relational repair. In turn, I argue, creating and enhancing opportunities for participation in processes of relational repair facilitate better theories about and practices of care in a postcolonial context.

I locate the phenomena of intercultural crisis and repair in a broader academic problem of insufficient attention to postcolonial theories on the part of pastoral theologians. *My primary argument is that by attending to postcoloniality as our present-day context, pastoral theologians will have a more complex understanding of culture(s) that will in turn deepen the field's understanding of suffering exacerbated by colonialism and the possibilities of the healing work of empathy and mutuality.* My primary audience is scholars, students, and practitioners in the field of pastoral theology, to whom I am extending the psychology-theology conversation to consider postcolonial theories. In addition, this project comes out of my own participation in intercultural relationships; thus, I hope that it will prove relevant to those readers who find themselves in the midst of intercultural crises and seeking to repair or restore relationships.

MISUNDERSTANDING AS CRISIS

Consider the phenomenon of crisis. Rather than chaos, which describes a disorganized and unpredictable state, the root meaning of *crisis* is "turning point," after which point things get better or worse.[1] Developmental psychologist Erik Erikson certainly has this meaning of *crisis* in mind when he claims that developmental achievements are born from specific kinds of crises along the lifespan.[2] Crises call for response. In the context of theological education, seminaries offer resources in formation as a response to both predictable and unexpected vocational crises. Pastoral theologians call for self-reflection and imagination in response to crises of identity. One scholar calls for slowing down to invite imaginative, reflective listening in light of his claim that the hardest thing about being a pastor in the early twenty-first century is "confusion about what it means to be the pastor."[3] Pastoral theologians also offer new stories in response to the experience of participating in a discipline in crisis. Some argue that the label of crisis applied to the discipline of pastoral theology calls for the

---

1. "Crisis," 27.
2. Erikson, *The Life Cycle Completed.*
3. Barnes, *The Pastor as Minor Poet,* 4, 123–36.

response of ongoing work rather than a disciplinary stalemate that fails to do the work claimed as particular to pastoral theology.[4]

Pastoral theologians pay particular attention to crisis because pastors, trained pastoral counselors, chaplains, and ministers in other contexts are requested and expected to respond to a variety of crises in their vocation. Howard Stone, a pastoral theologian who focuses on crisis counseling, draws on Charles Gerkin to describe crisis as a "boundary condition" where a conflict emerges between infinite aspirations and the obvious conditions of finitude.[5] More and more, ministers are confronting the same kinds of developmental and situational crises as before but with the added factor of increasing recognition of diverse identities, life experiences, and cultural differences. The phenomenon of crisis that most concerns me and that has received little attention in the field of pastoral theology to date is that which arises around cultural differences. Cultural or intercultural dimensions accompany many specific kinds of crisis experiences.[6] Few pastoral theologians who address crisis explicitly attend to culture even while many call for the field to address cultural shifts.

Womanist pastoral theologians have done a better job of attending to immediate crisis situations with explicitly cultural dimensions.[7] Attention to culture(s) is not the role or responsibility of communities who have experienced the greatest marginalization; rather, attention to culture(s) is a shared responsibility of all ministers and pastoral theologians. Students often ask when they will know enough about a particular identity marker or life experience to minister responsibly around a particular identity marker or life experience. Men often ask whether they ought to refer all women to women pastoral counselors; heterosexual students often ask whether they ought to counsel homosexual congregants; white students often ask whether they ought to counsel Latino congregants. I contend that responsible ministry includes both preparation to be in community and to participate in care across differences while also building and maintaining a robust referral network in one's local community. A referral network in this sense is not a list of names but a network based in relationships among caring professionals in the local community.[8] Responsible

4. Dykstra, *Images of Pastoral Care*; McGarrah Sharp and Miller-McLemore, "Are There Limitations to Multicultural Inclusion?"

5. Stone, *Crisis Counseling*, 2.

6. See typologies of crisis in Switzer, *The Minister as Crisis Counselor*, 32–33.

7. For example, Ali, *Survival and Liberation*.

8. Kornfeld, *Cultivating Wholeness*, 41, 69–70, 92–94, 310–11.

ministry is ministry that acknowledges and proactively learns about difference. Provisional understanding in this sense is not an excuse to eschew relationships of diversity, but quite the opposite: to cultivate diverse networks of relationships within and across faith communities. Culture(s) not only affects all kinds of crisis experiences but also draws ministers to participate in responding to crises with attention to cultural differences.

While the *Oxford English Dictionary* describes crisis as a moment rather than a process, I use the terms *crisis* and *repair* to refer to processes within relational life that manifest various dynamics over time. I am most concerned with crises of understanding within relationships. Within a traditionally Western therapeutic tradition, a whole body of literature exists around the idea that counselors must develop multicultural competencies as essential to good and professional care to limit the risks of intercultural misunderstandings in the therapeutic hour.[9] Nonetheless, few pastoral theological resources engage a theory of culture. I redress this lack in pastoral theology by clarifying an understanding of crisis and repair that extends beyond traditional models in recognizing the intercultural nature of relationships.

CRISIS IN CONTEXT

Crises that occur within and between seemingly distinct communities always include layers of intrapersonal, interpersonal, and familial dimensions. Relational psychologies argue that each individuated person experiences a sense of self that includes a vibrant internal world filled with representations of other people and experiences. The internal world represents a matrix of relationships in which persons internally experience themselves and other people.[10] Social psychologists argue that greater connection to other people corresponds to greater personal uniqueness. These theories hold together the idea of individuated selves embedded in webs of interconnected relationships.[11] Process theologians argue that there is no distinct individuated person apart from one's relationships and overlapping connections with other people.[12] Philosophers and philo-

9. For example, McGoldrick, *Ethnicity & Family Therapy*. It is interesting to note the major transformations in content and form from one edition to another, given the increasing and increasing recognition of cultural diversity in the United States.

10. For example, Winnicott, *Playing and Reality*; Kohut, *How Does Analysis Cure?*

11. Sullivan, *The Interpersonal Theory of Psychiatry*; Mead, *Mind, Self & Society*.

12. Whitehead, *Process and Reality*.

sophical theologians also question the possibility of identifying a separate self apart from other selves.[13]

One way in which persons are deeply relational is within the internal world itself. Although impossible to isolate from the interpersonal context, intrapersonal crisis and repair—conflicts within one's self—often take a variety of forms. For example, object relations psychologist D. W. Winnicott argues that healthy persons experience real connections between a rich inner life and relationships with other people in the "external world." In contrast, unhealthy persons or persons experiencing pathologies might lead a rich inner life but experience limited connections between an inner world and real persons in external reality.[14] Layers of embeddedness in relationships blur stark boundaries between inner and outer experiences as two isolated states of being. Winnicott characterizes health according to depth of personal awareness of and active participation in real relationships with other people. Persons in all kinds of developmental stages experience crisis and repair in their internal worlds through their participation in a complexly relational life.

Consider the kinds of personal thinking or discussion within one's internal world that accompany major life transitions such as trauma, marriage, divorce, job change, birth, or death. Or, consider the rich interior life associated with more mundane yet still challenging experiences such as travel, parenting, and vocational discernment. Both extraordinary and mundane life experiences lend themselves to personal reflection in which persons internally interact with representations of other people, places, and experiences. The inner life includes crisis and repair around disconnection between expectations and experiences. The higher the stakes, the more crisis-like these disconnections can feel.

Intrapersonal crises involve conflicting perspectives within one's internal world. The popular activity of internet blogging allows persons to illustrate and communicate this struggle with others. For example, notice the many experiences and relationships included in the following blog:

> All of my adult life I have had friends and family tell me how amazing I am . . . The truth is that when they told me I was amazing I did not believe them. The other truth is that I was running myself into the ground trying to do everything, something that wasn't healthy for my children or for me. I was so busy trying to be more that I didn't realize how amazing I was

13. Burkitt, *Social Selves*; James, *Pragmatism*.
14. Winnicott, *Playing and Reality*.

already . . . Why is it that we can . . . see that "amazing quality" in everyone but ourselves? . . . That is why I am admitting today that I am pretty amazing! . . . We all need to look ourselves in the mirror and see how amazing we are. I have many women in my life that support, encourage, and inspire me every day and I simply don't tell them enough! . . . I wouldn't be as amazing as I am without all of you![15]

This blogger gives her readers—both known and anonymous—a sense of the ways in which her friends, family, experiences, and expectations dynamically reside within her internal world. Blogging does what letter writing once commonly did in expressing the internal world of one person to others. Consider the following excerpt from the published letters of someone more familiar to pastoral theologians:

I have just returned after a day spent in the same place which we visited eleven years ago. I have wandered through the chestnut woods where we took lunch and where, but for your watchfulness, I might have started a forest fire . . . I need not speak of the memories which these places brought back to me, memories full of unutterable sorrow for that which might have been. This I foresaw when I went . . . Then came a hopeful thought. Though I may not send you the few little flowers I have gathered and have sent them to Mother instead . . . I can tell you of the acres of growing flowers which I have found and of the thought of you which they have brought to me . . . And I am wondering if I may not have found to-day a better understanding of you and of the possibilities of our relationship one to the other.[16]

In this excerpt from a letter to a woman he loved, founder of modern-day pastoral theology Anton Boisen demonstrates that his internal world is populated by representations of other people drawn from memories and connected to his hopes and dreams. Both self-reflection and interaction with other people inspire new insights of self-awareness within the internal world. Certainly new insights gained by intercultural interactions also affect one's sense of self.[17] A process of intrapersonal repair involves interaction with real, external persons in order to inspire movement from a heightened sense of internal angst toward a sense of internal resolution, understanding, insight, or "being at peace" or one with external reality. A

15. Rigler, "Challenge and Hooray for Amazing Women." Online: http://katy-uncooked.blogspot.com/2009/08/challenge-and-hooray-for-amazing-women.html /.

16. Boisen, *Out of the Depths*, 145–47.

17. For a classic example, see Geertz, "Deep Play."

process of repair involves considering a dynamic continuum of movement and interaction within one's internal sense of self.

Healthy intrapersonal life always exists alongside relationships with other persons. Interpersonal crises involve two or more persons engaged in a personal relationship. Experiences of interpersonal crisis include the more mundane and the more challenging. Sometimes called interpersonal conflict based on a conflict-resolution model, interpersonal crisis includes disagreements, misunderstandings, or other minor or major harms between persons. Crisis elicits questions and self-reflection: Who am I? Who are you? How can we each understand our relationship with one another? How does our relationship fit into our experiences and beliefs about the larger world in which we live? A process of interpersonal repair calls persons to respond to these kinds of questions in a way that restores functioning in a "good enough" relationship.[18] Navigating multiple relationships contributes to even greater complexities of relational life.

Familial relationships characterize another dimension of relational crisis and repair. Consider the various cultures that both separate and enrich cross-generational relationships within families. Engaging in a political conversation within a family can exemplify what is shared and what is contested across generations. Family-systems theorists provide numerous ways of identifying stresses and strains, as well as sources of strength, across generations within the life of families.[19] Familial crisis and repair surface in mundane arguments over dinner and bedtime as much as in collective decision making in the event of determining how to care for a dying family member. Like all of relational life, familial life is complex.

Intrapersonal, interpersonal, and familial dimensions complexify relational life. All persons are embedded in multiple layers of relationships interacting with other persons and embedded in families in multiple ways. The complexity of relational life is incontestable despite continuous efforts to collapse this complexity for the sake of grasping it. Each inseparable dimension of relational life is deeply embedded in and connected to each other dimension. One's family of origin necessarily informs one's internal world. Internal worlds shape interpersonal relationships. Persons

18. I further develop the concept of "good enough" to describe healthy intercultural relationships in the following chapters. I adapt this concept from object relations theories, which use it to describe relationships (modeled on the infant-mother relationship) that recognize limitations, possibilities, and responsibilities of persons oriented in relationship with other people (Winnicott, *Playing and Reality*).

19. McGoldrick et al., *Ethnicity & Family Therapy*; McGoldrick, *You Can Go Home Again*.

are always moving into and out of multiple overlapping relationships. Inevitably, conflicts occur that demand decisions about whether and to what extent to respond. Participation in social, political, and cultural contexts further complicates and enriches responses to crisis.

INTERCULTURAL CONTEXTS OF CRISIS

Pastoral theologian Emmanuel Lartey's conceptualization of relationships as intercultural has become a central resource for the emerging intercultural paradigm within the field of pastoral theology. Lartey, a Ghanaian theologian trained in England who now teaches in the United States, draws on his diversity of lived experience to offer a compelling understanding of the dynamic nature of human identity and experiences. He expands classical anthropological theories that depict each person as like no other, like some other, and like all other people. Each person is unique in his or her embodiment. The individuated *I* exists in this particular body in this particular place and time. Each person is also unique in his or her embeddedness in particular contexts. An individuated person exists within a particular family network, however one understands *family*. Each person has a unique constellation of narratives that make up a particular life story.

At the same time, each individuated person is like some other people, sharing a "matrix of values, beliefs, customs and basic life assumptions."[20] As French philosopher and social theorist Pierre Bourdieu claims, families and subcultures embody particular habits and dispositions. Bourdieu argues that "different groups and classes will have a different habitus, which predisposes them toward specific types of practices and the development of particular lifestyles."[21] Other influential modern theorists like George Herbert Mead and Sigmund Freud affirm shared social spheres that originate in familial contexts and expand into larger spheres through new connections and communications.[22] While Lartey envisions individual uniqueness, he also considers persons as simultaneously involved in a matrix of communal relationships. Persons are both like no others and like some others.

Lartey further claims that each individuated person is like all other people: "We are all born helpless, grow from dependence toward relative self-management, we relate to other beings and to a physical environment

---

20. Lartey, *In Living Color*, 34–35.

21. Burkitt, *Social Selves*, 132–33; Bourdieu, *The Logic of Practice*.

22. Burkitt, *Social Selves*, 41.

and ten out of ten die!"[23] Physical and social development occurs in shared intercultural spaces in which persons connect to anyone and everyone else. Lartey's claim of common humanity resonates with Jacques Derrida's philosophy and Henry Stack Sullivan's psychology. Each of these theories lifts up the paradoxical nature of understanding persons as embedded within complex interpersonal relationships. In *The Gift of Death*, Derrida claims that death is the one thing that must be borne alone by persons.[24] According to Derrida, death unmasks the unique "irreplaceable self behind the social mask."[25] At the same time, perhaps Derrida would agree with Lartey that the fact of historical death (as well as birth) represents the unique equalizer of individuated persons who are, in this regard, paradoxically like all other people.[26]

Derrida claims the absolutely unique experience of each death; Lartey claims that all selves share in their participation in finitude. In a similarly paradoxical fashion, Sullivan claims that the more social persons become, the more individual persons become because of the unique interconnections upon interconnections within the fabric of each unique self.[27] Sullivan envisions a complex self as a social being situated historically and developmentally.[28] Both Sullivan and Derrida reinforce Lartey's depiction of the person or self as a constellation of overlapping spheres of like no, some, and all other persons or selves. All three embrace paradox. A claim of individual uniqueness is immediately paired with claims of universal similitude and vice versa.

This dynamic understanding of selves as interconnected beings in process brings together individual and social aspects of the experience of being in relationships. Lartey characterizes *health* as participation in differentiation and interaction among the three spheres. This understanding leads to an intercultural research methodology that "seeks always to have the others in view and therefore to hold all three in creative and dynamic tension."[29] Intercultural theory calls pastoral theologians to acknowledge

23. Lartey, *In Living Color*, 34.

24. Derrida, *The Gift of Death*, 1–34. See also Wolff, *Surrender and Catch*, 30–31.

25. Derrida, *The Gift of Death*, 36.

26. The situation is made infinitely more complex when we consider contestations throughout the history of religion and more recently in the discipline of biomedical ethics over the meaning and definition of birth and death.

27. From conversation with Dr. Barbara McClure in 2007.

28. Sullivan, *The Interpersonal Theory of Psychiatry*.

29. Lartey, *In Living Color*, 35. See also Lartey, *Pastoral Theology in an Intercultural World*.

the intercultural context of interpersonal relationships, unmask violence and oppression within interconnecting spheres, and work toward conditions that deepen fulfillment, liberation, and mutuality in intercultural relationships.

Acknowledging the intercultural context of interpersonal relationships includes resisting a static notion of culture. Intercultural caregiving practices are enhanced when we envision culture(s) as constantly changing, internally diverse, and internally contested. Pastoral theologians have only just begun to think about how culture(s) affects history, meaningful interplay between theory and personal narrative, ritual, empathy, self-awareness, life-giving and life-depriving practices of care and communal life, public witness, and interconnections of care and justice.[30] These themes emerged out of the 2007 annual Society of Pastoral Theology meeting on the theme of post-colonialism held in Puerto Rico.

A pastoral theological engagement with Victor Turner's structural anthropology of social relationships contributes a more robust theory of culture(s) to pastoral theology. Cultural differences shape dynamic negotiations around more or less obvious differences in identity construction, habits, values, claims of heritage, and shared memories and histories. I assume the pastoral theological tasks of acknowledging, unmasking, and working that Lartey suggests. I direct these tasks toward developing an ethics of mutuality that recognizes interculturality as an aspect of a pluralistic, globalized context. A complex context of pluralism that normalizes intercultural encounters presents even more opportunities for intercultural crises and demands a greater sense of responsibility for participation in responding to and repairing them.

VICTOR TURNER'S STRUCTURAL ANTHROPOLOGY OF CULTURAL CRISES

Anthropologist Victor Turner (1920–1983) argued that because crises are inevitable and important dimensions of all human relationships, coherent cultures develop rituals for repairing the damage caused by interpersonal conflicts. That Turner attended to cultural differences within his ethnographic methods makes him an important conversation partner in my study of intercultural crisis and repair. A British social anthropologist who trained in London as a student of Max Gluckman's Manchester School,

---

30. Several pastoral theologians address these and other themes in the *Journal of Pastoral Theology* 17/2 (Fall 2007).

Turner is affiliated with the same school as influential anthropologist Malinowski.[31] According to Victor's life partner, Edith Turner, their immersion in the social context of World War II and in the academic context of British structuralism inspired them to work together to find in literature and anthropology "any kind of idea which could encompass change" and resonate with an innate hopefulness in human experience.[32] The Turners used these resources to develop theories that reflect both individual experience and the life of larger social and political groups.

Victor Turner advanced theories of social process, ritual symbols, play, performance, comparative ritual studies, comparative symbology, political anthropology, and medical anthropology.[33] Turner also contributed an influential body of "specialized vocabulary," including the concepts of liminality, social drama, rites of passage, betwixt and between, and *communitas*.[34] These words and phrases have seeped into many areas of study and conversation. A central figure in the anthropology of religion, Turner is known, with Edith Turner, by his work articulating the profound complexity of religious symbolism within Ndembu culture in central Africa and by later work on Christian pilgrimage.[35] Turner is noted for extending an academic interest in literature and religion in his anthropological method to attending to ways in which "one's inner life provides a key to explaining the inner life of others."[36] According to one scholar, Turner "razed the wall between text-based or theologically based religious studies and the social sciences by resituating social sacrality within individual experience."[37] Turner constructed an understanding of a cross-cultural ritual process from his extensive fieldwork. He argued that his structural theory of ritual applies coherently to a wide range of experiences.

Like his contemporary modern academics, Turner grounds his understanding of all cultural contexts in Western theories.[38] This is a

31. Sullivan, "Victor W. Turner (1920–1983)," 161; Engelke, "The Problem of Belief," 6.

32. Engelke, "An Interview with Edith Turner," 844.

33. Sullivan, "Victor W. Turner (1920–1983)," 162; Jules-Rosette, "Decentering Ethnography," 160.

34. Weber, "From Limen to Border," 526. I explain communitas below.

35. Engelke, "An Interview with Edith Turner," 4; Sullivan, "Victor W. Turner (1920–1983)," 162.

36. Engelke "An Interview with Edith Turner," 8.

37. Sullivan, "Victor W. Turner (1920–1983)," 163.

38. I recognize this tradition of the Western academy in which I participate by using Turner's theories to understand dynamics of present-day intercultural relationships. I

problem. Postcolonial theories encourage naming this problem and charge academics to account for participating in and resisting traditional research methods and theorizing practices. Postcolonial theories connect to dominating interpretative lenses[39] the predominance of Western practices and theories of understanding all persons. These lenses harm rather than illuminate others' experiences. For example, the problematic term *non-Western* identifies others by what they are not, and defines Western as necessarily normative. Postcolonial critics ask academics to identify the extent to which we fail to recognize pluralities and difference and, correlatively, the extent of our participation in this nonrecognition for good *and* for ill. Pastoral theology is a discipline aimed toward understanding theologies that undergird practices of healing and minimizing harm. Therefore, as a discipline we have a moral obligation to heed warnings about problematic language rooted in our tradition as a Western academic discipline.

Given the challenges of Western representation, how might Turner's core concepts yield fresh and liberative understandings of intercultural crisis and repair? Turner structured his understanding of relationships in terms of a series of experiences between persons within discrete cultural groups.[40] He aimed for a universalizable understanding that he then tested through fieldwork in different cultural contexts. Turner recognized culture as complex and multidimensional. He also maintained possibilities of decoding, communicating, and understanding across cultural differences. *From Ritual to Theatre* (1982), published near the end of Turner's life, succinctly describes his structural understanding of human experiences. In the rest of the chapter, I construct a model of understanding intercultural relationships by weaving together three of Turner's structural theories. Turner opens up possibilities for understanding intercultural relationships that account for cultural differences within and across cultures.

hope that my appeal to intercultural experience in this book contributes to a more dialogical project than does a traditional one-way application of Western theories to explain the rest of the world. I also take up the methodological problem of voice across the chapters.

39. In later chapters, I elaborate this point through critical engagement with Frantz Fanon's notion of the Western *gaze*.

40. Turner, *From Ritual to Theatre*.

A PROCESS UNDERSTANDING OF CRISES AND RECONCILIATIONS

Turner developed a structure for understanding diverse forms of human experiences by exploring instances in which a breach between two or more persons threatened communal identities. Turner located what he called the *ritual process* within specific cultural groups. Through extensive ethnographic research, he explored ways in which relationships in particular cultures move between crisis experiences and reconciliations. He focused on ways in which cultures ritualize this movement. Turner's articulation of this kind of movement provides an important lens into the kind of intercultural relating in which most people live.

To the extent that he applies his theories to "tribal" societies, or social groups other than his own, Turner implies the possibility of intercultural understanding: "We should try to find out how and why different sets of human beings in time and space are similar and different in their cultural manifestations; we should also explore why and how all men and women, if they work at it, can understand one another."[41] Turner incorporated the possibility of intercultural understanding into his theories. He participated in this possibility by aiming for a structural understanding of ritual relevant to diverse cultural expressions. His own position as an anthropologist theorizing about structures of culture-specific rituals other than his own, while he and his family lived among the communities they studied, further exemplifies his assumption that intercultural understanding is possible. A synthesis of three of Turner's theories contributed to the following model of intercultural crisis and repair:

1. **Breach**
   Instance of Initial Split
2. **Crisis**
   Crisis of Identity, Understanding, Relationships
3. **Redress**
   Internal/External Split
4. **Reconciliation**
   a. Perceptual Core
   b. Past Images
   c. Renewal of Feelings
   d. Meaning
   e. Expression

   Overarching Process
   Separation → Transition → Incorporation

41. Ibid., 8.

Turner employed the concept of *social drama*, relying on his scientific and dramatic ways of understanding complex phenomena of social life. Social dramas structure experiences of disruption in relation to the normal workings of society.[42] Societies have ways of responding to conflicts among their members. Sometimes society's rules are widely accessible through legislation and social narratives; however, many social processes are informal and not immediately accessible to someone outside the system, so to speak. Turner tried to discern a form or structure for a common processual unfolding of social drama across diverse life experiences.[43] A disruption in normalcy, according to Turner, follows from initial breach to crisis to redress to reconciliation.[44] This sequence serves as a first interlinking structure of intercultural experience:

Initial Breach

Crisis Experiences

Redress

Eventual Reconciliation

German structuralist Wilhelm Dilthey inspired Turner to develop stages in the reconciliation phase. Turner conceived of reconciliation as a dynamic process that develops from perceptual core to evocation of past images to corresponding feelings to meanings that link past and present to expression.[45] I explain these concepts in more detail below. The expanded reconciliation phase serves as a second interlinking structure of intercultural experience:

Perceptual Core

Evocation of Past Experiences

Corresponding Feelings

Meanings that Link Past to Present

Expression

Turner envisioned each of these stages as distinct dramatic processes within societies. In the following paragraphs, I clarify these two interlinking structures of intercultural experience.

Crisis is an inevitable part of all human relationships. Families, small communities such as rural congregations, and even larger communities

42. Ibid., 10.

43. Engelke "An Interview with Edith Turner," 846.

44. Turner, *From Ritual to Theatre*, 10–11.

45. Ibid., 11–15.

experience disruption in the form of conflict. This claim links Turner's understanding of relationships to present-day intercultural, feminist, psychological, and postcolonial theorists I explore in later chapters. Along with these theorists, Turner considered crisis to be a normal, even productive part of social life. Postmodern theorists and Turner share the claim that crisis and conflict—if resolved justly—can contribute to healthy ways of relating. Turner first focused on precipitating events that he called breaches. He then outlined a ritualistic process in which divergent members of society participate in concrete stages of relational repair. While Turner was hopeful that relationships can move through these dynamic stages, he recognized that the process itself likely leads to additional personal and communal crises.

Turner described a *breach* as an event that transgresses "normal" social relations. Breaches interrupt the flow of relationships in such a way that demands a response.[46] (For example, consider the kinds of habituated responses in-person and in media representations in present-day United States airports among those privileged with access to air travel when security breaches occur. While breaches may occur among strangers, Turner focused on the phenomenon of breach within established relationships in which persons have amassed shared time(s), space(s), and histories. Parties invest in relationships through the play between shared commitments and experiences of detachment.[47] The breach leads to a crisis in which persons involved in the particular social constellation experience disruption. They might experience a tangible sense of brokenness within previously established relational bonds. This can accentuate already present conflicting emotions and uncertainties about the future. Philosophers such as Judith Butler point out that disruptions often activate emotional experiences of awe, wonder, or astonishment.[48] Turner considered a breach to be a prereflective event that initiates series of crises within relationships. Turner identified the hinge between a breach event and a crisis experience to be intentional reflection that usually includes recognizing uncertainty.

A relational breach leads to experiences of *crisis* that initially appear to limit possibilities of recovering anything similar to the relationship's previous status.[49] Therefore, Turner characterizes a breach as an event

46. Ibid., 10.

47. See Jules-Rosette, "Decentering Ethnography."

48. See for example, Judith Butler's description of the experience of wonder in light of disruption in her foreword to *The Erotic Bird: Phenomenology in Literature* by Maurice Natanson, ix–xiv.

49. See Turner, *From Ritual to Theatre*, 10–11.

that necessarily involves experiences of loss. A breach of trust within friendship or among business partners can draw parties into crisis about the identity and future of the relationship and the persons involved. Even a perceived breach of trust often introduces doubt into the future viability of relationships. A breach can also accompany an impassioned disagreement, particularly around often contested subjects like religion and politics, which tend to be intimately tied to conceptions of identity. Differing conceptions of identity and human nature can quickly come into conflict when least expected. Experiences of crisis can easily lead to splinters within relationships previously felt to be "just fine." While Turner locates splits among intracultural bonds, crises of misunderstanding also abound in intercultural relationships, especially in relation to cultural differences. At the point of intercultural breach, experiences of crisis can split along cultural or subcultural lines.

Paradoxically, while crisis experiences arise because of reflecting on breaches, they also narrow possibilities for reflection. In intercultural relationships, splits might introduce, highlight, or even seem to cement various insider-outsider dynamics. Crises reveal differing cultural values, norms, and rules that may have been hidden or unapparent to persons involved in the relationships prior to the breach.[50] Crises also bring attention to normally unexpressed cultural values, norms, and rules. According to Turner, crisis is not only a time of splitting within relationships, but also a time that sparks internal reflection on the experience of breach and core values.

Turner viewed splitting within relationships as a continuing feature of the ritual process. He considered the *redress* phase a sometimes theatrical, public forum that addresses social behavior.[51] For example, consider the formal courtroom drama that promises to redress breaches in a United States American context. Communal values, norms, and rules find expression through ritualized dramatic social responses. Relational brokenness along cultural, subcultural, familial, gendered, racialized, and other seemingly distinct lines can lead to exclusive forms of ritualistic redress. For example, one family enacts redress in such a way that persons outside the family do not participate or might even be unaware. At the same time, this familial process affects and is deeply connected to social relationships between members of this family and other families. While Turner argued

---

50. Disruption often characterizes a starting point for learning and for pedagogical reflection (for example, hooks, *Teaching to Transgress*).

51. Turner, *From Ritual to Theatre*, 11.

that redress is a shared, communal, public event, it also necessarily occurs, at least initially, in a limited and privileged space among persons who share particular understandings of social structures for response and redress.

While redress is an initial communal response to crisis after the breach event, it is still only a beginning. Both experiences of crisis and efforts toward redress highlight various fault lines in relational matrixes within and across cultural differences. Efforts toward redressing relational breaches also accentuate the particular breach. Turner thus considered *reconciliation* to be a structured, communally embodied process of response. As noted above, Turner proposed a theory of reconciliation that unfolds as stages within the social drama, progressing from perceptual core to evocation of past images, to connection to feelings, to meaning, to expression. According to Turner, each subphase of what I am calling a larger ritualistic process of repair has a particular structure that draws divergent participants progressively more deeply into the communal process. Each subphase intensifies the risk that the relationship will move away from rather than toward eventual reconciliation.

Turner, following Dilthey, considered the first stage of reconciliation to be the ability to identify a *perceptual core*, or the disruptive experience itself.[52] The perceptual core of a breach is in some ways the pre-reflective human experience of pain that triggers the pit-in-the-stomach or angry interpretation: something is terribly wrong. For example, consider the breach that occurs when a retirement or medical diagnosis[53] disrupts a family's or society's core narrative of identity around leadership of elders. This is a prevalent situation with local church, denominational, or seminary leadership transitions, especially when these changes come in the wake of crises.[54] Cultural factors contribute to the appropriate way to name, speak about, and reflect on this interruption. Cultural-specific rules and customs make intercultural understanding difficult and intercultural misunderstanding likely. Further, intercultural uncertainty is even more pronounced when forced disempowerment is a contributing factor in a family's or society's need to respond in the midst of crisis. For example, like other "developing"

52. See ibid., 13–14.

53. See Blaine-Wallace, "The Politics of Tears," for one of many examples of the need to address family leadership transitions prompted by a family elder's medical diagnosis.

54. For example, see studies of church leadership in the wake of Hurricane Katrina in New Orleans (Blue, "Spiritual Mothers and Midwives") or New York immediately after September 11, 2001 (Swain, *Trauma and Transformation at Ground Zero*).

countries, histories of forced relocation within Suriname contributed to the context of the misunderstanding stories analyzed in this book.[55]

As in the redress phase, articulating the perceptual core in an intercultural breach appears to be culture-specific because of the need to appeal to language. The raw communal experience of crisis is destabilizing and threatens to cement impasses while opening new possibilities. This is one reason why the pastoral theology seminary classroom is not the place to analyze raw experience, even while teaching the theological significance of self-aware ministry that finds appropriate outlets for recognizing and attending to the minister's raw experience.[56] Reconciliation's perceptual core is full of existential questions: Why does the future suddenly seem so fragile? Who are we if we cannot be in relationship? What is relationship without understanding? Was it really ever as good as I thought it was? Existential questions perpetuate cycles of crisis in the internal world.

Turner claimed that identifying the present perceptual experience *evokes images of the past* with unusual clarity.[57] The present state of relationships is compared to a past vision of stable, sustainable, or at least unproblematic status quo. On a precipice of possible change, persons must navigate and evaluate temptations to settle back into past structures. This is as old as the Israelites contemplating turning back to oppressive conditions just when change—albeit uncertain and necessarily difficult work— is not only possible, but already beginning to be embodied (Exodus 14). Even today, persons facing crisis remember "the way it used to be" or "the old days" or "the early days" with unusual clarity. Moments of remembering highlight connections while also making palpable the risks of further estrangement and miscommunication within relationships.

In an intercultural context, personal memories of culturally specific and interculturally shared past experiences pervade this process. Evocation of past memories in relation to an identifiable perceptual core solicit connection while also interrupting culturally specific rituals of redress. Differences in cultural values, norms, and rules reveal vastly different ways of being, speaking, acting, and embodying that can feel incommensurable. This divergence coexists in contrast to clear, even romanticized, images of past intercultural harmony evoked in the perceptual moment. For example, consider the ways in which after the events of September 11, 2001, some United States Americans remembered past intercultural global

---

55. Walsh and Gannon, *Time Is Short*.

56. Cooper-White, *Shared Wisdom*.

57. Turner, *From Ritual to Theatre*, 14.

harmony, while others saw the event as unmasking a naïve, romanticized vision of prior global harmony.

Turner, again relying on Dilthey, claims that past images *renew feeling states* associated with the experience of remembering.[58] Persons, families, friends, and communities begin to remember by accessing feeling states that predate the breach. Feelings express *both* culturally specific *and* shared intercultural communal ways of relating. The convergence of past memories in the present act of remembering also accentuates crisis.

Turner claimed that *meaning* links the past to the present by distinguishing between the "value" and the "meaning" that can emerge en route to more complete reconciliation. The distinction between value and meaning here is that meaning is a process of making sense of various values that often are not thought of as ordered and/or connected.[59] Reconciliation is more complete when it involves parties—from the various splits that the crisis accentuates—into the process of meaning making. If, with Turner, we consider reconciliation's end as an articulated memory that respects multiple perspectives and is therefore accessible across differences, then the meaning-making process invites different ways of speaking different experiences into robust conversation. Eventually with sustained attention to and participation in the meaning-making process, something new breaks in. A new possibility, word, image, or understanding creates the conditions for an open future with respect to this particular strained relationship within this particular intercultural moment.

Turner highlighted *expression* as the ultimate and somewhat elusive stage in reconciliation. Expression completes a cyclical, processual turn within the larger social drama.[60] Turner differentiated between initial attempts at expression and more integrated, longer lasting, creative, artistic interpretations of reconciliation.[61] Consider the difference between monuments erected in the immediate aftermath of a tragic loss compared to those that are more permanent and enduring, yet no less meaningful. For example, in the recent event of the devastating earthquake in Haiti, immediate forms of expression included primarily mixed media news reports and documentary-style communal processing. In time, films, monuments, and other artistic expressions will strive to make meaning of something so senseless and tragic in forms incorporated into larger social narratives across cultural differences.

58. Turner, *From Ritual to Theatre*, 14.

59. Ibid., 14–15.

60. Ibid., 15–19.

61. Ibid.

Such expression is not quickly achieved; in fact, according to Turner, inevitably premature efforts toward expressing reconciliation intensify interpersonal splits and move relationships away from more complete reconciliation.[62] Efforts at more inclusive participation continue to highlight the limits of interpersonal and intercultural understanding. The drive toward consensus among divergent voices also illustrates the dynamism always present in and among all cultures. Turner considered expression to be reached when persons within and across cultures who are both near to and far from the particular moment of initial breach can agree that a specific monument, film, or other artistic expression conveys what all of our words and efforts have failed to do: there is a past to lament and a future open to new possibilities.

Turner organized social dramas by appealing to cyclical patterns of intracultural and intercultural experiences. After an initial breach, persons can move in intercultural relationships through time and space toward reconciliation. Turner wrote: "If our cultural institutions and symbolic modes are to be seen . . . as the crystallized secretions of once living human experience, individual and collective, we may perhaps see the word 'experience' itself as an experienced traveler through time!"[63] Turner understood movement from breach toward reconciliation as a normal and inevitable rite of passage within coherent and well-structured cultures. In this sense, his use of the word "experience" suggests intercultural sharing in a discernible idea that plays out in culture(s). Trying to understand across the different ways in which experience plays out in cultures contributes to problems of intercultural crisis and repair. What might it mean to consider Turner's description as a developmental stage in intercultural relationships? To consolidate Turner's claims about relationships, I suggest that his understanding of intracultural rites of passage provides a third interlinking structural understanding of intercultural experiences:

Separation

Transition

Incorporation

62. Future research could explore whether reconciliation is always between persons or also between persons and events. For example, in relation to September 11, 2001, do persons reconcile with the event in a separate process from reconciling with others who may have contributed to the event, which may never occur? Another example of reconciling differently with person and event arises in the international uproar over the release of the primary Lockerbie bombing suspect in August 2009.

63. Turner, *From Ritual to Theatre*, 17.

Turner's influential theory of liminality adds an additional dynamic to the unfolding of social drama in which breaches cause separation between persons. The transition, or liminal space, emphasizes the flowing and processual nature of ritual that opens persons and groups to a sense of freedom, creativity, and possibility.[64] The next section consolidates the three interlinking structures to propose a model of understanding intercultural experience.

A FRAMEWORK FOR UNDERSTANDING INTERCULTURAL MISUNDERSTANDINGS

A structural understanding of intercultural experience draws on what I consider to be Turner's three interlinking structures of the social drama. In an imagined landscape of intercultural experience, relationships move through stages of intercultural understanding. Each stage tends to draw participants back to crisis, which then calls again for personal and communal response, even if the response is to opt out, as I propose below. Intersecting cycles back to crisis point to the ever cyclical, never quite stable or certain intercultural experience. Reconciling processes drive toward fuller and more concrete expression even while participants remember, re-story, and imagine possibilities.

The case studies of intercultural crisis and repair in the next chapter exemplify how a breach in relationship (separation) prompts a lengthy time of deep ambiguity (transition) with respect to future possibilities. A new insight can allow for mutual transformation of understanding that invites diverse participation. I assess this goal in the later analytical chapters. Eventual reconciliation, even if provisional, invites meaningful exchange where diverse persons are capable of recognizing a multiplicity of cultural identities (incorporation). The prospect of sharing in experiences of reconciliation deepens intercultural relationships by increasing possibilities for mutual understanding.

Possibilities for mutual understanding exist in a context of good enough intercultural relationships. "Good enough" is an idea from object relations theory that mothers (and othermothers[65]) will fail and that these empathic failures or "optimal failures" in a loving environment can

64. Sullivan, "Victor W. Turner (1920–1983)," 161–62.

65. Bonnie Miller-McLemore, drawing on womanist theologians, considers "othermothers" to be "anyone who cares for kids and is changed by it" (*In the Midst of Chaos*, xvii).

facilitate healthy development. The classic example is the mother of a new-born who eventually cannot immediately respond to the baby's cries. A good enough mother fails to respond *immediately all the time* but does not fail to respond as quickly as she can. In contrast, mothers (or other-mothers) who aim for perfection and do not tolerate failures constrict possibilities for a healthy developmental environment. I adopt the concept of *good enough* as an analogy that to theorize about care in a context of intercultural relationships is to theorize about good enough intercultural relationships. This is most poignantly the case when we can recognize the realities of postcoloniality that impinge on self-understanding and inter-personal relationships.

Can Turner be diagnostic in the common case of intercultural crisis? The model I propose below envisions that good enough intercultural rela-tionships exist in contexts defined by (1) a processual understanding that experience is moving, rather than static or excluded from moving, (2) in which potential for repairing responses increases by inviting greater par-ticipation in the movement, and (3) that includes an imagination capable of balancing flexibility and continuity in a relational matrix of complex commitments and detachments. Given the inevitability of conflicting per-spectives within intercultural relationships, perhaps the best practices of care are those practices that draw conflicting parties into participating in relational repair. Consider the following model:

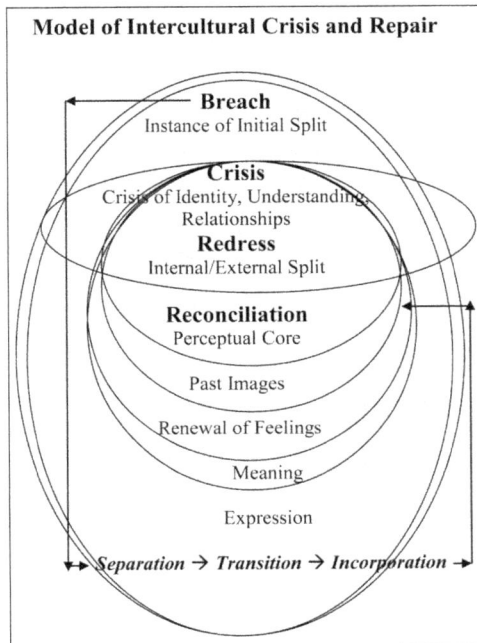

Model of Intercultural Crisis and Repair

Breach
Instance of Initial Split

Crisis
Crisis of Identity, Understanding, Relationships

Redress
Internal/External Split

Reconciliation
Perceptual Core

Past Images

Renewal of Feelings

Meaning

Expression

Separation → Transition → Incorporation →

A two-dimensional model necessarily fails to account for the complexity of life experiences. Therefore, in the above depiction, the circles serve as reminders of the multi-dimensional processes of interacting human experiences unfolding in time and space all the time. Models like this are helpful in processes of intercultural meaning-making toward reconciliation when conversation is needed and part of the problem is the inadequacy and even destructive nature of language.

Turner proposed that reconciliation at its best invites what he called spontaneous communitas, where he relied on Martin Buber to envision "a sense of unity [that] is achieved without the dissolution of individuals."[66] One scholar describes Turner's communitas as "the ritual leveling process containing the potential for new social arrangements, new forms of imagination, of ritualized play."[67] New possibilities emerge in instances of communitas in which diverse persons participate with "attentiveness and affirmation" in relation to one another.[68] In other words, new possibilities become available in and across cultures even when the idea of new possibilities is suppressed.

Whether *communitas* becomes spontaneous and full of potential, normative and reifying of established institutions, or ideological depends on the unfolding of opportunities created by the instability of crisis.[69] Turner named this hinge *liminal space*, where possibilities of both dangerous and "vitalizing" experiences coexist with possibilities for violence and repair and where "liminal entities" are "betwixt and between" normally recognizable forms of community.[70] Here, he distinguished *communitas* from everyday community by identifying ritualized spaces and times of "sacredness of that transient humility and modelessness" in which persons participate.[71] Whether participation tends toward reification or awakening new possibilities depends on collective wisdom in navigating *communitas's* "regenerative abyss" of "untransformed power."[72] Turner's efforts to model and structure liminal space raise tensions over how structure

---

66. Sullivan, "Victor W. Turner (1920–1983)," 163; Turner, *The Ritual Process*, 126–27.

67. Weber, "From Limen to Border," 528.

68. Alexander, "Correcting Misinterpretations of Turner's Theory," 38.

69. Turner, *The Ritual Process*, 132; see also Alexander, "Correcting Misinterpretations of Turner's Theory," 30.

70. Turner, *The Ritual Process*, 95, 108–11; Alexander, "Correcting Misinterpretations of Turner's Theory," 30.

71. Turner, *The Ritual Process*, 97.

72. Ibid., 139.

and possibility come together both in preparation for and analysis of experience.

Good enough intercultural relationships account for the institutional brokenness of postcoloniality, allow for participation of multiple perspectives, permit uncertainty and ambiguity, and resist the perfectionist and ideological idea that relationships can or should maintain a solidified status quo. These features exceed any two-dimensional representation of even a complex theory; therefore, it is important to consider ways in which models both illuminate and constrict understanding. How does a careful examination of Turner's anthropology of experience both enlighten and constrict liberative possibilities in understanding intercultural crisis and repair?

POSSIBILITIES OF INTERCULTURAL UNDERSTANDING

Like all models, Turner's structural anthropology of human experiences contains strengths that open up interpretive possibilities and limitations that restrict them. Strengths include Turner's broad applicability, his embrace of movement as an integral part of relational life, and his hopefulness that relationships can move between crisis and repair. Limitations include his Western biases, such as the idea of the anthropologist as outside observer with sufficient expertise to understand and accurately describe any coherent culture. Other limitations include Turner's ideas around identifying and measuring successful relationships and his lack of attention to contexts in which a real impasse leads to violence and furthers crisis rather than repair. How can such a model of intercultural crisis and repair be open to postcolonial criticism?

Sociologist Bobby Alexander accuses many Turner scholars of minimizing the transformative possibilities of drawing on Turner to understand social strife. In response to scholars who argue that Turner's structural understanding can justify oppressive hierarchies, Alexander draws on case studies to show that liminal space can be inspired by and can inspire resistance.[73] Like Alexander, I also find Turner to be a helpful resource in identifying potential spaces for liberative intercultural encounters. Turner's theories provide tools for understanding how persons might respond to intercultural crisis. His work can help persons in conflict meet an intensified and marked possibility of violence with an agenda of

---

73. Alexander, "Correcting Misinterpretations of Turner's Theory," 39. See also Alexander, *Victor Turner Revisited*.

reform by unmasking embedded misunderstandings and inviting participation in destabilized moments. This is why Turner (like so many anthropologists and religionists) focused on ritual's potential to bring together
divergent persons by suspending a sense of concrete time and space in
favor of, even if momentary, a multidimensional understanding: "Ritual
not only replicates structures of experience (the 'social drama'), it also
reshapes experience."[74] In an intercultural geography, what are the poten-
tials for resisting and reshaping oppressive social powers and traditional
hierarchies?

A methodological challenge is to consider how pastoral theologians
might draw on postcolonial theorists to destabilize intellectual spaces in
order to unmask misunderstandings and latent oppressions while inviting
new possibilities without reinscribing the same old power placeholders in
the center(s). Alexander is helpful in pointing out that one methodological move is always to be ready to investigate the extent to which academic
responses intend redressing societal oppression. However, I depart from
Alexander by offering mutuality instead of a "drive to inclusivity" as a
goal.[75] A drive to inclusivity risks minimizing intercultural embodiment
by colluding in the institutionalization of articulating social reality at the
expense of silencing diverse voices and experiences. I agree with Alexander in turning to liberation theology but find that additional conversation
with postcolonial theorists is important for articulating and maintaining
tensions when trying to understand intercultural experience.

Turner's theory of ritual antistructure is still valuable in the study of
religion because of "religion's potential to serve as a significant force for
social protest and social-structural change within . . . Third world countries . . . and countries like the United States."[76] Religion also has the potential for harm in these contexts. While Alexander sees the potential for
the relevance of Turner's theory to religious studies today, he maintains a
distinction between developed and developing countries that we can now
recognize as problematic with the help of postcolonial theories.

Other theorists agree with Alexander that Turner can be read as
foreshadowing the postmodern turn and a deeper recognition of postcoloniality. Alexander argues that Turner has been misread around claims
that social rituals reinscribe oppressive social hierarchies. Instead, Alexander corrects this misreading using a case study of a black Pentecostal

74. Alexander, "Correcting Misinterpretations of Turner's Theory," 41.

75. Ibid., 39–40.

76. Ibid., 42.

congregation to argue that Turner considered rituals to open liminal spaces that "relax" social hierarchies and allow for possibilities of social change and transformation.[77] Engelke affirms that throughout his writings, "Turner did indeed primarily want to show how ritual was creative, not a means of confirming the social status quo."[78] Other theorists point to Turner's inclusion of reflexivity within his structural understanding of social drama.[79] Turner's reflexivity displays a pragmatic invitation to discern what matters by imagining consequences.

In 1995, Donald Weber echoed critical voices, such as Renato Rosaldo, to argue that scholarship using the physical site and metaphor of the "border" has advanced Turner's concept of liminality in a way that is more adequately responsive to current social realities.[80] While some praise Turner for envisioning a liminal structure with inherent potential to recognize marginal persons and inspire social protest,[81] Weber doubts the continued influence of Turner's structure of social drama because of a latent imperialist tone that prizes consensus, sets a goal of resolving social conflict, and lacks the legitimate option to refrain from participating in social drama as a form of marginal protest.[82] Weber claims that Turner misses "a conception and recognition of culture as *political* contestation: the battle over narrative power, the fight over who gets to (re)tell the story, and from which position."[83] Weber argues that theorizing "borders" extends Turner's methodological insistence on both human experience and interdisciplinary study to an orientation more open to various forms of hybridity, multiplicity, and ambiguity.[84]

Within the same year that Weber was writing on Turner, Bennetta Jules-Rosette argued that Turner contributed to "decentering ethnography and repositioning the postcolonial subject" by shifting the ethnographer from an "omniscient stance" to an "empathetic interpreter in a cross-cultural dialogue."[85] Jules-Rosette argues that Turner must be read as a cru-

---

77. Ibid., 26, 34, 40–41.

78. Engelke, "An Interview with Edith Turner," 8.

79. Sullivan, "Victor W. Turner (1920–1983)," 162; Jules-Rosette, "Decentering Ethnography," 173.

80. Weber, "From Limen to Border," 525.

81. Sullivan, "Victor W. Turner (1920–1983)," 162; Alexander, "Correcting Misinterpretations of Turner's Theory," 29.

82. Weber, "From Limen to Border," 526, 529–531.

83. Ibid., 532.

84. Ibid.

85. Jules-Rosette, "Decentering Ethnography," 160–61.

cial figure in the transition from a colonial to a destabilizing postcolonial anthropology that focuses on dynamic processes surrounding personal narratives.[86] She further asserts that Turner considers the Ndembu not as "passive colonial subject" but rather as "active agents in social change" among whom many voices participate in an ethnographic dialogue or trialogue.[87]

Jules-Rosette raises the question of whether and how the academic can learn from his or her subject of study. She envisions a destabilizing ethnographic practice that matters in response to the suffering implicit in the human condition, even as envisioned by practitioners who unwittingly participate in a colonial order because of the very nature of Western academia.[88] Is Jules-Rosette right that ethnographers can participate so well in the social drama through their own struggle that liminal possibilities transcend barriers of culture, class, ethnicity, knowledge, or power in the emergence of "a new, plural reflexivity"?[89] Can Turner's theories help us imagine a mutuality that "overcome[s] the dichotomy between commitment and detachment" in academic practice?[90] Weber inspires a postcolonial challenge worth our consideration: Does using Turner's theory obscure or enlighten borders? Can a model based on Turner reconcile authentic social experience with the ambiguities of hybridity? Is there another side to Turner's imagined liminal threshold? Do Turner's theories of social experience correlate to postmodern projects that try to resist the concrete and to postcolonial projects that try to unmask our habituated forms of oppression?

CONCLUSION

The proposals and questions of this chapter arise from lived experiences of intercultural crisis and repair. In reflecting on intercultural experiences, Turner provides a helpful lens to resist strategic dehumanization, which later chapters theorize with reference to a dominating "gaze." Anthropology comes "alive in human interaction" in a way that allows human experience, particularly ritual experience, to emphasize the play within

86. Ibid.,162–63.
87. Ibid., 164, 168.
88. Ibid., 174.
89. Ibid., 175–76.
90. Ibid., 177.

the usual "coldness of academic demand."[91] Engelke points out that methodologically, Turner performs the faith that the other with whom he is in relationship not only has something to teach him about anthropology but also has the power to impart transformative wisdom regarding the inner life.[92] In this way, Turner frames a structural understanding of intercultural relationships that draws participants into risky liminal spaces full of possibilities. The following chapter continues to investigate the extent to which a model of good enough intercultural relationality based on Turner might open possibilities for a pastoral theological engagement with postcolonial theories.

Each of the experiences at the beginning of this chapter presented crises in intercultural understanding that threatened to sever relationships and evoked intense feelings. In chapter 2, I look at these and other experiences more closely to move us toward recognizing the prevalence of intercultural misunderstanding so that we can better understand and practice theology in our postcolonial context.

91. Engelke, "An Interview with Edith Turner," 845.

92. Engelke, "The Problem of Belief," 8.

2

Misunderstanding Stories in Context(s)

ANY BREACH IN THE flow of intercultural understanding occurs in shared space shaped by converging contexts. We each bring our culturally specific understandings of ourselves and other people to our relationships. Our shared stories are constantly in flux around the subtexts and personal narrative threads each of us contributes to spinning throughout our lived experiences. Breaches can be difficult to understand because of the tensions and translation work that accompany healthy intercultural life together. Staying in relationship after a breach in understanding requires attention to shared contexts and personal and communal histories. This chapter provides a thick description of one shared context—MoiKonde, an Afro-Surinamese village in the Republic of Suriname, South America—where the examples of misunderstanding I draw on throughout the book occurred.

My role was that of a Peace Corps volunteer between one period of graduate study and another. The stories in this book are woven from my journals and subsequent reflection with friends from MoiKonde. Our relationship was not that of researcher-subject; rather, constantly aware of our different yet intersecting cultural identities, we worked within a model of sustainable international intercultural partnership. I chose to apply for graduate work from the heavy heat of a zinc-roofed house in MoiKonde. I began to craft an academic trajectory while seated at the same porch table and surrounded by the same friends represented in the misunderstanding stories—friends who remain central to my experiences in the village. However, I did not take stories from MoiKonde with me to graduate school as objects of study. I did not live in MoiKonde for two years as an ethnographer, pastoral theologian, anthropologist, cultural critic, or graduate student; rather, I took on these academic roles immediately following a two-year immersion in intercultural friendship that surpassed my expectations of the relational depth possible across cultural differences. The stories that I reflect on here are ingredient to my identity and are not external objects of fascination. In my studies, I have paid attention to ways in which stories of intercultural possibilities and misunderstandings bubbled up in the midst of my reading other things for other purposes. I kept remembering and kept being affected, caught up, by these intercultural stories. I allowed them to check my reading and writing. They disrupted theories I was learning. I telephoned friends in the village. Sometimes I would get through, and we would have a conversational reunion. Stories thickened. When I reflect on living in community in MoiKonde, I remember deep connections as well as misunderstandings.

When I decided to write about intercultural misunderstanding and to draw on stories of my experiences in MoiKonde as examples, I returned to the village in hopes of having a face-to-face conversation with village leaders to ask their permission for me to approach our shared experiences formally, on paper, in my studies. After long and eventful travels, there I was in the midst of sweet expected and unexpected reunions. There had been births and deaths. Children had grown. Some friends had left the village for the city where they hosted me in their new homes. I sat on the porch of our old home that is my friend's current home. Spiritual leaders in the village ritually blessed my visit and work.

I was able to see Captain, the leader of the village. He continued the practice I remembered of allowing me, inviting me, to look at him while we talked. This was a cultural honor. *He said that he would like to eat with me but was sorry that I didn't eat rice. Oh, I said, I do eat rice and like it. I would be honored to share rice with you. But, he said, my rice is plain. Do you eat plain rice? Yes, please let us share plain rice. We did.* Captain sat in what I had always thought of as his normal spot right in front of the window with the curtain that moved with the breeze and rain and that can be moved when people come to the window to greet him or consult with him. I sat in a plastic chair on the wood plank floor (his house was raised a few feet off of the ground by design and from erosion) beside the small table, which was covered with fabric crocheted around the edges—a bowl of plain rice in the shared space between us, next to the ceremonial medicines that ritually blessed him as village leader even as, while spooning plain rice into my bowl and his, he gave his blessing to my intentions to write. Later I would return to the *Gadu Osu* for a second invitation to ritual blessing. The *Gadu Osu* is a house that is among the most sacred sites in the village and into which we had been invited only once before on the morning that we left the village after two years of communal life there.

Three years after moving back to the United States, I returned to MoiKonde for face-to-face encounters, not knowing how it would unfold or if I would even be able to meet with village leaders, who often travel with or without notice for governmental, ceremonial, ritual, and healing-related purposes. I went not knowing who would meet me and what would happen when I encountered shared memories in formerly shared spaces. I went to share my thoughts on what I felt had been our experience together and to ask permission to write. I returned to acknowledge my provisional understanding of our shared experience.

Engaging thick description of a shared context requires careful attention to the kind of provisional understanding I advocated in chapter 1. Both academic scholars of pastoral theology and practitioners of pastoral care and counseling know the importance of provisional understanding in listening to and interpreting lived human experiences in partnership with other people. In relation to writing about my experiences of misunderstanding stories in MoiKonde, I am simultaneously story listener, story interpreter, and storyteller. Navigating these multiple roles presents a difficult conundrum: to tell stories of shared experiences that include others' stories risks colluding in colonization of other people; *and* not to tell stories of shared experiences that include others' stories risks colluding in the old academic idea that I am or could ever be an isolated, neutral observer who does not participate in the formation of ideas through networks of relationships with other people. I contend that all who theorize about and practice pastoral care have to navigate this delicate tension in our work.

My stories continually interact with *your* stories. This is why the development and maintenance of good boundaries is crucial to "good enough" pastoral care. Especially as the discipline moves toward more communal and more intercultural models of mutual partnership, professional ethics is crucial.[1] Pastoral theology and care embody a theological posture of

---

1. Cooper-White, *Shared Wisdom*, 58–60; Gill-Austern, "Engaging Diversity and Difference," 30.

acknowledging our finitude and ambiguity as human beings. Given that the field of pastoral theology begins the work of theology by attending to experiences of suffering, *and* given the immediacy of suffering for practicing good enough pastoral care, none of us understands perfectly. No one of us has access to the many voices needed to tell the stories about shared spaces that lead to mutual understanding because as finite human beings, all of our understanding is provisional and partial.

This book interweaves theory with narratives from personal intercultural experience to aid in provisional understanding oriented toward the possibility and goal of mutual intercultural understanding. One single-authored book or one set of rich experiences cannot complete this process. Rather, I hope to model the courage and vulnerability required for cross-contextual fluency even while acknowledging the limits of my perspective and situatedness. My work in community with my neighbors in MoiKonde raised postcolonial concerns. The misunderstanding stories I describe in this chapter are each situated in Suriname. By drawing attention to complex legacies of colonialism in that place, I suggest themes relevant for intercultural relationships in a variety of contexts. Acknowledging misunderstanding stories opens questions of identity (chapter 3), vulnerability (chapter 4), and empathy (chapter 5) as important for personal investment in and scholarship of intercultural relationships more broadly. In this chapter, I reflect on the role of context, voice, narrative, and history in relation to breaches of understanding in intercultural relationships.

PROCESS OF TELLING MISUNDERSTANDING STORIES: FRAMING EXPERIENCE WITH LANGUAGE

Brief summaries merely hint at the contextual complexity of intercultural misunderstandings. In chapter 1, I offered the following brief summaries of misunderstanding stories: In one instance, I intervened in my home when a mother began to strike her daughter with my broom. In another, I arranged for a group of new Peace Corps volunteers to learn about cultural taboos in the village setting, inadvertently breaking a cultural taboo in the process. In another, I returned to my village home and learned that four young girls had not only stolen from me but had also been publicly beaten in my absence for their crime. Finally, in a conversation with some young girls, I realized some of the difficulties of engaging histories of slavery and colonialism. Each of these four experiences presented crises in intercultural understanding that evoked intense feelings and threatened to sever relationships. In this chapter, each case prompts contemplating possibilities of relational repair across cultural differences in a postcolonial context.

These experiences, in which I was a participant, demonstrate *inevitabilities of misunderstanding* and *possibilities of understanding* within intercultural relationships. Victor Turner's dynamic model of breach-crisis-redress-reconciliation that I introduced in chapter 1 provides language to texture a thick description of cases. I use the term "relational repair" to point to ways in which persons involved in intercultural crises participate in movement from the disruption of misunderstanding toward the mutual understanding that can be found in reconciliation. I understand intercultural experiences from a multiperspectival approach that brings theological, psychological, postcolonial, and anthropological perspectives together in dynamic interaction. Lived experiences of intercultural misunderstanding focus this theoretical project.

Cases that begin rather than end in crises are particularly illuminating because they demonstrate possibilities for intercultural misunderstanding to unfold into what Turner called a *processual movement* toward relational repair. Desire, commitment, and vulnerability in relation to the history and future of the intercultural relationship affect possible responses. If relational crisis is inherent to intercultural relationships, it is important to recognize that breaches in understanding may serve to restructure relationships in fundamentally different ways for better or for worse. While this is no reason to justify suffering or to exemplify misunderstanding as a virtue, "a crisis can mean that possibilities previously unavailable are now close at hand."[2] Examining situations of crisis within committed intercultural relationships provides an avenue to consider that possibilities of more mutual understanding might be close at hand.

The crises I highlight occurred in the *context of established yet still unfolding intercultural relationships*. Participation in intercultural relationships is at stake in experiences of relational breach. In each case, cycles of trial and error allow for new possibilities of inviting or limiting participation and communication. Each experience of breach involves processes of delicate negotiation, including calling for the creation of new rituals. Stories of intercultural misunderstanding and subsequent social repair offer opportunities to evaluate whether Victor Turner's social drama helps deepen understanding of complex intercultural misunderstandings in a postcolonial context.

2. Butler, *Liberating Our Dignity*, vii.

The process of telling misunderstanding stories often begins with a brief summary as tellers try to put a disruptive experience into language. Pastoral theologians know that rushed description often exacerbates misunderstanding and almost always blocks listening for what is going on.[3] In the midst of crisis, there are sound reasons to heed the wisdom of systems theorists: don't just do (or say) something, stand there.[4] Only later can we slow down and examine our own narratives, open to the possibility of having misunderstood even the narratives in which we participate. Verbatim and case-study reporting are pastoral practices often used in pastoral theology to open narratives to deeper, more sustained reflection.

In the following section, I offer a more detailed iteration of the same four case studies presented in summary form above. I repeat the telling in different forms in hopes of unpacking some of the cross-contextual complexity. Rather than as serving as data from academic fieldwork, these stories, in all their narrative complexity, speak to the qualitative dimension of friendly partnering. Then, I reflect on the act of telling and retelling such shared life experiences in narrative form. As Søren Kierkegaard demonstrates on the first page of *Fear and Trembling*, retelling the same story in different ways can lead to imagining new possibilities that matter tremendously.[5] A postcolonial pastoral theology is receptive to complexity and can accommodate multiple versions of shared narratives.

PROCESS OF TELLING MISUNDERSTANDING STORIES: REFLECTIVE RETELLING

I write out of a commitment to my neighbors in MoiKonde to tell about significant moments of intercultural misunderstanding as a narrative thread in the two consecutive years of our shared encounter. Rather than telling their story, I have covenanted to tell our story, an account of our coming to get to know each other, even as I recognize the limits and vulnerabilities that accompany my self-aware position as storyteller in the larger process of provisional understanding that exceeds this book. The narrative fragments included here are my attempt to tell a complex intercultural story of shared experience without assuming that

---

3. Hunter, "Ministry in Depth," 6–10; Weil, "Reflections on the Right Use of School Studies with a View to the Love of God," 114–15.

4. Friedman, *Friedman's Fables*, 11.

5. Kierkegaard, *Fear and Trembling*. Kierkegaard here tells the Abraham and Isaac story in four different ways.

my perspective on the experience is actually shared; rather, I narrate toward shared experience. Complex problems located in Suriname but not unique to one country contribute to contextual understanding. I engage postcolonial literature that calls for shared participation in reflection on shared problems, attempting to respect local contexts without abandoning global responsibilities.

My life partner and I lived in MoiKonde in Suriname for two years as United States Peace Corps volunteers. We were continually reminded of our lack of knowledge of others and ourselves at the same time that we were offered invitations to experience local knowledge and wisdom. Rather than only helping others from our powerful, educated, North American position, we gradually learned about mutual intercultural encounter through exploring possibilities of sustainable, partnered, locally owned development with our new neighbors. In the context of our learning-to-encounter, the following descriptions of a breach in intercultural understanding continue to impact me and to inspire further reflection on these misunderstanding stories.

Communal Context of Intercultural Crises and Relational Repair

While we were away for one month to the United States, five girls between the ages of eight and twelve broke into our house by prying open the boards of the back window, and stole several items. We learned this during a New Year's Day phone call from a friend in the village. Another layer of breach is our friend's identity as a member of a different indigenous group who married into the family of a village elder. Layers of insider/outsider dynamics complexify the context. We knew the girls, the daughters of our closest neighbors, well. The Peace Corps organization offered to move us to another village. In the midst of comprehending the breach, we decided to return to the village to attempt to reconcile with our neighbors. We are committed to being neighbors here, we said, to learning how to be neighbors here in the experience of confusion, hurt, and conflict. I learned that the site of deep conflict is ripe with possibilities. The layers of cross-contextual, intercultural misunderstanding were so complex over such a long time that the rest of the book traces this misunderstanding story as it moved toward reconciliation.

Intervention in Possible Child Abuse as Cultural Taboo

After living for a couple years in a context with a complicated history of cultural exchange and conflict, we hosted a gathering that included representatives of several cultures and subcultures. While we were playing together, one of our friends became upset, for whatever reason, at the way her daughter was acting. She reached for the nearest implement—a broom in the corner—with which to reprimand her. Just as the mother moved toward the child and raised the broom to hit her daughter, I intervened. Spontaneously, I reached out to grab the broom from the mother's hand. I heard myself saying (or did I just think it and remain silent?): *You cannot harm this child in my home. Not in my home.*

Silence instantly pierced the room. From the look on my friend's face, I realized that my action in front of her children and our neighbors had likely heightened an already tense interaction. I had unintentionally violated accepted norms of adult interactions in relation to children. Yet I also believe that hitting other people, particularly children, is always wrong and should be prevented. But I find it difficult to articulate my reasoning in a way that respects my friend or makes sense across the obvious and not so obvious cultural differences. How do we discern what is happening in this moment? Does it matter that I am in our own home? On what do we base judgments about which actions are right or wrong? Was the mother wrong for starting to strike her child? Was I right to intervene in the mother's parenting?[6]

Prevention of Cultural Taboo and Intercultural Misunderstanding

When we had been living in the village for a year, I was asked to teach a group of new Peace Corps volunteers some cultural taboos I had learned that pertained specifically to women's embodied experiences. To prepare, I engaged in conversation with women in the village and reflected on my own experiences living in the village community. The new women volunteers, who would soon move to villages culturally similar to the one in which I was living, gathered in our home for conversation. (For one month of the three-month-long training period, Peace Corps trainees live with a host family in a village culturally similar to the village in which the trainees will be assigned as volunteers. The village where

---

6. This scenario also appears in McGarrah Sharp and Miller-McLemore, "Are There Limits to Multicultural Inclusion?"

I lived was a training site for the Peace Corps.) After my presentation, I escorted the group of women on a tour of the village, taking care to indicate markers of sacred village locations that must be avoided during menstruation. I led the group toward the *Gadu Osu* (which translates as "House of God"), a place of great importance to the village that must be avoided during menstruation in order for it and the medicines held within to remain pure and potent. I noted that I had never been invited into the sacred space surrounding the *Gadu Osu*, and that only a certain few seemed to enter the physical structure in the center. I was not about to cross the threshold of this sacred space with a group of strangers. As we neared the marker of the sacred space, the matriarch of the village, MaLespeki, ran toward us, *kisi winti*, or in the manner of spirit possession. She called me her enemy and bade us leave the sacred space lest we, the white man, continue to invade and destroy the sacred spaces of the village and its ancestors. I quickly moved the group away from the *Gadu Osu* to another place so that they could wait for me while I went to speak with MaLespeki's daughter and to explain what I had been doing and to inquire as to how I could apologize to her.

After encountering MaLespeki's objection to the white "male" invasion of the sacred space she protects (what was I to make of MaLespeki's gender reversal?), I engaged a series of conversations apologizing and accounting for my behavior. I realized that I had initiated an intentional act of trying to prevent future disrespect in other villages in a manner that unintentionally caused disrespect toward the very people who protected me in my village home. Even though I did not lead the group of women into these precise sacred spaces (for I had not ever been invited into them and would not be invited into them until my last morning in the village at the end of two years), nevertheless I drew near to them and indicated their existence along with my perceptions of meanings and taboos associated with these sacred spaces. What did it mean to act responsibly within my role as an educator for future volunteers? I knew well that people choose to inhabit and embody the role of Peace Corps volunteer in a variety of ways that I consider to be more or less empowering. Who was I to teach about sacred practices about which I was only beginning to learn, and of which I can be sure I did not understand? How might I respond to fierce resistance from MaLespeki, who represented and literally embodied the village? How did this experience embody levels of power and resistance in roles, memories, and sacred spaces? While the village came to be a second home for me in meaningful community with my new neighbors, I only gradually learned of complexities of this home for the people of the village.

Intercultural Crises, Slavery, and Problems of Colonial History

After a long day of difficult work in the peanut fields with village women and girls, I organized the harvest for the long walk home by preparing to hoist upon my head my large basket, which was heavy with peanut plants freshly tugged from the soil. My friends had taught me to roll a cloth into a long coil to provide a cushion between my head and the heavy basket in order to strategically distribute the weight atop my head. A fleeting thought crossed my mind when I remembered hearing about a sermon from a village preacher who likened the coiled cloth to God's work in the life of the community. Cloth ready, I hoisted the basket up high, strapped my small pack together, and began the journey home with friends. I sang, danced, skipped, and exchanged stories with Mia and Ella, two of our young neighbors, on the way home, gratefully feeding off of their seemingly ever flowing energy. Along the dirt road we started talking about traveling, about what my home in the United States was like, and about places they would like to go one day. So questions arose: Were we the fifth and sixth United States Americans that the villagers had ever met? How do we represent the US, much less the complexity of the reality and romanticized memory of our home? Previous volunteers in this village had come from California and Florida. We were from the rural and urban South. How do we represent our country? What is our home? I described my home and then asked whether either would want to go to the United States one day.

"Haaa!" Mia laughed. "What, so they will chain me up as a slave?"

When I asked what she meant, her younger sister, Ella, explained to me that black people who look like them get locked up in slavery in America. Knowing they had several relatives in the Netherlands, I asked whether they would want to go and visit there one day.

"Oh, sure," said Ella, "we will love to go to the Netherlands one day."

When I explained that there was no more legal slavery in the United States, Mia paused for a minute and then asked, "Would I be able to live freely in America?"

After realizing the misunderstanding of village girls about slavery in the United States, we incorporated African American history into English classes at the village elementary school. Could the most fitting intercultural educational tool be to sing spirituals together? "Hambone, Hambone" . . . "I'll Fly Away" . . . "Swing Low, Sweet Chariot, Coming Forth to Carry Me Home"? . . . Songs of embodiment and at the same time of fleeing and flying and freedom . . . I encountered difficulties and complexities describing the United States as a place of freedom and equality for all persons: what a mismatch between the ideal and the real! Could my young friends really come to my home country and live freely? How could I understand their perception of the Dutch as a hospitable, tolerant people who would welcome them from Suriname, a former Dutch colony, and their perception of US Americans as intolerant and necessarily oppressive? I was aware of my responsibility to help my friends discern ultimately unclear distinctions between histories and mythologies, between perceptions and actual experiences. What are real and imagined opportunities for intercultural freedom?

Each of the above stories exemplifies a breach in intercultural understanding around subthemes of private property, child discipline, menstruation, and history. Each raised deeper questions about cross-contextual, communal consequences of a betrayal of trust, about colonial representation, about hospitality in the midst of conflict and crisis, and about the role of questions in clarifying misunderstanding. Each story activates intercultural tensions and translation work already providing the substrate of meaningful intercultural partnership.

These experiences were both moving and disturbing. I had become comfortable (too comfortable?) with the achievement of provisional intercultural understanding that had already far surpassed my expectations and imagination. While I regularly experienced a somewhat uncomfortable and at the same time invigorating shift in understanding—a new insight (learning new layers of meaning with respect to language, literally at the level of words, phrases, intonation, and naming)—experiencing this shift within the texture of intercultural friendship was somehow more shocking. I learned and remembered that I understand neither myself nor the community that I encountered.[7] Drawing on Turner, I describe these above experiences as starting with breaches—simultaneously helpful and

---

7. In her ethnography of class representations among high school girls, Julie Bettie realized that "the uncertainty I felt about representing Mexican-American girls' lives led me to believe that I had a false sense of security about my ability to represent white voices" (Bettie, *Women without Class*, 25). Bettie cautions against overconfidence in claiming to know or understand the meaning and reality of the experience of any person or group, including myself and the groups in which I claim membership.

uncomfortable instances that open partners in intercultural relationships to deeper levels of mutual understanding. Fertile, disruptive experiences of intercultural crisis in understanding provoke new questions.

How do we hear, interpret, and tell stories in a postcolonial context? *Whose history explains the embrace of the Dutch and fear of United States citizens by Mia and Ella?* How do power and position affect representations that then come to define what we think of as the actual past? How does the power of strategic historical dehumanization influence identity construction over time, from colonial pasts to hoped-for decolonized futures?[8] *Whose history is behind MaLespeki's protection of sacred space against the white man?* How do we come to represent gendered, raced human beings to each other? How do I recognize and lament these trappings and live in relationships interculturally, recognizing limits to understanding? How was I to reconcile my interpersonal interactions with MaLespeki and my role educating about her to a group of other women? How does our disruptive, transformative exchange reveal kinds of poverty that result from the legacy of colonial dehumanization? Whose cultural values trump in examining situations of conflicting norms? On what grounds? Who negotiates values across cultures, and how? How do intercultural misunderstandings encompass and cross spheres of private and public—guarded and open—spaces, property, and senses of home?

Questions flow in the midst of breaches in intercultural understanding, and even more so in subsequent reflection on misunderstanding stories. These questions prompt academic struggle with claims on space and representations of space as owned and powerful. How I think about history is deeply connected to how I think about physical space. This connection is especially pertinent to those who have been made to be a wandering people and yet who have staked firm claims on foreign grounds and continue to establish generative lifestyles of survival there. Saakiki women still bury their placentas in the ground, living with this land for now while remembering how other lands and sacred burials have been taken from them over and over again across time and space.

---

8. It is important to note that both interpenetrations of time and our ideas about linear time influence how we construct and structure lived experience (see Connolly, *Pluralism*). Fanon defines *decolonization* as "the encounter between two congenitally antagonistic forces that in fact owe their singularity to the kind of reification secreted and nurtured by the colonial situation" (Fanon, *The Wretched of the Earth*, 2).

CONTEXTUAL UNDERSTANDING:
THE EXAMPLE OF SURINAME

Modern European histories describe the Republic of Suriname on the northern coast of South America as a place rooted in colonialism and plantation-based slave labor. From British to Spanish Jewish to Dutch colonialism, this history bears witness to interpersonal violence and in-equality in the forms of slavery, indentured servitude, and entrenched race-based social hierarchies. While geographically part of continental South America, Suriname participates in Caribbean culture. Suriname has hosted Carifesta, the Caribbean Festival of the Arts, and participates in Caricom, the Caribbean Community and Common Market.

Suriname, formerly Dutch Guiana, was founded in 1651 by the British and ceded in 1667 to the Dutch in exchange for what is today Manhattan, New York.[9] Independent from the Dutch rule since 1975, diverse Surinamese peoples still negotiate historically submissive roles in relation to the former so-called mother country, both within and outside Suriname's borders. The dehumanizing orientation, described later in the chapter as the *gaze*, of the former master over the formerly colonized and presumably weak servant survives political independence and formal na-tional equality. In name, Suriname has developed from undiscovered land to prosperous colony to struggling, independent, so-called Third World country to now part of the global South. This hierarchical trajectory can mask continued struggle. For the bountiful natural resources within its land and waterways, many outside, powerful nations clearly view the small country of Suriname as a place of exploitation for the sake of im-mense economic wealth.[10]

The MoiKonde people are one of many communal groups who have been displaced numerous times throughout their cultural history. Violent-ly forced from Western Africa to the colonies for slave labor, these "wild Negros" or "Maroons" were separated from their families and dispersed onto plantations, rebelled, and were then exiled in the Amazon rainforest, becoming migratory in response to intense sustained military campaigns against them. During the same historical period (in marked contrast to MoiKonde, but not surprisingly), Dutch immigrants to New York describe thorough efforts to maintain their own familial structures, professions,

9. Price and Price, *Stedman's Surinam*, xi–xii; Walsh and Gannon, *Time Is Short*, 37; Resch, *Only in Holland*, 114; Wekker, *The Politics of Passion*.

10. For example, ALCOA and Cambior represent just two multinational mining companies with stakes in Surinamese land.

and even household belongings so that their experience mirrored the experience of people residing in Holland.[11]

According to postcolonial theorist and literary critic Jenny Sharpe, "the term *Maroon* is believed to be derived from *cimarrón*, a Spanish term for 'wild' or 'untamed' originally used for domestic cattle that had escaped into the bush."[12] Writing in 1917, Thomas E. Penard describes Maroons: "There are . . . so-called *Boschnegers* (Bush Negros), descendents of Negros who escaped from slavery in the early days, and, in defiance of the authorities of the time, set up independent communities in the wilderness, retaining many of their African customs and beliefs."[13] Penard goes on to invite his colleagues to explore this culture, not from the "hardships," "dangers," "wildness," and "practically unknown" interior, but from the comforts of the capital city, where, according to him, emancipated slaves retain authentically Maroon customs and beliefs. Tensions remain to this day between descendents of escaped slaves in the "interior" villages and descendents of emancipated slaves in the capital city of present-day Suriname.

Throughout recorded Surinamese history, one finds evidence of the colonial tool of inciting tensions between colonized groups of people. As early as the seventeenth century, colonial powers pitted the Afro-Surinamese against each other for the sake of so-called individual freedom and the fulfillment of basic needs.[14] Anthropologists Richard and Sally Price, who devote their academic careers to ethnography of Maroon history, culture, and art in Suriname and French Guiana, record the earliest political independence of Surinamese Maroons, who were granted "freedom" in exchange for turning against "future Maroons":

> In 1760 and 1762, the two largest groups of maroons (the Ndjuka and the Saramaka, settled along the upper Marowijne and Suriname rivers, respectively) had won their independence by treaty, after a century long guerrilla war against the colonists. But the succeeding decade witnessed unexpected and lively hostilities involving newer maroon groups that lived just beyond the borders of the flourishing Cottica and Commewijne plantations, trapped between the slave societies of the coast and the

11. Singleton, *Dutch New York*.

12. Sharpe, *Ghosts of Slavery*, 4.

13. Penard, "Surinam Folk-Tales"; online: http://www.zoonomen.net/bio/biop .html/, which notes that Penard was born in Suriname and immigrated to the United States.

14. Fanon recognizes this as a common colonizing strategy (*The Wretched of the Earth*, 107).

free Ndjukas and Saramakas (who, as part of their treaties, were pledged to turn over to the colonists any new maroons they encountered).[15]

Colonial military officer John Gabriel Stedman, whose journals provide a historical narrative of colonialism in Suriname, considered this kind of "forced friendship" to be dangerous in that the Ndjukas and Saramakas were provoked to violent rebellion against torturous enslavement by the very same Europeans who now sought their trust via this treaty.[16] Stedman also describes the "Neeger Vrijcorps," a group of slaves who were given various forms of payment, including their freedom, in exchange for their participation in military exercises against neighboring Maroons. Stedman recounts battles between freed and escaped slaves that included seemingly endless strings of exchanged insults.[17] In my experience, verbal insults remain an important part of conflict *and* conflict resolution among present-day Saakiki contexts.

The aforementioned treaty forced freed Ndjukas and Saramakas to vow to remain ever at a "proper distance" from the city and the wealthy populous.[18] Stedman described victories against Maroons that rooted them out of their place, never allowing them to return to their "same spot."[19] According to colonial history, Surinamese Maroons divided into six tribes that correspond to African ancestry and hiding "spots" in the Amazon: Saramaka, Matawai, Kwinti, Ndjuka, Aluku, and Paramaka.[20] Outside powers have continued to displace the tribes from spot to spot throughout time.

In the 1960s, the American aluminum company ALCOA built a hydroelectric dam that created a huge reservoir and forced many Surinamese Maroon communities to relocate to government-established transmigrated villages. At this time, MoiKonde formed as a site of relocation where Aukans came to live in closer proximity to Saramakan villages, resulting in the emergence of Saakiki as a slightly different

15. Price and Price, *Stedman's Surinam*, xix.

16. Stedman, *Stedman's Surinam*, 27.

17. Ibid., 214–15.

18. Ibid., 32.

19. Ibid., 220.

20. Price and Price, *Co-wives and Calabashes*, xxix–xxxi. Price and Price use the term *djuka*, which I have changed to the more respectful *ndjuka*. Literally, *djuka* translates to *dju kaka* or "feces of the Jewish slave master." While this term is still used in Suriname today, *ndjuka* is the preferred linguistic adaptation to talk about the same cultural group (see Shanks, *A Buku fu Okanisi anga Ingiisi Wowtu*).

language. Before the land was flooded, Americans John Walsh and Robert Gannon were sent by international animal-protection agencies to save thousands of animals from the floodwaters in and around villages that were soon to be submerged permanently. When they visited a forcibly relocated transmigrated village for the first time, they noted with shock, "The new settlement no longer looks like a Bushnegro village . . . no longer did the people take pride in *their* village. It wasn't theirs; it was the government's."[21] Visually, transmigration villages differ from traditional villages in that standard-issue village houses are organized in long, straight rows rather than in family clusters.

Oral histories of the Saakiki record cultural intermingling between Aukans (Ndjukans), who were forced to live in transmigration villages, and Saramakans, who were already living in villages surrounding the transmigration sites. MoiKonde villagers trace familial lineages to a point of higher elevation that was not flooded by the ALCOA dam, which is still home to three densely populated villages across the humanmade lake (named Prof. W. J. van Blommestein Meer) from the relocated transmigration villages. We lived in community with a transmigration village that traces its familial linkages to villages across the reservoir. Traveling by motorized dugout canoe across the humanmade lake requires a highly skilled driver who can navigate through what used to be the forest canopy that now reaches just above the water level. The canoe navigates the skeletal canopy where thousands of dead trees stick out of the water and serve as a powerful reminder of what has been displaced and buried beneath.

As recently as the late 1980s, Afro-Surinamese groups fought each other to their mutual detriment.[22] A politically motivated civil war continued to pit Surinamese Maroons against each other, resulting yet again in devastation and death throughout the interior of Suriname. In spite of their repeated forced displacements, the Saakiki value land and cultivate relationships with the land through ritual. Embodying an African cosmological understanding that the physically dead continue to participate in community with the physically living, the Saakiki engage in elaborate ritual, especially in transitional times, in relation to embodied life.[23] Ritual

---

21. Walsh and Gannon, *Time Is Short*, 51–52.

22. See Brana-Shute, "Love among the Ruins," 198. See also "The World Factbook: Suriname."

23. Jackson, "Remembering the 'Disremembered,'" 140–41. Norton provides an account of Saramaka ritualized placenta burial (*U Da Sembe Fa Aki*, 117–23). Sally Price's work with Saramaka women illuminates ways in which Saramaka places are gendered (Price and Price, *Co-wives and Calabashes*, especially chapter 2). See also

acts "symbolize the connection of people to places and also establish a connection to past, present, and future generations of the community (as a place and as a group)."[24] Yet, debates over rights to ever increasingly valuable land, rich with natural resources such as gold, rare timber, and medicines, threaten to dislocate Saakiki communities once again, exacerbating complex present-day postcolonial problems rooted in unjust colonial social structures.

RECOUNTED COLONIAL HISTORIES
AS "THE HISTORY"

The preceding section summarizes European history of Surinamese Maroon communities. Yet, activities of writing and reading history are necessarily representational and therefore plural rather than singular. In the foreword to a newly released volume on the 2009 Quadricentennial celebrations commemorating Henry Hudson's "discovery" of the Hudson River, Russell Shorto envisions how concrete historical texts mediate the interaction between authors and readers. He writes, "The role of the historian is to deliver the past into the present. The reader takes it from there."[25] What happens in the experience of this hand-off? The metaphor points to an activity in which historians "simply [hand] over intact" packaged material from a past generation to a future reader.[26] Histories evoke memories and make new interpretations and connections possible. The editor of this volume considers "ways historical reexamination becomes a vehicle for the transmission of cultural values."[27] This text and others, such as Edward Said's classic *Orientalism*, reexamine history from a perspective of power, or from above.[28]

In the effort to understand colonial histories, we must consider the interplay between stories, storytellers, and readers. Rather than disputing history fact by fact, a hermeneutic of suspicion is helpful in challenging

---

Thoden van Velzen and van Wetering, *In the Shadow of the Oracle*; and Kalilombe, "Spirituality in the African Perspective" that all discuss place as negotiated between the visible embodied humans and invisible yet ever-present ancestors.

24. Norton, *U Da Sembe Fa Aki*, 138.

25. Panetta, *Dutch New York*, xii.

26. *A Dictionary of Education*.

27. Panetta, *Dutch New York*, 2–3.

28. Said, *Orientalism*.

the illusion of a "disinterested history 'for its own sake.'"[29] For example, historical texts often use the categories of colonizer and colonized at the same time that they deconstruct "unstable boundaries" between these categories.[30] According to biblical scholar Wayne Meeks, "We cannot help making up the best history we can." He argues that we make up history in order to "assist the Logos of God" to respond in a world of suffering.[31] Rather than simply delivering packages given by one generation and offered (or marketed) to another, we participate in the unfolding construction of histories. This unfolding happens in and between cultures. Rather than a one-way delivery, stories transform storytellers, audiences, and communal understandings of the past, present, and imagined futures.

Histories are told, unearthed, lamented, retold, and embodied. Pragmatist theories connecting knowledge and histories have influenced pastoral theology as the study of psychology and religion that begins in storied experiences of suffering. For example, Charles Sanders Peirce valued doubt as the beginning of all learning. Valuing doubt recognizes inevitable possibilities of error and suggests practices of self-correction. Peirce urged attending to the "irritation of doubt" to resist tendencies to fix knowledge in complete, unquestioning ways.[32] William James, a pragmatist who helped develop modern psychology, claimed that knowledge is always mediated rather than immediately accessible. In other words, facts are always interpreted and experienced through and in light of particular individual and communal values, resulting in communal and experiential processes of discerning meaning.[33] Because "pure" facts are absolutely inaccessible, James encouraged questioning the consequences of our actions and interpretations as a measure of the truth of our knowledge. John Dewey, another pragmatist and contributor to modern forms of Western education, recognized our common desire for "perfect certainty" and suggested investigating the case(s) at hand via moral inquiry.[34] However, like James, Dewey imagined that we train our vision not only for responding to this particular moment but also for thinking critically about conse-

29. Crossley, "Defining History," 10.

30. Dube, *Stitches on Time*, 13–14.

31. Meeks, "Assisting the World," 151–62.

32. Peirce, *The Collected Papers of Charles Sanders Peirce*. See also James, *Pragmatism*, 29; Anderson, "Peirce Again."

33. On fact-value distinction, see James, *Varieties of Religious Experience*, 21–24; Carrette, "The Return to James," xxxix–lxiii. For James's pragmatic method see James, *Pragmatism*, 28, 30, 43, 97.

34. See Dewey, *Quest for Certainty*.

quences that interpretations hold for future action.[35] Peirce, James, and Dewey each emphasized the value of experience as an important source of unfolding knowledge.

Pragmatism, scholarship on history, pastoral theologies, current trends in narrative ethics and therapies, and postcolonial theories emphasize interplay between histories and memories.[36] So does Victor Turner, who cautioned Western scholars to be more explicit in recognizing that "we never cease to learn our *own* culture, which is always changing, let alone other cultures."[37] Turner interpreted cultures using his concept of the social drama, in which play and improvisation generate narratives from experiences of breach that initiate intercultural crises in mutual understanding.[38] In relation to personal experiences, scholar James Crossley claims that "the fragmentation of history has opened the way to studying the history of almost anything and everything on their own terms, from slaves to the mental construction of landscape."[39] Postcolonial theories rewrite and reimagine narrative possibilities in order to correct exaggerations and oppressive projections that infantilize, hyper-sexualize, and even demonize "primitive" persons and cultures.

We can also look to more explicitly postcolonial perspectives to better understand the interactions between stories, readers, and storytellers that undergird colonial histories as conditions for lingering postcolonial struggle. For example, Frantz Fanon also resists the notion of history as gift passively received from accredited historians:

> The problem considered here is one of time . . . I will not make myself the man of any past. I do not want to exalt the past at the expense of my present and of my future . . . I am not a prisoner of history. I should not seek there for the meaning of my destiny . . . No attempt must be made to encase man, for it is his destiny to be set free . . . The body of history does not determine a single one of my actions. I am my own foundation. And it is by

35. Dewey, *Quest for Certainty*, 67–73.

36. For at least twenty-five years pastoral theology has envisioned human beings and personal experiences as texts that matter for both method and practice (Gerkin, *The Living Human Document*). See also such diverse resources as Mucherera, *Meet Me at the Palaver*; Neuger, *Counseling Women*; Wimberly, *African American Pastoral Care*; Charon, *Narrative Medicine*; Talburt, "Ethnographic Responsibility without the 'Real,'" 80–103.

37. Turner, "Social Dramas and Stories about Them," 144.

38. Ibid., 157.

39. Crossley, "Defining History," 9.

going beyond the historical, instrumental hypothesis that I will initiate the cycle of my freedom . . . That it be possible for me to discover and to love man, wherever he may be . . . Why not the quite simple attempt to touch the other, to feel the other, to explain the other to myself?[40]

Fanon rightly demands a voice in representing his person and his story. He resists being "overdetermined from without" by colonizing representations. Drawing on Fanon and developmental psychological theories, pastoral theologian Tapiwa Mucherera charts how indigenous peoples have been portrayed in history from sources of intrigue to the wretched of the earth when "the colonizers forgot they were the foreigners."[41] Together, we must face the problem that a singular illusion of colonialism in world history was published without respect for the voices of the many people unjustly and violently colonized. Religion played a vital role in masking injustice and violence by appealing to the worth of advancing civilization through mission.[42] Postcolonial theorists like Fanon need to be heard and respected. Fanon's work teaches how to unmask violence that many, appealing to published texts, seem to consider over with colonial independence.

Postcolonial theories point to the interplay between histories and memories that unfolds in culture(s) and that is usually mediated through published texts, even a text like the book you are reading. The aims and consequences of this interplay turn on questions around voice. Responsible writing that respects postcolonial criticism must be explicit about the tensions and dangers of writing both historically and today. For example, postcolonial theories focus on habituated reading practices and institutionalized assumptions about genre, literature, and writing itself.[43] These theories are postcolonial in that they point to the literal and literary ways in which "cultural production . . . engages, in one way or another, with the enduring reality of colonial power."[44] Feminist political theorist Uma Narayan defines a *colonialist representation* as "one that replicates problematic aspects of Western representations of Third-World nations and

---

40. Fanon, *Black Skin, White Masks*, 226–31.

41. Mucherera, *Meet me at the Palaver*, 3.

42. Narayan, *Dislocating Cultures;* Grau, *Rethinking Mission in the Postcolony.*

43. Ashcroft et al., *The Empire Writes Back*, 186–87. See also King, *Orientalism and Religion.*

44. Ashcroft et al., *The Empire Writes Back*, 195.

communities, aspects that have their roots in the history of colonization."[45] Narayan points to history as both problem and source of lingering "pro-colonial" stances, particularly the most dangerous kinds that are masked as good will from above without any hint of uncertainty or reflective engagement with on-the-ground relationships and accompanying diverse perspectives.[46] Narayan reexamines historical texts to reveal particular cultural practices that have been reified in dehumanizing colonialist representations as timeless, natural, Third-World ways of life with undertones of Western moral and cultural superiority.[47]

Practical theologian Stephen Pattison recognizes that "in practical theology, heavily influenced by the social sciences, postmodernism and liberation theology, there is no such thing as a view from nowhere, a text without a context, subtext or pretext, or an essay without an author formed of dust and social forces."[48] Yet, we could do more to emphasize the political nature of the way we remember narratives—our own and those of others with whom we inhabit the world. Oppressive political agendas shape histories and collective memories. We all participate in the politics of structural forgetting.[49] Theologians, such as womanist theologian Katie Cannon, call for an "emancipatory historiography" that directs historical analysis toward a more profound understanding for a more accurate and thus liberative remembering.[50] As part of structural strategies of forgetting, memories become "tucked away in family and local history" in a way that lives on and can be recovered.[51] A key strategy of dehumanization is to invest in habits of forgetting in order to mask that these habits often work to justify violence.[52] How are the forgotten within dominant narratives remembered? Postcolonial theories urge the following task: "work to remember the forgotten so that those traditionally marginalized in history should no longer be seen merely as a "problem" to be solved for those with power. History from below shows how people participate in making

45. Narayan, *Dislocating Cultures*, 45.

46. Ibid.; see especially chapter 2, "Restoring History and Politics to 'Third World Traditions.'" See also Cole, "The White Savior Industrial Complex."

47. Narayan, *Dislocating Cultures*.

48. Pattison, *The Challenge of Practical Theology*, 13.

49. For example, see Frazier, *Memory, Violence, and the Nation-State in Chile*, 85–116; Freire, *Pedagogy of the Oppressed*.

50. Cannon, "Emancipatory Historiography," 81.

51. Frazier, *Memory, Violence, and the Nation-State in Chile*, 86.

52. Mitchell, *Plantations and Death Camps*, 32–33, 64–66.

their own history, participate in creating their own identity, and can even participate in shaping broader ideals and attitudes."[53]

Pastoral theologians have long viewed persons as living human texts embodying narratives of resilience. A postcolonial pastoral theology recognizes the importance of remembering and validating memory in relation to lived experiences as vital to a contextual (and unfixed) understanding of histories. Speaking of histories in the plural is a resistive strategy of remembering and respecting the voices, agendas, and risks constantly negotiated in telling historical stories.

COLONIAL LEGACIES: HISTORIES, MEMORIES, AND RITUALS

The misunderstanding stories sparked by breaches in intercultural understanding described above occurred in a small Surinamese Maroon village in the Amazon Rainforest in Suriname. The village is a community of descendents of West African slaves of Dutch plantation owners who have been literally uprooted time and time again throughout their cultural history. Despite relentless colonizing efforts, MoiKonde endures the poverty and harsh conditions that accompany continual oppression and marginalization. I lived in MoiKonde, a Saakiki village, in a role afforded to me by my privilege and power as a representative of the United States government. As a Peace Corps volunteer, I participated in the luxury of choosing to live in the impoverished village at the local level of income knowing that I could at any time radio a helicopter to take me *home*. Yet, the Saakiki people of MoiKonde invited us, white United States Americans, into their midst to share in a two-year encounter that affected both me and the village.

A description of a people's complex physical and cultural history raises questions of recognition, representation, and resistance. Remembering intercultural experiences prompts questioning *whose history is operative in everyday lived reality*. Postcolonial theories help Western academics see ways in which colonial histories have been much more about making the West than about "discoveries" of "new" lands and peoples.[54] The history of Suriname presented in the previous section referred to modern European history published in English, relying on Stedman's colonial journal

---

53. Crossley, "Defining History," 22. See also Chambers, *Whose Reality Counts?*; Spivak, *Thinking Academic Freedom in Gendered Post-Coloniality.*

54. See Fanon, *The Wretched of the Earth*, 15, 53, 58, 157.

and modern interpretations of it. My depiction of Surinamese history also draws from Saakiki oral histories. Both of these sources are important; neither is complete nor independently authoritative.

Recognition of multiple sources points to a tension between postmodernism and projects of respecting and participating in recovering absent, invisible, and oppressed voices. Postmodernists warn academics to resist hegemonic master narratives as necessarily incomplete accounts that privilege the experiences of the powerful, exclude diverse voices, and perpetuate myths of fixed identities.[55] We must participate in the important unfinished task of trying to recover alternative accounts of histories in protest and response to colonizing textual and visual representations. This often includes intentional, engaged silence in order to hear or overhear voices so long unheard. Representing history automatically problematizes a sense of "the" (or certainly ownership of "the") definitive history. Narrative practices, such as multiple tellings, can also resist the idea of a final, complete history.

In the context of Surinamese Maroon histories, using psychoanalytic film theory and Stedman's representation of black slave bodies found in the drawings and plates that populate his lengthy journals, literary scholar Mario Klarer "unearths" eighteenth-century techniques for representing stories in particular ways for particular ends.[56] Klarer argues that through detailed representations, Stedman aligns with other narrative efforts of his time to focus readers' attention on "erotically charged black female slaves punished by cruel overseers."[57] The reader is invited to partake in the *gaze*, becoming an "agent of power" who is assured of "*his* sense of completeness [and therefore has] a deeply pleasurable experience" of reading.[58] Klarer emphasizes the *gaze* as gendered: the white male reads white male representations of voiceless, suffering, tortured black females as a beautiful brokenness. Ironically, Klarer identifies Stedman's invitation to readers to "*see* the '*real* thing'" happening in Suriname as part of his larger project of "compassion for the oppressed, exploited, and tortured African slaves."[59] Klarer explains that Stedman's technique of representation serves

55. For example, see Loomba, *Colonialism/Postcolonialism*, 204–12; Dirlik, "Reading Ashis Nandy," 266; Young, *Postcolonialism*; Farley, *Deep Symbols*.

56. Klarer, "Humanitarian Pornography," 570.

57. Ibid., 562.

58. Ibid., 562, 564, 570, emphasis mine.

59. Ibid., 571–73 (italics added). Others link art to representation of actual social contexts, particularly of Dutch visual artistic renderings of blackness (see Blakely, *Blacks in the Dutch World*, 79–81).

to persuade fellow colonizers to join the abolition movement by "mak[ing] people look [and] bringing human misery to people's attention."[60]

While Klarer works to unearth previously silenced stories and narrators, he does not confront the connections between pain and pleasure that he digs up. Rather than "bring[ing] the dead back to life," feminist postcolonial theorist Gayatri Chakravorty Spivak argues that "the unlamented corpses of colonized cultures must be lamented anew" by women, who traditionally lead communal practices of mourning.[61] Here we remember MaLespeki's gender reversal with her reference to white men as agents of continued colonialism, even when speaking to a group exclusively of women. As a white woman, I must consciously negotiate tensions about voice and representation that MaLespeki raises for all of us. I am simultaneously colluding and trying to partner so as to resist collusion. This is one way of understanding the difficulty of mutual listening in our postcolonial contexts.

Along with Klarer, Spivak recognizes the tragedy in which glorifying and *gazing* upon past tortures perpetuates colonial ends. Tragic images that describe broken black (usually women's) bodies as beautiful continue to pervade mixed media.[62] For example, a recent exhibit at the Metropolitan Museum of Art includes John Greenwood's "Sea Captains Carousing in Surinam" as one of several formative "American Stories." The *New York Times* identifies this painting, depicting naked black women serving finely clothed white men, as a comic painting.[63] The 2009 exhibit "keeps slavery—the most irreducible fact of American history—before us in ways that illuminate both past and present."[64] Spivak takes the crucial ethical step of calling for academic responsibility: stories must not only be unearthed but also lamented. She argues that even if global liberation for all were realized, there would still be an urgent need to rewrite cultural history from below.[65]

60. Klarer, "Humanitarian Pornography," 574.

61. Spivak, *Thinking Academic Freedom in Gendered Post-Coloniality*, 17, 28. Fanon observes this same loss: "The classic mourning tears are hardly any longer to be found in Algeria" (Fanon, *A Dying Colonialism*, 117).

62. Sharpley-Whiting, *Black Venus*. On gendered and raced representations, note controversy around the depiction of Lebron James as the first black man on the cover of *Vogue* magazine. See, for example, Associated Press, "LeBron James' 'Vogue' Cover."

63. Smith, "One Nation, in Broad Strokes."

64. Ibid.

65. Spivak, *Thinking Academic Freedom in Gendered Post-Coloniality*, 8–9.

Traditional accounts of slave women's agency in Suriname also need to be unearthed and lamented as a key part of provisional cross-contextual understanding. Jenny Sharpe considers slave women's stories to be buried within histories recorded by powerful white male masters. She employs the metaphor of ghost to voice stories into survival and views her task to include digging stories out of recorded histories to give them a "proper burial." She argues that "slavery continues to haunt the present because its stories, particularly those of slave women, have been improperly buried."[66] Sharpe introduces the modern reader to Afro-Caribbean slave women's narratives that move "between past and present, history and fiction."[67] In his review of modern black writers and slavery in Latin America, author Richard Jackson refers to this kind of movement as an "African mythology . . . that breaks down walls between the past and the present, between the living and the dead, between fact and fiction, and between myth and reality."[68] Like Sharpe, Jackson urges recovering stories to disrupt what we in the West have been taught to think of as fixed forms of linear time and space.

Postcolonial theorists, scholar-activists, and hundreds of thousands of people around the world work toward what Fanon called decolonization:[69] "No attempt must be made to encase [humanity], for it is [humanity's] destiny to be set free. The body of history does not determine a single one of my actions. I am my own foundation. And it is by going beyond the historical, instrumental hypothesis that I will initiate the cycle of my freedom."[70]

Tensions surface within Fanon's liberative declaration. Just as we must ask whose history is this history, deconstructive and restorative efforts must also avoid throwing dirt over actual experiences with neither proper respect nor communal lamentation. While "I am my own foundation" expresses a right to self-determination that Fanon advocates must

66. Sharpe, *Ghosts of Slavery*, xi.

67. Ibid., xii.

68. Jackson, "Remembering the 'Disremembered,'" 141. Other sympathetic points of view attend to "walls" between fact and fiction for the sake of comparing structures of historical or ahistorical "selves." Ashis Nandy argues that the difference is how human beings access and construct memories (Nandy, "Themes of State, History, and Exile in South Asian Politics," 160).

69. Hawken, "To Remake the World." For examples, from the 1950s through post-9/11 reports, of particular groups who claim inspiration from Fanon, see Bhabha, "Foreword," vii–xli.

70. Fanon, *Black Skin, White Masks*, 230–31.

be taken if not given, we humans are still historical, contextual, storied peoples with fallible memories. We are *caught* in communities of thickly intertwined liberative and oppressive systems.[71]

PROCESS OF TELLING MISUNDERSTANDING STORIES: SURRENDER-AND-CATCH

Intercultural misunderstanding occurs within relationships oriented toward understanding in the presence of differences. When we human beings try to connect in meaningful and not so meaningful ways, we miss each other. This can lead to crises of identities and the resultant feeling that the future of our web of relationality is somehow threatened. Yet, risking breaches in understanding is ingredient in committing to intercultural relationships in the first place. Just after the time period in which Fanon was writing, radical sociologist Kurt Wolff offered a puzzling theory of the risks involved in relationships in *Surrender and Catch*.[72] These theorists make an interesting pair relevant to postcolonial challenges today. According to Wolff, to participate in intercultural relationships is surrender, which is, to the extent possible, to anticipate that disruptive moments will happen and will require a particular kind of participation. We must pause to recognize that surrender is a precarious theological concept and practice in a postcolonial context that recognizes that surrender has been misused in the name of religion to collude in dehumanization of women and "other objects" of missionary pursuit.[73] I contend that, with this caveat in mind, Wolff's idea of surrender-and-catch can help frame retelling of misunderstanding stories that depends upon the mutual respect oriented to the possibility of mutual understanding that Fanon cries out for above.

According to Wolff, surrender-and-catch suggests both a framework of attending to a breach in understanding *and* an interpretive framework following a breach in understanding. Surrendering to disruptions—in Turner's terms, being in the raw experience while being caught in the convergence of memories, histories, and imagined futures—involves six

71. For example, the academy tends to keep trying to capture experience by writing words and speaking languages to the exclusion of other perhaps more performative or embodied forms that might not be recognized as legitimate or reputable scholarship. And yet, theologically, the written word often symbolizes a site of embodied communion.

72. Wolff, *Surrender and Catch*.

73. Miller-McLemore, "Practising What We Preach," 51–52; Grau, *Rethinking Mission in the Postcolony*.

embodied practices of attention. First, I can expect to be totally involved or caught up in the occasion of surrendering at the point of disruption and caught up in myself, my act or state, and my partner. Second, I can expect to be required to put my assumptions into question when I experience a new insight as disruptive. Third, everything within my awareness becomes connected to the experience of disruption. Fourth, I can expect that I will try to identify with anything and everything I can imagine that *must*, in this occasion, be known, understood, considered. I will want to know more and will think that knowing more will help me understand better and more quickly. Fifth, I can expect that with this intense level of participation with others oriented toward mutual understanding, I risk being hurt, and I risk hurting. Sixth, I can expect to be caught up paradoxically in *cognitive love* in which in the immediacy of my wanting to know more (*not* to master but to learn with) and to understand more, I can expect to be "thrown back" on what I really am, which is what I share with every other person.[74] Here, the goal of more knowledge and more understanding is for the purpose of embodied learning, which is inherently morally demanding because it suggests that *I* will be moved in the process in relation to *you*. Philosopher Richard Zaner points to forms of false surrender: surrender aborted, as when an idea of value has too great a hold on the would-be surrenderer to let itself be suspended or questioned; or surrender betrayed, wherein too much is surrendered, including even the possibility of surrender itself.[75]

The "catch" is that surrender is unpredictable but happens in the ongoing flow of relationships. "The 'catch' is that there are simply no ways of commanding its occurrence; and it can neither be willed, nor reasoned into happening."[76] On one hand, misunderstanding stories merely instantiate tensions always and already present around differing norms, values, and conceptions of space, place, and time. On the other hand, misunderstanding stories surprise me when breaches in understanding emerge in the midst of what I experience as mutual intercultural partnership. Disruptions *move* us in the midst of otherwise sustained, committed connections. Considered in the framework of surrender-and-catch, both disruptions and connections can honor rather than collapse differences. The catch is both a bind (i.e., a "catch-22") and an experience of being caught up in disruption.

74. Reframed from Zaner, "The Disciplining of Reason's Cunning," 373–75.
75. Zaner, "The Disciplining of Reason's Cunning," 373–75.
76. Ibid., 375.

Through intercultural surrender-and-catch, participants play a part in creating new possibilities (and receiving a being-created-ness).[77] Paradoxically, being caught calls me to pause even as it begs for a response. Active response comes not as intentional orientation to do something but to relax these intentions by pausing to ask questions, open to learning. For example, when students start to recognize and name dimensions of their previously unacknowledged privilege in the seminary classroom setting, this is often a disruptive experience. One seminary student recently asked what he should do to know whether he was being unintentionally harmful in his use of language in his reference to persons whose identity differs from his own. What we have to do is to ask, to bear to stay engaged in conversation while bearing to hear the response, and to be caught up in what follows. Wolff invites us into wonder: a breach in understanding disrupts *me*, and *I* must share with *you*. The unstable surrender-and-catch makes new understanding necessary, urgent, and possible. It is a wonder to ponder the possibilities of communicating understanding and understanding communication across cultural differences:[78] "Cognitive love thus at its root assumes the form of questioning: asking, examining, challenging, doubting, reconnoitering, exploring, sounding-out, rummaging, prying, peering, unearthing—*whatever* it takes to 'find out,' to resolve (i.e., to get *free-from* the not-knowing and thus to become *free-for* genuine knowing and the 'relevant speech and right action' which must then follow)."[79]

Surrender-and-catch recasts social experience by theoretically making room for the fragmentation of the idea of the isolated individual.[80] This profoundly disrupts a stable notion of "the history" by inviting the urgent work of unearthing and lamentation discussed above. In distilling Wolff's theory of surrender-and-catch, Zaner attends to "social arrangements that kill and mutilate millions of human beings and diminish all of us as human beings."[81] To respond actively to the violent categories that pit human beings against other human beings is to participate in relationships in such a way that I risk being caught up in recognizing you as free

---

77. See also Scarry, *The Body in Pain.*

78. See Zaner, "The Disciplining of Reason's Cunning," 382; Wolff, *Surrender and Catch*, 19–31.

79. Zaner, "The Disciplining of Reason's Cunning," 384, italics and parentheses in original.

80. See Wolff, *Surrender and Catch*, 24; Zaner, "The Disciplining of Reason's Cunning," 386.

81. Zaner, "The Disciplining of Reason's Cunning," 369.

to respond or not to respond.[82] Surrender-and-catch recognizes the importance of personal and representational freedom that Fanon identifies as structurally denied to colonized human beings. Yet, careful attention to moving into such of liberating human dignity (fraught with implicit colonialist drives to liberate others) through practices of recognition is needed long after colonial structures of social life have been declared over by treaty, legislation, or pronouncement. This way of seeing can bolster a more liberative framework of understanding the work of partnering.

Surrender-and-catch also recasts the misunderstanding stories described above as intercultural experiences of being caught by *and* caught up in breaches in understanding. Consider the following four stories from my experience as a Peace Corps volunteer in community with neighbors in MoiKonde, a small Afro-Surinamese village in the Amazon rainforest of Dutch-speaking Suriname in South America:

When I returned to the MoiKonde, I learned that four of my neighbors' children had been publically beaten and exiled from relationship with me after breaking into my home while I was away. *We were caught in an intercultural, postcolonial crisis.*

When my friend saw her eleven-year-old daughter playing on my porch instead of helping with the evening chores, she angrily reached for my broom. I grabbed the broomstick out of her hand in front of her children before she could strike her daughter with it. *We were caught in an intercultural, postcolonial crisis.*

With permission of village elders, I was identifying sacred markers and taboos to encourage a new group of volunteers to respect sacred spaces and practices. The matriarchal spiritual leader, who was also my neighbor and friend, raised her staff and scolded me for being the white man violating her people once again. *We were caught in an intercultural, postcolonial crisis.*

During the three-mile walk home from an exhausting day of peanut harvesting, I asked some village children about their hopes for their future. They told me they thought they would be successful if they could leave their village, which is in a former Dutch colony, to live in the Netherlands and become fluent in Dutch culture and language. I asked if they would ever want to come to America. They told me that America is a frightening place where they would be forced into slavery and would never be free. *We were caught in an intercultural, postcolonial crisis.*

82. Ibid., 367–69, 388–89.

These misunderstanding stories continue to generate difficult questions about cultural differences around private property, child discipline, cultural taboos, and cultural memories and histories. They point to and exemplify what I call intercultural crises. Framing these complex stories in terms of surrender-and-catch leads to a reformulation of my thesis: *A postcolonial pastoral theology attentive to intercultural crises of understanding involves reimagining classic themes in pastoral theology in conversation with postcolonial theories and with reference to experiences of misunderstanding stories.* In the remaining chapters, I therefore expand classic themes to probe identity crisis (chapter 3), possibilities of shared vulnerability (chapter 4), and intercultural empathy (chapter 5) in relation most prominently to the first misunderstanding story because of its complexity and lengthy process of relational repair. In addition, the breach included both a breach in trust and a breach in understanding the consequences for the future of intercultural life together in partnership.

Pastoral theology needs a more complex conception of culture(s). Postcolonial theories reorient how we attend to suffering by helping us realize some of the ways in which we participate in violence in even well-meaning and thoughtful attempts to engage multiculturalism. Intercultural relationships can also redefine empathy. Here is another reason that pastoral theologians need to engage postcolonial theories. Concrete experiences of intercultural crisis call for theories of empathy that recognize the many intercultural misunderstandings and histories of violence that provide the context for occasional moments of intercultural understanding. Finally, attending to dynamics of intercultural relationships deepens pastoral theological theories of mutuality by widening possibilities for better participation in interpersonal and intercultural justice. Such reimagining requires careful negotiation of multiple roles of story-listener, story-participant, story-interpreter, and storyteller.

To approach shared human experience through the critical lens of surrender-and-catch is to invite the risk of the unknown and predict that the unpredictable awaits. Pastoral theologian Mary Clark Moschella writes that "the very sharing process itself can become a catalyst for greater mutual love and theological commitment."[83] Three years after living in MoiKonde, I returned to the village to seek counsel from Captain. I returned inviting mutual dialogue. I returned to share what I could from my perspective and to invite dialogue to "instigate reciprocal learning,

---

83. Moschella, *Ethnography as a Pastoral Practice*, 215.

growth, and transformation."[84] I was thrown back on myself—*Who am I? Who are we? What am I asking? Why am I here? Why did I leave? Am I resisting seeing the disruptive suffering by idealizing intercultural relationships?*—in the midst of deeply relational cognitive love in community with children, spiritual leaders, MaLespeki, women, friends, and Captain.

My conviction that participating in intercultural relationships matters deeply continues to motivate my writing. To use a methodological metaphor, why ought I continue developing a path along a precarious road filled with predictable and unforeseen pitfalls? First, academic responsibility requires hermeneutical risk. Nancy McWilliams tells the story of D. W. Winnicott claiming that he interprets so that his clients know that he is awake and so that they know he can be wrong.[85] Early liberationist and educator Paulo Freire claims that to wash our hands of the struggle between the powerful and the powerless is not to be neutral but to side with the powerful.[86] Perhaps the question is not whether to participate but how. Reflection with commitment yields insight and hope of more complex, even mutually transforming, interactions.[87] A method that attends to postcoloniality—without reducing intercultural experiences to one particular understanding to be fit into my method, but considering it an orientation to questions that open method to new and more liberative possibilities—is one oriented toward learning "from below" that resists claiming an expert position in applying individualistic, achievement-oriented, abstract knowledge "from above." The above stories of intercultural misunderstanding embody the complex legacy of colonialism within my lived experiences and relationships of friendship. Suriname is a postcolonial context of shared lived experience. However, historical interpretations "from above" are continually in play with lived experience across diverse contexts.

IMPLICATIONS FOR A POSTCOLONIAL PASTORAL THEOLOGY

As a pastoral theologian, I see the field in relationship to shared experiences in intercultural community with Mia, Ella, MaLespeki, and my neighbors, friends, and partners living together in MoiKonde. There is no

84. Ibid., 214.

85. McWilliams, *Psychoanalytic Case Formulation*.

86. Freire, *Pedagogy of the Oppressed*.

87. Graham, *Transforming Practice*.

question that the field must move toward more communal and intercultural models, theories, theologies, and practices. However, according to Joretta Marshall, the communal-contextual paradigm has a ways to go and the intercultural paradigm in the field of pastoral theology is just emerging.[88] We have work to speak more boldly about "'unspeakable' things in classrooms, in scholarship, and in the church with a language that is clear and compelling, yet open to possibilities that are not yet seen."[89] The shift to a broader and more complex understanding of care practices suggests that persons cannot understand one another without attending to our multiple contextual connections and disconnections in relation to partnering within and across familial, institutional, historical, and cultural differences. It is time for a pastoral theological engagement with our current situation of postcoloniality. I write this book out of the school of pastoral theology that considers theology and psychology in dialogue.[90] Pastoral theology occupies a particular place within theological studies. It is not applied theology. It is a theological commitment to prioritize human suffering as a source for theological reflection. Pastoral theology adopts an interdisciplinary method of study to understand and responsibly offer care in the face of suffering.

How do I assess the truth of my proposals and the integrity of my narratives of shared experience in MoiKonde? Methods in pastoral theology, which reside in the much broader fields of the humanities and social sciences, generally tend toward qualitative research and tests of theoretical adequacy. However, there is no agreement regarding what counts as an appropriate test of verification. Even methodological verification based on minimal harm varies according to particular and cultural understandings of harm.[91] Some argue for validity according to internal coherence, consistency, or attention to what makes sense.[92] This method can be criticized for a lack of attention to or appreciation of mysteries, ambiguities,

---

88. The December 2009 issue of the *Journal of Pastoral Theology* and the 2009 Society of Pastoral Theology annual meeting both called for deeper engagement with the communal-contextual and intercultural models, while also embodying what these models could look like in practice.

89. Marshall, "Models of Understanding Differences, Dialogues, and Discourses," 31.

90. Jonte-Pace and Parsons, *Religion and Psychology*, 1–10.

91. For examples, see McGarrah Sharp and Miller-McLemore, "Are There Limits to Multicultural Inclusion?"

92. Browning, *A Fundamental Practical Theology*.

and uncertainties.[93] Others argue for validity according to adequacy and relevance to experience, including experiences of particular groups of persons.[94] Still others argue for validity according to accounting for complexity of persons in relationship to the world as an interdependent pluralism.[95] Validity can also be assessed according to the ways a theory promotes psychological flexibility, functionality, or movement toward *versus* away from relationships.[96] All of these methods value evidence measured in metaphors or models of right relationship of selves with selves, others, God, and the world. The ultimate validity test must be exercised in practice. In this book, I practice negotiating multiples roles of story-teller, story-listener, story-participant, story-interpreter in the process of provisional understanding as preparation for moving toward mutually recognizable shared stories aware of the current context of postcoloniality.

Scholars have just begun to adopt the term *postcolonial* in the last ten to fifteen years to account for structural imbalances that affect traditional ways of theorizing.[97] Postcolonial theories encourage action and reflection directed toward power imbalances that can be traced to unjust hierarchies established by historical colonialism. Pastoral theologians need to attend more to some of the central themes that emerge from these theories. For example, *alterity*, having to do with the other, represents the idea that colonialism developed and instituted practices of *othering* some people as essentially different. These practices have become so engrained and habitual that they contribute to a version of natural history that has reordered the world of human beings. With the artist's brushstroke, the novelist's rhetoric, and travel journals full of so-called exotic stories, European explorers, for example, convinced a larger population that African tribal persons were other-than-fully-human *by nature*. Social and psychological norms became redirected in support of dehumanization justified by appealing to common good. Procedural justification for oppression and sometimes even destruction is all too prevalent in world history, extending to our day. In fact, we can trace patterns of dehumanization across historical events of mass violence.[98] Othering *kinds* of diverse peoples as

93. Keller, *On the Mystery.*

94. For example, see Glaz and Moessner, *Women in Travail and Transition;* Ali, *Survival and Liberation;* Isasi-Díaz, *En La Lucha.*

95. For example, see Barbour, *Religion and Science;* Thatamanil, *The Immanent Divine;* Knitter, *The Myth of Religious Superiority.*

96. Gay, *Joy and the Objects of Psychoanalysis;* Winnicott, *Playing and Reality.*

97. Young, *Postcolonialism.*

98. Mitchell, *Plantations and Death Camps.*

less than human—of a different kind—leads to tragic examples such as genocide, colonialism, and human trafficking, when certain human beings are forced into expendable bodies. Destructive rhetoric persists across cultures in discourses that "produce" so-called inferior others, connecting histories of violence to our present-day postcolonial contexts. Pastoral theology as a discipline that begins in the practice of attending suffering is uniquely poised to engage the work of unmasking patterns of dehumanization historically and today.

Colonial histories and postcolonial historical recoveries shape practice by contributing to the context of all present-day intercultural misunderstandings. Some claim that it is possible to recognize colonial violations as time bound. In these narratives, the historical end of colonialism not only liberated former colonies but also unmasked colonialism's inherent structural problems. It is not uncommon to read matter-of-fact statements such as the following: "The search for opportunity and dignity for all people has made progress, as colonialism has ended and democracy has spread, and more workers enjoy more of the results of their labors."[99] Postcolonial theorists warn against this kind of false optimism in the midst of many forms of oppression that long outlive colonial rule; and I am persuaded by postcolonial theorists who point to the enduring legacies and consequences of colonialism evidenced in lived experiences all over the world, including in diverse communities within the United States. Pastoral theologians must take this postcolonial argument seriously as it plays out in pastoral practices, theories, and ethics. Colonial histories and postcolonial historical recoveries continue to affect the psychic and social structures that organize relational life.[100] *Structural oppression*—the social structures established to justify dominating and violent actions—has not disappeared; rather, strategic habits of forgetting continue to justify oppression in subtle and unfortunately habitual ways.[101] Postcolonial theories work to unmask clever forms in which these structures and their discourse of alterity endure beyond the historical end of colonialism.

Pastoral theologians must expand traditional theories of relationality to account for postcoloniality if we as a field are serious about resisting injustice. To be about solidarity in suffering and possibilities of healing, pastoral theologians must continually work to identify and resist the way our theories collude with a destructive *gaze*. *Gazing at* others rather than

99. Lovin, *Christian Ethics*, 57.

100. See Smith, *The Relational Self*.

101. Hill Collins, *Black Feminist Thought*; Ali, *Survival and Liberation*.

being with human beings across diverse contexts is a practice that enlists us in habits of forgetting to shore up structural oppression. Here language is problematic, because to recognize the pertinence of structural oppression can lead to forgetting that human beings have to work to support these structures. Structures don't act, oppress, or resist; human beings do. Beverly Mitchell reminds us that "social structures and systems may be demonic or diabolical in the way in which they deface people, but these systems and structures are created [and maintained] by human beings."[102] We *gaze* when we impose our own narratives on neighbors, overlooking diverse voices and refusing to participate in certain relationships. *We* language is instructive here, as *we/they* or *us/them* dichotomies evidence these habits embedded in language. *We* cannot see an other individuated *I* because of *our* overwhelming tendency to sort others into kinds that *we* already know and understand. We allow ourselves to forgo any actual encounters, surprises, vulnerabilities, or new possibilities by being lured into the false predictability of profiling. Telling misunderstanding stories is one way intentionally to open to surprise, but it requires vulnerability, courage, and acknowledgement of provisional understanding.

Postcolonial theorists argue that a dominating gaze affects how we consider interpersonal interactions to be embedded in larger systemic political histories. Edward Said's *Orientalism* argues that the gaze not only affects interpersonal relationships but also serves as a tool of locality that fuses whole communities to particular geographic locations. You and I *gaze* by unreflectively buying into colonial and colonizing mythologies about geographies and histories. The gaze continues to fix persons and places in particular global power-powerlessness relationships. Not only is this gaze a product of historical colonialism, but it is also a practice of present-day scholarship! Thus, academic reflection itself must pay particular attention to resisting collusion in a dominating gaze within its own practices, processes, and privileges. The gaze denies personal and communal worth across cultural differences. Models of neighbors or partners provide more liberative language for resisting habits of forgetting that lead to the illusion of a normalized and ethically neutral practice of gazing.

Pastoral theologians have long been concerned with mutuality and empathy as important dimensions of best practices of care in a variety of settings. Post-Freudian psychological theorists highlight relationality as an aspect of the human condition, well-being, and human development. Postcolonial theorists consider how violence might contribute to

102. Mitchell, *Plantations and Death Camps*, 125n16.

postcolonial problems *and* solutions. Correlating interdisciplinary resources helps construct attention in practice accompanied by a theoretical response that recognizes the simultaneous depth of crisis and opportunity for mutual learning that surrounds misunderstanding stories. However, a pastoral theological method does not stop at correlating interdisciplinary theories in order to understand a contemporary problem. Theological, psychological, and postcolonial theories work together to offer a critical edge in an interdisciplinary response to experiences of intercultural breaches in understanding. A method of critical correlation recognizes the limited nature of theories of human relationships, allowing contemporary problems to hold weight for academic theory. Postcolonial theories challenge pastoral theologians toward responsible scholarship more attentive to intrapsychic and social contexts of postcoloniality and that transforms rather than necessarily abandons traditional wisdom. I approach these tasks with theoretical rigor that partners traditional Western theory with postcolonial theory. A second layer of partnering through telling misunderstanding stories is crucial to this academic task. This is the work of the next chapters.

3

Narrating Identities in Crisis

Who am I? is a basic question that confronts human beings in the midst of life experiences. Who are we? also confronts us at expected and un-expected times and places, particularly in response to communal and process-oriented movements within traditionally individualistic ways of understanding human beings and networks of relationships. In our postcolonial and intercultural contexts, occasions for misunderstanding stories are increasing, which opens up more possibilities for identity and relationship crisis. Experiences of crisis in relationships almost always open space for raising questions of identity. That is not to say that iden-tity questions are always voiced into open spaces or that invitations to ask questions about identities are always welcome. A desire to preserve the illusion of a once and for all set identity from which I can imagine future trajectories and reconcile past experiences can be gripping. However, as soon as one considers time as a dimensional phenomenon in which both past and future always bear on the present, we can remember again how absurd is the idea of a once and for all static identity that never moves and never shifts. Appealing to experience, we can recognize that all of us without exception are constantly shaped by and shape our individualized and communal identities in a constant state of becoming. Paradoxically, change is constant, uncertainty a certainty.

Life experiences always affect identities. Stories stay with us, literally becoming incorporated into our *self-structure*,[1] the scaffolding that gives shape and support to the stories we tell about who we are—our identity narratives. Opportunities for growth and change in identity can be chosen through education or other investments in learning or can happen involuntarily through experiences of loss or life transition. Pastoral theologians appeal to developmental theories because of the way in which these theories structure metanarratives of identity that account for who we are, how we've lived, and how we've endured. Developmental theories also structure predictions of who we are becoming, how life will continue to unfold, and what kind of endurance we will individually and collectively need for the journey ahead. Remember that pastoral theology and good enough pastoral care start with the human experience of attending suffering in community. Most seminarians will study theories of human development at some point in theological education as a way of helping to discern and predict the care needs, the challenges that contribute to or exacerbate suffering, and the practices of healing relevant to persons of different ages and stages of life. But there is a problem.

Consider the following illustration. "Two Languages, Many Voices" refers to a segment of interviews that ran on National Public Radio in the fall of 2011. While the special news series focuses on the experiences of Latinos in the United States in particular, many Latino Americans interviewed raise important questions around the intersections of identities and intercultural realities of a twenty-first-century world that everyone needs to hear and engage. In one interview, Cuban American and Columbia University professor Gustavo Perez Firmat describes how he turns to genres of writing like poetry and memoir to help make sense of his experience that "words fail him" in both Spanish and English. He evokes the Czech proverb, "learn a new language, get a new soul," and asks: is it such a good idea to have more than one soul?[2] He does not ask about developing from a more "primitive" soul to a more "developed" soul; no, he is raising a question of recognizing multiple valid threads in a complexly woven identity.

The breaches described in the last chapter that initiated misunderstanding stories for me within intercultural relationships in MoiKonde raise questions of identity in the midst of my participation in an intentional learning process around cross-contextual fluency. Learning a new

1. "Self-structure" is a conceptual term from Kohut's self psychology.
2. National Public Radio, "For a Bilingual Writer, 'No One True Language.'"

language indeed affects identity. As a partner in intercultural relationships, I experienced questions and crisis in relation to my identity, the identities of my friends and partners in MoiKonde, and how to identify the character of our life together. For example, when Mia and Ella asked me if they would be free in America, I was at once Peace Corps volunteer in the midst of intercultural friendship, disrupting the isolationist privilege that can prevent intercultural relationships of mutuality, *and* privileged citizen of a country with a complex history of enslaving and colonizing people just like Mia and Ella. Even if Mia and Ella recognized me as an exception to what I have historically represented, and even if I recognized Mia and Ella as exceptions to how "people like them" have been historically represented, I still must wrestle with embodying the perceived norm of US imperialism through my identity as a US citizen. Being an American means radically different things in different circumstances. Recognizing the complexity of representation raises questions of multiple identities. Is it such a good idea to recognize more than one soul?

Above, Firmat is speaking out of his intercultural experience as an *exile* in America, a common category claimed by immigrants to the United States. I write as a former partner in the work of sustainable community development with neighbors in MoiKonde, a small Saakiki village in the Republic of Suriname, South America. I agree with Firmat, who argues that multi- and intercultural stories must be written and voiced into liminal spaces, what Turner calls betwixt and between.[3] Theological and sociological concepts and practices of *home, belonging, community,* and *language* become more nuanced in conversation with the intercultural nature of contemporary *identities.* Further, identity crises that accompany misunderstanding stories in intercultural relationships provoke *wonder* around the phenomenon of sharing in the human condition across cultural differences. At the same time that I recognize intercultural relationships as part of my mundane reality, I am also astonished: How is it possible to share in human experience across such wide expanses of cultural difference? How is it possible to recognize multiplicities even within my own soul?

Questions of identity often bubble up in the midst of life as persons and communities move and grow. However, scholars of postcolonial psychology caution that the stories of development, growth, and change

---

3. Firmat, *Literature and Liminality.* See also the concept of neplanta in Gloria Anzaldúa's *Borderlands,* signifying a state of perpetual "torn between ways" where the process of conversation can flow from a crying out and can navigate identity borders toward hope rather than despair or endless frustration (Anzaldúa, *Borderlands,* 100).

offered by developmental theory can easily collude with strategies of dehumanization. In other words, the study of developmental theory can represent the privileged development of some human beings afforded through strategies of oppression of other human beings contained in and masked by developmental theory as ideology. This chapter explores questions of identity and identity crisis through analysis of developmental and postcolonial theories.

Stories of disruptive moments within intercultural relationships can be described in terms of breaches in intercultural understanding. As chapter 2 discussed, such breaches invite a flow of questions into experiences of disruption. I continue to adapt Turner's trajectory to structure story-telling as a process that moves from breach in understanding toward a renewed relationship of reconciliation that incorporates the breach experience and includes experiences of and reflection on identity crisis. The following section retells another piece of one of the misunderstanding stories introduced in previous chapters to illustrate identity crises that flow forth from an experience of breach in intercultural understanding.

A NARRATIVE FRAGMENT OF IDENTITY CRISIS IN MISUNDERSTANDING STORIES

Like our neighbors in MoiKonde, we lived outside in the shade of trees or in open-air thatched-roof porches or cooking structures almost all the time, as the zinc metal-roofed houses only cool in the evenings. Even when we were inside, we regularly conversed through open windows with our friends in the neighboring houses as if we were sitting across the room from one another. Conversations across houses and in shared outside spaces filled each and every day: "Fa waka anga yu tide mamatain?" (How are you this morning?) "San yu boli gi mi tide ba?" (What are you cooking today for us to share?) "San pasa anga a pikin?" (What happened that is making a child cry?) "Yu opo Abaamai?" (Are you awake yet, Abaamai? Or, in the evening, Are you still awake, Abaamai?) In MoiKonde, we learned to live communally as an everyday practice. In MoiKonde, we learned to live communally as a way of understanding and therefore seeing reality. Who am I? I am astonished at the invitation to learn to live in community. Who are we? We are different yet live together as neighbors. Can we sustain this intercultural relationship of life together in community?

Learning to live communally is in constant tension with recognition of difference. This is found in our names. Naming ceremonies in MoiKonde provide an important framework for intracultural and intercultural hospitality. Bestowed to us in a formal community meeting within days of our arrival, we were given new names: Abaamai and Abaapai. Literally translated as "from across," our new names made it impossible to forget the differences we were navigating on a daily basis. With these names, we were welcomed into a communal way of life with constant opportunities to learn to live well in this context. With these names, we literally embodied the translation work of intercultural partnership required to do so. Who am I? Who are we? We cross and live across from each other, and yet we are learning to be neighbors.

The highly communal way of life was facilitated by our willingness to learn through making linguistic mistakes in word choice, pronunciation, and use of metaphor; through mistakes about cultural practices of where to walk; through mistakes about appropriate dress for corresponding cultural ritual; through mistakes traversing spaces with respect and safety, especially when navigating the rainforest with our neighbors. These mundane and even humorous disruptions characterized the atmosphere of learning that made communal living possible.

The highly communal way of life that we were continually learning and that we had come to appreciate was severely disrupted when we returned to the village after several weeks away in the United States. Each morning, the routine greeting (one must formally greet each and every person one passes in the morning, midday, and evening, even if simply walking through the woods to a bathing area to brush one's teeth) now occurred in awkwardly navigated shared spaces. Great distances cut through our small neighborhood. We could feel these fresh rifts but could not understand. I don't understand how to be Abaamai, and yet I am Abaamai. Who am I? Who are we? Can we sustain this intercultural relationship of life together in community?

Unexpectedly, we constantly crossed the line. Any effort to reconcile seemed to offer yet another invisible treason. How do we identify and navigate the unstable status of previously shared spaces?

While we were away, we learned that the daughters of our neighbors, the very children and families with whom we lived in community, had broken into our home in our absence.

We were able to recognize differing norms of insider/outsider information sharing when we learned that we were not supposed to have received the news of the breach. The insider community had apparently experienced a second breach and crisis when the message was communicated to us by our friend, who also finds himself as somewhat of an outsider who has married into a prominent family in the village. Who are we?

The breach created by the violation of private property (also a contested concept in such a communal way of living) was not the difficult breach to navigate, however. The difficult breach to navigate was a breach in understanding how to recover from the violation of trust within the intercultural relationship.

We experienced the crisis of failed attempts to communicate with the girls, their mothers, their siblings, the larger community, schoolteachers, the school headmaster, and elders of the village. Our efforts to communicate intensified the crisis, as they did not match with the norms of communication for the village. We could almost see and certainly could feel the mismatch. We could not yet imagine how best to proceed given this painful recognition. Could we sustain intercultural relationship of life together in community? Who are we to play a part in so doing?

UNDERSTANDING IDENTITY CRISES THROUGH DEVELOPMENTAL STAGE THEORY

A breach in understanding leads to crises of identity. Framing questions of identity with language—who am I? and who are we?—in and of itself can intensify experiences of identity crisis. Psychoanalyst Erik Erikson's influential developmental psychology considers identity crisis as the pivotal phenomenon that encourages growth throughout the lifespan. While the particular aspect of one's identity in question changes throughout life, Erikson maps periodic serious questions around identity as developmental tasks necessary for maturity. Erikson is only one example of a developmental theorist who affirms that identities change over time with life experience and age. Developmental psychologies will always be popular because of their predictive assumptions that map the kinds of challenges one will likely face over the course of life. The same perception of predictability that makes development theories so appealing is also their limit in the assumption that life unfolds over a more or less linear trajectory of predictable peak and valley experiences from the more identifiably immature to the more identifiably mature. Before critical engagement with this dilemma, let us briefly review Erikson's developmental psychology.

Erikson proposes a stage-by-stage model of chronological and psychological development that insists on the influence of real changes prompted by encounters between human beings. Erikson seriously considers complex yearnings for growth, learning, and movement from one phase to another within relationships across cultural groups. He values growth potential even while he is mindful of the identity struggle that facilitates change. Influenced by biology and psychoanalytic constructions of identity, Erikson asserts a continuum of human development in a process that unfolds in nine discernible stages from birth to old age in specific patterns and accompanied by significant transitions between each stage. Experiences of conflict, or experiences of a "core crisis,"[4] characterize the transition to each new stage of development. For psychological development to occur, each stage-specific core crisis requires resolution. Subsequently, each resolution involves a human being making choices directly related to the question, who am I?, which then moves human beings from stage to stage. In this theory, each time a human being successfully navigates the identity crisis of a major life transition, a new virtue is generated.[5] Not just any virtue, but a lifetime of negotiating developmental transitions generates a specific progression of predictable virtues, each virtue necessary for the next developmental transition: hope, then will, then purpose, then competence, then fidelity, then love, then care, then, finally, wisdom.[6] Successful negotiation of identity crises over the lifespan leads to human survival and to emergence and endurance of character as ingredient to identity formation. Over time, a strong sense of self comes to be embedded in and supported by a particular contextual network.

Navigating identity crises through developmental stages involves a sense of participating in the human condition and belonging to communal groups. Basic human needs of encounter and belonging have a dynamic relationship. The phenomenon of encounter moves human beings toward inclusivity by foregrounding the relational nature of persons that allows for growth and change through their interactions. The phenomenon of belonging moves human beings toward exclusivity by emphasizing

---

4. Erikson, *The Life Cycle Completed*, 80.

5. We must "consider how emerging human strengths, step for step, are intrinsically beset not only with severe vulnerabilities that perpetually demand our healing insight, but also with basic evils which call for the redeeming values of universal belief systems or ideologies" (ibid., 60–61).

6. For example, Erikson theorizes that *basic trust* formed in the relationship of an infant with his or her parents conflicts with *basic mistrust*. When an infant resolves this conflict in his or her relationships with others, the virtue of *hope* is generated and incorporated into this child's identity. Like other psychologists, Erikson refers to only the mother because of the modern understanding of the mother as primary caretaker. As later stages suggest, the encounters through which children resolve the core crisis of trust versus mistrust affect other developmental transitions as well. For example, Erikson argues that parents often experience growth of children in a way that contributes to their own stage-appropriate core crisis.

commonalities that contribute to the creation and maintenance of groups. As in the anthropological theories employed by pastoral theologian Emmanuel Lartey reviewed in chapter 1, Erikson recognizes the tensions between navigating one's identity always in relation to all human beings, some human beings, and no other human being. In terms of symbolic interaction represented in play therapy with children, Erikson distinguished between common meanings available to all, special meanings available to discrete groups, and unique meanings of life experiences, language, and material reality available to *me*.[7] Human beings need the mediating language required by *both* moments of encountering often prone to misunderstanding *and* possibilities of mutual understanding found in belonging to groups. Theorizing that encounter and belonging are fundamental to what it means to be human leads to moral obligations to attend to these categories of experience in discerning and practicing pastoral care and constructing pastoral theologies.

Each new interpersonal encounter begins not with practicing care or recognizing inherent goodness or human dignity, but rather with a mutual sizing up.[8] In the narrative fragment above, I noted that new names were bestowed on us soon after our arrival, but not immediately. This gave time for the kind of mutual sizing up that precedes understanding. Human beings require some time to get to know one another; in the best of cases, social structures provide the space and time for the practices of acquaintance that accompany relationships of mutual care.

Spatially, in the middle of Erikson's stage theory is not midlife but rather adolescence as the height of identity crisis. Adolescence follows successful navigation of the preceding four stages of infancy, early childhood, play age, and school age. The challenges of adolescence are a necessary hurdle to experiencing the four subsequent stages of young adulthood, adulthood, old age, and the ninth stage characterized by transcendence.[9] While each stage turns on an experience of crisis, Erikson designates *identity crisis* as the core crisis of adolescence in which human beings realize the need for recognition by their community. *Recognition* as a process that involves a human being and her or his community(ies) of belonging is key both to provoking and to resolving experiences of identity crisis. Adolescence as a stage of peak identity crises is full of mutual sizing up.

---

7. Erikson, *Childhood and Society*, 219.

8. Ibid., 49.

9. Erikson, *The Life Cycle Completed*, 56–57, 123ff.

A human being needs to be recognized for who she or he is and has chosen to be. At the same time, the identified community(ies) of belonging needs to be perceived as recognizing this human being for who she or he is and has chosen to be. In the best circumstances, negotiating identity crisis in a way that recognizes a developing sense of identity, communicates a developing sense of identity, and receives communal responses of affirmation or rejection around a developing sense of identity is challenging for adolescents. The best circumstances occur when communities of belonging allow for a broad range of identity expression. The most difficult circumstances to negotiate happen when socially sanctioned roles are so narrow as to constrict possibilities of being recognized at all. Postcolonial theorists name experiences of this pervasive dynamic *non-recognition*. One legacy of colonialism is strategic forgetting in relation to the goodness of human beings, who necessarily display a broad range of identity.

In general, this developmental psychology theorizes that human growth is a process by which society supports human beings' efforts to integrate internal conflicts with external contexts.[10] However, writing in 1950, Erikson recognized the unequal access available to children to participate in US American identity because of our being schooled into prejudices through social structures, media representation, parenting, and formal education.[11] Systemic injustice regulates social roles, responsibilities, and opportunities differently for different human beings by reinforcing misunderstanding through repeated narratives that may sound, but need not be, true.[12] The mutual sizing up within human encounters is an attempt to probe integrity of another person, to question whether he or she is experimenting with playing a role or whether he or she is moving into a socially acceptable identity.[13] Relationships of mutual care develop when attentive, expectant presence can be maintained over and against the social suspicion often instituted through historical schooling.[14] We are all susceptible to getting so caught up in the mutual sizing up that we risk real harm when any of us misunderstands our own and others' identity narratives.[15]

10. Erikson, *Childhood and Society*, 211, 77.

11. Ibid., 237–46.

12. Ibid., 331.

13. Ibid., 49, 235–36.

14. Ibid., 421–24. While conversation with theories of social schooling advanced by Michel Foucault would be interesting here, this work is beyond the scope of this book.

15. For example, the 2012 tragic killing of Trayvon Martin in Florida, which

NARRATING IDENTITY CRISIS TO WHAT END?

Developmental psychology as modeled by Erikson must be recognized for both its contributions and its limitations. Erikson exhibits a deep regard for intricacies of human beings who continually move, change, and grow throughout the lifespan. Developmental psychology reminds us that children require caretaking by persons more developmentally mature, persons who have wrestled with conflicts and found in them the virtues and strengths of hope, will, purpose, competence, fidelity, love, care, and wisdom. While helpful in thinking about the transitions from childhood to adulthood, Erikson's stage theory fails to consider the role of adversity on development, or the ways in which these ordered virtues bolster the courage required throughout the lifespan when social structures fail to support experiences of identity crisis.[16]

Developmental psychology categorizes human beings in archetypal stages of "normal" development. While Erikson's theory is based in clinical observation and is populated by stories of clinical encounters, he decides to "attempt to do without narrative"[17] to develop an overarching system of normative development that either stalls out or progresses to each subsequent stage without exception.[18] However, he does allow for two qualifications. First, as an example of the potentiality in each of us and the good ends to which so-called advanced development can be directed, Erikson allows for great adult persons in history, such as Gandhi, Martin Luther, and Martin Luther King Jr. to skip intermediate stages, contributing wisdom before their chronological old-age stage. Second, Erikson and his wife, artist Joan Erikson, developed a ninth stage, roughly defined as dealing-with-old-age, as they literally outgrew their previously theorized eighth stage of old age, adding additional nuance to adult experience as

---

sparked international attention, shows how appearance and caricature can lead to harm, even death, when interpreted incorrectly (for example, see Fung, "Geraldo Rivera: Trayvon Martin's 'Hoodie'"; Lomax, "Who's Going to Sing a Black Boy's Song."

16. Miller-McLemore, *Let the Children Come*; Brennan, *The Vocation of the Child*.

17. Erikson, *The Life Cycle Completed*, 24. Erikson writes of the status of clinical experience as a "clinical 'specimen' as a springboard for theoretical discussion" (*Childhood and Society*, 49).

18. Erikson claims that "as we proceed to the next proceeding stage it should above all prove to have been developmentally indispensable for the later stages" (Erikson, *The Life Cycle Completed*, 66). Interestingly, a recent leadership development theory inspired by Erikson makes the same claim—that mastery of each level is required for attempting to negotiate the challenges of the next level. The author claim that "so far, we've found no exceptions to this pattern" (Joiner and Josephs, *Leadership Agility*, 12).

varied over time as well.[19] Erikson allows his own experience to expand the number of stages of generalized stage-based development. However, he fails to extend similar flexibility to human beings in general, asserting the reality of bounded, step-by-step human development with the exception of a few great adult persons. At best, it is unclear how Erikson accounts for the many who, for whatever reason, lead less linearly organized lives.

Attentive to injustices in his post-World War II social context around race, ethnicity, gender, nationality, and religious identity, Erikson theorized the importance of culture for psychological development in ways radical for his time.[20] However, his developmental schema still makes individualistic, privileged experience normative for successful development. Oppression is often characterized as a deliberate denial of an individuated person's or discrete cultural group's sense of identity by the imposition of a rigid order onto lived experience. Wisdom, the virtue Erikson assigns to old age, often appears in human beings and discrete groups experiencing oppression, even in children, whom Erikson places at the other end of the developmental spectrum, well before the structural possibility of wisdom as a virtue. In 2004 the Dutch Parliament named Anne Frank the "greatest Dutch person in history."[21] Her identity as a Jewish child was systematically denied within an oppressive and ordered privileged identity.[22] And yet many consider Anne Frank a child "wise beyond her years" in her ability to record and reflect upon her experience of oppression during the Holocaust. Resistance to oppression often includes the kind of wisdom that helps maintain "some order and meaning in the dis-integration of body and mind."[23] Systematic theologian Beverly Mitchell recognizes the wisdom required to maintain a sense of human dignity in the midst of the violence of identity-based oppression.[24] Erikson seems to consider counter-narratives that challenge his linear, age-based theory of development, such as children who need or have wisdom or generativity in the face of

19. Liebert, "Seasons and Stages," 20.

20. Erikson, *Childhood and Society*; Liebert, "Seasons and Stages."

21. See Associated Press, "Dutch MPs Want to Give Anne Frank Posthumous Citizenship."

22. Mitchell, *Plantations and Death Camps*.

23. Erikson, *The Life Cycle Completed*, 64—a description of "old age."

24. Mitchell, *Plantations and Death Camps*. As another example, Erikson also fails to extend exceptions to sick children who live a lifetime in a shorter number of years and who often experience the role reversal of caring for their parents during their own dying process much earlier than expected.

social oppression, as outliers.[25] Many crisis experiences, both internally and externally provoked, do not occur at "age-appropriate" times and so do not bear their fruits according to a chronological schema. Norms meant to guide human development for all may in reality be experienced by a privileged few. At a theoretical level, Erikson respects the cultural location and relational nature of human beings; but in describing how his theories unfold in lived experience, he defines a norm that excludes those socially unrecognized as having power to assert their place on his continuum or to contest the normative narrative implied by the continuum. Erikson sacrifices personal stories to create a complete system of development. But his "attempt to do without narrative" instead leaves his system radically incomplete because the theory fails to account for how power works in systematic oppression, where the least powerful and sickest among us have few structural opportunities to belong; but it also labels anyone who is not developing "normally" as deviant and unsuccessful.

What is the best use of developmental theories as a basis for age-appropriate predictions of identity and crises in identities? Analysis of Erikson's developmental theory suggests that attention to relational human beings who encounter and belong at the expense of narrative fails to account for the suffering due to the complex ways in which structural oppression affects opportunities in lived experience. Developmental theories should instead supplement narratives of human beings embedded in intercultural contexts. Intercultural understanding is best tested on the edge of experiences where narrative becomes a vehicle for recognizing misunderstanding and for realizing possibilities of mutual understanding. This is especially the case with misunderstanding stories in which human nature, uncertainty, and possibility intersect.

To what end do we tell and retell narratives of identity crisis? Appealing to Erikson as an influential model of developmental psychology, we tell

---

25. For example, he tells a story of how he was moved in a particular experience with a client, a young African American boy whom he asked to construct an imaginary movie scene on a small table. Erikson had already drawn some conclusions from years of collected experiences with this exercise with other clients and discerned patterns of differences between the kinds of scenes constructed by boys in comparison with girls. However, the scene constructed by this particular child was different from all others. The African American child constructed his scene under the table. Erikson concludes that this child "offers stark and chilling evidence of the meaning of his smiling meekness: he 'knows his place'" (Erikson, *Childhood and Society*, 98–99). Erikson's developmental theory continues to be compelling. However, postcolonial psychologies expose and oppose developmental theories that create situations like this one, where it is not only possible but seemingly the natural order of life events that even children experience an oppressive, prejudiced, hierarchical context of life possibilities.

and retell stories of identity crisis as a way of narrating a successful journey through major life transitions. However, postcolonial theories have exposed that developmental psychology has been used to create and cement identity crisis in such a way that successful resolution is only available to those with structural power and is therefore afforded to some human beings by way of instituting identity crisis as a strategy of dehumanizing other human beings. Understanding this dilemma within a compelling model of human development that has structured best practices of pastoral care in the past can help reorient the telling and retelling of narratives of identity crisis toward more liberative and empowering ends that resist strategies of dehumanization.

Pastoral theologians have always considered the ethics of care, albeit in more or less explicit ways. It is important for us to keep reflecting on the goals of story-telling, story-listening, story interpreting. In this book, I tell and retell misunderstanding stories for the purposes of more liberative and empowering partnerships across cultural differences that resist the dehumanizing strategies that structure our postcolonial world. However, it is significant that my role as a partner in development work, even development work oriented toward sustainability and modeled on friendship, is also problematic.

Consider the misunderstanding story introduced in earlier chapters in which I intervened in child discipline with my friend. In terms of identity crisis, new questions emerge. First, what and who was I witnessing? I was seeing the particular child-rearing/disciplinary practices of one mother. At the same time, I was seeing a culturally sanctioned and common form of child discipline. At the same time, I was seeing the legacy of colonial violence. At the same time, I was seeing my friend and I was seeing a cultural other. At the same time, I was resisting unquestioned moral categories and I was complicit in colonizing strategies. The cross-contextual complexity of this situation challenged my cross-contextual fluency. What does a liberative and empowering practice of translation founded on a model oriented toward mutual understanding look like when disrupted in all of these ways?

This set of questions raises another set of questions around how we witness in moments of disruption. Who was I when I was witnessing this disruptive breach in understanding? The breach was disruptive, in part, because it activated an identity crisis within me as I was learning to recognize my own multiplicity in the process of cross-contextual fluency.[26] In

26. Cooper-White, *Shared Wisdom*; and Cooper-White, *Many Voices* theorize

this experience, I was seeing myself as a neighbor and friend. At the same time, I was seeing myself as a participant in a highly communal way of life that challenged my US-American notion of privacy. At the same time, I was seeing myself as the person in charge of my private domestic space. And I was seeing an opportunity to exercise my moral convictions about justice and human rights. At the same time, I was infringing on the process of partnership by taking on my role as an official representative from a country whose narrative includes "our" more evolved sense of morality in relation to child-rearing practices. In spite of my best intentions, I felt a colonizing impulse to "civilize" "this woman" in this moment of crisis. At the same time, I was appalled by and resisted this impulse. Conditions were ripe for experiences of identity crisis.

Misunderstanding stories raise challenging questions about identity. To frame identity crisis with language activates even more identity crisis. Who am I? Who are we? Telling and retelling misunderstanding stories raises postcolonial dilemmas shaped in part by developmental theories. In the following section, I appeal to a postcolonial perspective on developmental psychology to probe ways in which the idea of "normal" human development has worked as a dehumanizing strategy that has supported historical colonialism and that lives on in its legacy.

MISUNDERSTANDING STORIES OF (HUMAN) DEVELOPMENT WORK

Legacies of colonization have lingering psychological consequences within the human family. Writing in response to legacies of British colonialism in India, postcolonial theorist and psychoanalytically trained Ashis Nandy debunks the prevalent colonial idea that cultural development moves from child to adult and from the feminine to the masculine. These colonizing myths trap some human beings in representations of dark-skinned, weak, female-bodied (although typically hypersexualized) children "in need" of being governed by the white masculine adults, who represent ideals of identity-formation. As Fanon suggests, the colonial *gaze* is raced. Nandy adds that the colonial gaze is gendered and aged. Colonial gazing facilitates seeing not human beings but instead representations of dehumanized raced, gendered, aged bodies. Colonialism works by training whole communities to see and appreciate one vision of healthy development in terms of whiteness, maleness, and developmental maturity while masking the violence

---

multiplicity from a pastoral psychotherapeutic perspective.

Misunderstanding Stories

done via inscribing visible identity markers with varying developmental capacities.[27] *The Intimate Enemy: Loss And Recovery of Self under Colonialism* (1983) by Nandy shows how developmental theory supports strategies of dehumanization embodied in these practices of gazing.

Nandy introduces gender and age as colonizing categories of inner life and interpersonal relationships, surveys literary responses to colonial heritage, and draws on Gandhi to problematize linear notions of gender, time, and history.[28] For example, aggression, achievement, control, competition, and power are not only stereotypical representations of colonizing forces but also represent mature adults in Western developmental psychology as well as in the historical accounts that funded the colonial imagination. In contrast, "the notion of the African as a minor, endorsed at times even by a Livingstone, took very strong hold. Spaniards and Boers had questioned whether natives had souls: modern Europeans cared less about that but doubted whether they had minds, or minds capable of adult growth. A theory came to be fashionable that mental growth in the African ceased early, that childhood was never left behind."[29]

Nandy demonstrates how colonized human beings came to be represented as children. We saw in Erikson that children and even adolescents require caretaking by persons recognized as more mature, in persons who have found virtues in successful resolution of identity struggles. In schema like Erikson's, Nandy shows how colonized human beings were represented as adolescents. On one hand, colonial projects sought to reform human beings who were recast as child*like*: the "innocent, ignorant but willing to learn, masculine, loyal and thus 'corrigible.'" On the other hand, colonial projects sought to repress human beings recast as child*ish*: the "ignorant but unwilling to learn, ungrateful, sinful, savage, unpredictably violent, disloyal, and thus 'incorrigible.'"[30] Opportunities for recognition normally available in identity crises were denied to colonized persons as they were actively excluded from communities of belonging and restricted to narrow subservient social roles. Nandy exposes not only the juvenalization of colonized human beings but also the fundamental devaluing of

27. Copeland, *Enfleshing Freedom.*

28. Of note, while Nandy addresses gender as a colonizing category, he also nonetheless employs the masculine pronoun to refer to humanity throughout the text. Since the book was published in 1983, in the early years of inclusive language, we can evaluate this practice in terms of collusion with seemingly inescapable colonizing categories and also in terms of a starting point for transcending them.

29. Kiernan, quoted in Nandy, *The Intimate Enemy*, 15n24.

30. Nandy, *The Intimate Enemy*, 16.

their personhood in such a way that distorts what any developmental stage theory would suggest as part of the normal growing up.

Dehumanizing representations impede recognition in two ways. First, such representations perpetuate habits of gazing at other human beings in a way that prevents recognizing their personhood. Second, they mask complicity in the violence of colonialism by disguising violence as a good in the form of cultural caretaking: "good for them," "good for us," "good for all."[31] In the West, colonizing violence has been justified by historically lauding the colonizer as a responsible salvific adult who imposes superior ethical codes upon inferior "blank slate" children in desperate need of education for *their* own good lest *they* remain undeveloped and devalued.[32] Nandy points out that colonialism also devalues elders, traditionally esteemed for embodying the pinnacle of progress but who atrophy through colonizing forces that dehumanize elders with strategies that suggest "these people" also desperately need salvation from younger, stronger, more stable adults.[33] Myths of progress—fueled by racism, ageism, and sexism—work by suggesting false avenues of development for colonized human beings, dehumanized through integration into colonial metanarratives as permanently immature.

Colonialism as moral, psychological, spiritual, and physical development work, particularly in the form of global mission, depends on strategies of dehumanization directed at human beings who come to be seen as objects and not as neighbors. In other words, it uses Western notions of development to refuse recognition to the other and by that very refusal seeks to forestall the development it pretends is already impossible. The circular logic here intentionally disguises a grand misunderstanding story as truth, thus institutionalizing a paternalistic form of misunderstanding. Strategies of dehumanization can force colonized human beings to entertain the impossible choice between two violent and therefore fundamentally disempowering options: denying their identity to assimilate or recognizing their identity with the knowledge that this will incite violence.

---

31. K. Samuel Lee nuances complicity itself with intercultural significance, calling attention to the care with which we must engage complicity in relation to cultural identities. (Lee, "Engaging Difference in Pastoral Theology").

32. Nandy, *The Intimate Enemy*, 14–15.

33. Ibid., 16–17; See Roland, *In Search of Self in India and Japan*, 308, where Roland describes the cultural appropriateness of elders embodying greater wisdom and spiritual achievement. Developmental theorists like Erik Erikson or James Fowler, Carol Gilligan or Lawrence Kohlberg, also depend on a notion of age progression with implications for corresponding sexual identity.

We can understand lingering consequences of these colonizing "choices" in practices of exclusion that range from legislated marginalization to calls for assimilation to ignoring the personhood of others who represent the formerly colonized by simply refusing to see them as sharing in humanity.[34]

The second part of Nandy's argument in *The Intimate Enemy* is a study of human resilience in relation to the psychology of colonialism. Through competing narratives of how human beings navigate colonial representations, he argues that oppressors necessarily and consistently discount the oppressed as nonhuman and thus automatically less able to participate in conversation, move into an open future, or become incorporated into any other practice of so-called "civilized" society.[35] Psychological splitting facilitates colonialism through the illusion that the world is neatly and necessarily divided between "like me and therefore recognizably human" and "not human like me and therefore legitimately dehumanized." However, he explains, while the oppressors must dehumanize those whom they subjugate, the mindset of oppressed human beings is that they survive and live in the presence of a human oppressor. Nandy insists on a preferential option for the oppressed, but not out of the kind of biblical grounding of liberation theologies.

> The essential reasoning is simple. Between the modern master and the non-modern slave, one must choose the slave not because one should choose voluntary poverty or admit the superiority of suffering, not only because the slave is oppressed, not even because [the slave] works (which, Marx said, made [him or her] less alienated than the master). One must choose the slave also because [the slave] represents a higher-order cognition which perforce includes the master as a human, whereas the master's cognition has to exclude the slave except as a "thing."[36]

Oppressed human beings often *recognize* oppressing human beings as fully human as a survival strategy by perfecting strategies of cross-contextual fluency and negotiating dehumanizing rules through careful practices of resistance, such as maintaining a cohesive sense of self in the face of colonizing violence. Indeed, the *choice* to recognize the oppressor as human is all the more developmentally advanced, as it were, if it

---

34. Gill-Austern, "Engaging Diversity and Difference"; McGarrah Sharp, "Globalization, Colonialism, and Postcolonialism"; Volf, *Exclusion and Embrace*.

35. Nandy, *The Intimate Enemy*, xiii, xv–xvi; see also Lal, *Dissenting Knowledges, Open Futures*.

36. Nandy, *The Intimate Enemy*, xv–xvi.

is, in fact, easy to dehumanize the oppressor who so consistently masks violence as a good. In Erikson, recognition given and received in adolescence is precisely what allows us the capacity to recognize others. Yet some unrecognized members of the colonized group develop the capacity anyway—that is, without first receiving recognition from their oppressors. Nandy radically inverts modern hierarchies by envisioning dehumanized human beings as the ones living in reality while the so-called master has become trapped in inner self-conflict fighting a projected, split enemy-self in the form of the other, whose suffering he justifies as a necessary good. Even with this reversal the psychological consequences of colonialism perpetuate practices of non-recognition throughout the human family.[37]

Nandy examines psychological colonialism and gives preference to the subjectivity of dehumanized human beings. But he resists the academic impulse and pressure to deliver a neatly packaged theory that presents final answers.[38] Instead, he not only deliberately leaves loose ends and untidy places in this text, but he also immediately problematizes each concluding section with critical and challenging questions.[39] Nandy includes an explicit warning to those of us who, even in the name of post-colonialism, work in hegemonic text-based academic circles: "A living culture has to live and it has an obligation to itself, not to its analysts. Even less does it have any obligation to conform to a model, its own or someone else's."[40] We share in the responsibility to engage the role of representations in perpetuating suffering. Nandy's psychology of colonialism resonates with the field of pastoral theology, which attends suffering and reflects on healing with similar methodological commitments such as valuing lived human experience, critically evaluating the relationship between practices (including religious practices) and psychological health, participating in interdisciplinary conversations as a learning process, and recognizing the value of identity crisis within academic study.[41]

---

37. He writes, "Ultimately, modern oppression, as opposed to traditional oppression, is not an encounter between the self and the enemy, the rulers and the ruled, or the gods and the demons. It is a battle between de-humanized self and the objectified enemy, the technologized bureaucrat and his reified victim, pseudo-rulers and their fearsome other selves projected onto their 'subjects'" (Nandy, *The Intimate Enemy*, xvi).

38. Nandy, *The Intimate Enemy*, 97.

39. For example, see Nandy, *The Intimate Enemy*, 48, 63.

40. Nandy, *The Intimate Enemy*, 82.

41. Dykstra, *Images of Pastoral Care*, 1–14.

DEVELOPMENTAL IDEOLOGY AND
MISUNDERSTANDING IN THE (HUMAN) FAMILY

Developmental psychology has served as a paradigm for healthy growth within relational human beings across the lifespan; yet, it is based on inherent biological and social struggles of "normal" growing up. Postmodernity exposes just these kinds of normative claims embedded in and assumed by modern theories of personhood. Erikson envisions healthy development in terms of human beings who move predictably from living with a given identity at birth, to making a series of choices to resolve identity crises at each developmental transition, to finally in old age giving back to others. In fact, Erikson claims that when all goes well in this trajectory, "Death . . . can be made [a human being's] final gift" of generativity and generosity to the world.[42]

While it may be inspiring, even therapeutically helpful, to maintain an ideal healthy life cycle, developmental norms patterned on trajectories of privilege limit opportunities for recognition.[43] When recognition is available to some human beings at the expense of non-recognition of other human beings, the structural death of personal and social opportunities over a lifetime is not a gift. In this sense, developmental psychology can be used to frustrate rather than facilitate mutual understanding. Stated another way, developmental psychology can contribute to misunderstanding stories, especially when we recognize how powerfully developmental narratives structure many international and intercultural relationships in dehumanizing ways. Pastoral theologians have critically engaged problems of non-recognition in relation to women and children within family life.[44] However, problems of non-recognition extend more broadly in the human family.

By analogy, development work suggests that healthy development within the human family moves from so-called "primitive" cultures through a series of identity crises to so-called "developed" cultures.[45]

42. Erikson, *The Life Cycle Completed*, 126.

43. Van Eys, "Who Then Is Normal?" 12–13.

44. For example, see Stevenson-Moessner, *In Her Own Time*; Miller-McLemore, *Also a Mother*; Witte et al., *The Equal-Regard Family and Its Friendly Critics*.

45. Historically, this movement was represented in the philosophical idea of the great chain of being, represented in writing and art. Among the over eighty striking drawings embedded within Stedman's journal display through art his paradoxical stance toward plantation culture, including a rendering of three naked women yoked together with thick rope. Stedman's drawing represents a white woman in the middle leaning to one side on a representation of a South American indigenous woman, and

Colonial projects prioritized "the human over the nonhuman and the subhuman, the masculine over the feminine, the adult over the child, the historical over the ahistorical, and the modern or progressive over the traditional or the savage." [46] We see this pattern reproduced in words, images, and flesh, as living colonized bodies were literally displayed in museums in the (ironically) so-called mother countries. Most famously, Sarah Bartmann, the so-called Hottentot Venus, was displayed mostly naked as a museum exhibit forced to embody as a site of dehumanizing fascination that was rendered in drawings and reinforced dehumanization in the colonial imagination. [47] Even in his drawings of his relationship with Joanna, Stedman initially depicts her as naked and later as clothed, but in both cases many times smaller in size in comparison with his own self-portrait. The cover of acclaimed Suriname author Cynthia McLeod's *The Cost of Sugar* includes William Blake's "A Surinam Planter in His Morning Dress," depicting a half-naked, barefoot slave woman serving a drink to a well-dressed white man three times her size. [48] Colonizing hierarchies that became embedded in the transhistorical Western sense of self as well as in masked identities of colonized human beings continue to appear in media and other representations. [49] Problematic representations endure today.

In 2011 I visited the Netherlands for the first time. As a white United States citizen, I was much more familiar with Suriname than with its representations in the Netherlands, its former colonizing country. Representations of my partners and friends from Suriname jumped out at me throughout the visit through images. Thankfully, I partnered with women's studies professor and scholar of Suriname history and culture Gloria Wekker, who helped me navigate this disruptive experience. Imagine my surprise to see in person a monument that had been installed in 2006 in Amsterdam memorializing Anton de Kom, the Surinamese nationalist exiled to the Netherlands who became part of the Dutch resistance movement in World War II, who died in a Nazi concentration camp, and whose

---

to the other side leaning on a representation of an African woman. The caption under his eighteenth-century drawing reads "Europe Supported by Africa and America." (The image appears in *Stedman's Surinam*, 317). Stedman's journal includes over eighty drawings, which were converted to engravings from Stedman's own original drawings by a variety of eighteenth-century artists (Price and Price, "Introduction," xxxv).

46. Nandy, *The Intimate Enemy*, x.

47. Sharpley-Whiting, *Black Venus*. See also Gaskell, "Ethical Judgments in Museums," for a broader range of ethical considerations in relation to museum exhibits.

48. McLeod, *The Cost of Sugar*.

49. Nandy, *The Intimate Enemy*, xi–xiv; Sharpley-Whiting, *Pimps Up, Ho's Down*.

political activism and writings influenced the vote for independence in Suriname in the 1970s. Rather than the suits and hats he was known for, there he was, represented as a naked black man emerging from black stone. According to a recent reflection, "the Dutch sculptor had rendered him for posterity as a half naked noble savage, an 'honour' that would never befall a white politician or writer."[50] This representation in stone continues to dehumanize de Kom, who in his 1934 *We Slaves of Suriname* had written, "It took a long time . . . before I had freed myself of the obsession that a Negro was always and unconditionally the lesser beside any white person."[51] When one is open to the shared woundedness that colonialism still marks on human relationships, witnessing such dehumanizing representations is deeply troubling.

Exhibits at the Ninsee, the national organization whose mission is to facilitate recognition of the history of slavery in the Netherlands, were more familiar in that they respected and represented Surinamese as human beings. However, recognition, for example, in the form of a national memorial to Dutch slavery installed in 2002 continues to evoke national debate in the Netherlands about how to bridge a past that is so psychologically challenging across multiple perspectives.[52] In Suriname, in the United States, and in our postcolonial context in general, embodiment is problematically inscribed with representing varying social power and privilege. When will we acknowledge rather than continue to perpetuate colonizing representations of human beings?

Today development is measured in terms of overall health, other biological factors such as life expectancy, economic wealth, educational opportunities and literacy rates, inequality indicators, and technological and other measurable advancements. Every year since 1990, the United Nations has released a "Human Development Report" that takes into account these kinds of data to identify needs and opportunities in countries throughout the world.[53] The word *development* is embedded in the language of global relations where the so-called developed world is charged with the responsibility to help the so-called developing world "mature" through economic aid, debt relief, public health and other medical initia-

50. Oostindie, *Postcolonial Netherlands*, 119, see also ibid., 97; also personal conversations in front of the monument with Dr. Gloria Wekker in May 2011.

51. Quoted in Oostindie, *Postcolonial Netherlands*, 149. I have not yet been able to locate a translated copy of the primary text but look forward to engaging this primary text in future research.

52. Oostindie, *Postcolonial Netherlands*, 148–59.

53. The development reports can be found online: http://hdr.undp.org/en/.

tives, infrastructural improvements, education, environmental awareness, the spread of democracy, and other initiatives. Christians have considered international global missions to be a moral and theological imperative.[54] In MoiKonde, we witnessed a range of governmental, nongovernmental, international, and religious development initiatives. Of course, we also participated in an international sustainable development initiative representing the US government abroad. Reflecting on this experience, development work can be structured in more or less empowering ways.

However well intentioned, the analogy of development is often oriented toward non-recognition and therefore perpetuates misunderstanding stories. With Erikson's developmental framework in mind, Nandy's postcolonial criticism of developmental theory helps unmask inherent problems with the analogy. Colonialism fixed colonized human beings and countries in adolescent identity crisis with colonizers claiming the authoritative and paternalistic title of "mother country," providing justification for the "caretaking" posture of the "more mature" colonizer. But this is a misrecognition, which thereby functions as non-recognition and aims to render passage out of cultural adolescence impossible by the very refusal of recognition. If this sounds somewhat circular, that's because it is. In other words, colonialism uses developmental ideology to block the very thing development turns on: recognition.

IMAGINING MUTUALITY

Mutual understanding is difficult even in the best situations. Conflicting cultures and differences across languages combined with categories of inclusion and exclusion contribute to identity crises that can impede understanding one's own experience and the experiences of others. Appealing to experience, we know that life trajectories are often thicker and messier than nine identifiable stages would suggest. Developmental theory is at best an ambiguous analogy for global relations and remains highly complex given the layers of deeply embedded structural oppression that characterize the present day as postcolonial. To foster possibilities for transcending developmental or other traditional categories, leaders in faith communities must be willing both to engage persons who embody narratives counter to normative theories and to participate in the creation

54. Here we can make a correlation to Erikson's development as his most advanced virtue of wisdom is the only developmental virtue identified in the New Testament to describe the life of Jesus (Stevenson-Moessner, *In Her Own Time*, 2).

of new places of and analogies for liberative, empowering relationships in which human beings across a range of differences and struggling with a range of identity crises can experience belonging.

Alternative models for intercultural relationships are more liberative than developmental psychology. Some, such as a model of equal regard[55] or a model that focuses on capabilities of what one can be or do in context,[56] can still be problematic because they assign familial roles or measure human capabilities across cultural differences. One model likens development work to lubricating gears so that intercultural conversation unfolds naturally.[57] Models that recognize movement and uncertainty in intercultural understanding are more promising.[58] I advocate a model of sustainable partnership facilitated through narrative strategies and oriented toward mutual recognition.[59]

Narrative combined with critical dialogue and the value placed on provisional understanding in this book offer insight regarding how to hold normative developmental theory in tension with embodied narratives that transcend normative categories. As one scholar writes, "Stories are never perfect answers, but they allow us to ask the questions in different ways and try on different responses."[60] Narratives help facilitate recognition of human experience as difficult to categorize.[61] One way to counter the generalizations about human development embedded in modern society is to tell and retell stories by accounting for details of experience, networks of relationships, interpersonal and intercultural encounters within social systems, and feelings and worries, particularly what can be identified as

---

55. Witte et al., *The Equal-Regard Family and Its Friendly Critics.*

56. Nussbaum, *Women and Human Development.*

57. Kristof and WuDunn, *Half the Sky,* 242. Contributors to a critical review of *Half the Sky* demonstrate just how difficult it can be to envision even this model as mutually empowering ("Global Gender Inequality and the Empowerment of Women. Discussion of *Half the Sky*," Review Symposium).

58. Ackerly, *Universal Human Rights in a World of Difference;* Narayan, *Dislocating Cultures.*

59. Future research could expand this model in connection with global partnerships recognized for their more mutual approaches, such as microlending and partnering in health initiatives.

60. Fuchs-Kreimer, *Parenting as a Spiritual Journey,* 128. The trickster theme is another way of considering multiplicity within stories while subverting the concept of "right answer" (Edwards, "Structural Analysis of the Afro-American Trickster Tale").

61. Zaner, *Conversations on the Edge.*

one's own. Telling and retelling stories allows secrets and silenced grief and pain to find a voice through which to emerge.[62]

Theologically, telling and retelling stories is the healing and prophetic work of lamentations. Lamentation is a spiritual practice not often identified as a resource for navigating experiences of identity crisis. Identifying lamentations as a justice-making practice, pastoral theologian William Blaine-Wallace writes the following: "The grieving and aggrieved need a predictable and consistent audience for telling and retelling their stories, over and over again . . . [because] there is no telling how often stories of sorrow and tragedy need repeating in order for a new perspective, a glimpse of meaning, an unforeseen path, a previously unimaginable forgiveness, a once-closed future to open."[63] Blaine-Wallace refers to the need for this kind of narrative lamentation that recognizes the identity crises of everyday life, including the losses and gains of developmental changes.[64] Full and complete emergence of stories as ways of thinking about experience continues to escape even those who pay careful attention to narrative nuances; therefore, Blaine-Wallace and Zaner and you and I continue to tell and retell stories. Narrative serves as a vehicle for interpretation and reinterpretation of shared experience that has the power to affect systems and open new possibilities of understanding.

To resist the colonizing use of developmental psychology is to tell and retell counter-narratives that resist and disrupt Western notions of linear time that unfold neatly on a more or less predictable developmental trajectory. Nandy recommends we focus on immediate social needs, combined with disrupting linear notions of time to emphasize the "all-embracing permanent present, waiting to be interpreted and reinterpreted."[65] Disruptive narrative strategies of poetry and laughter become practices of resistance that can appropriately trouble colonizing dualistic categories[66] by breaking out of exclusive dualisms and moving toward recognizing multiplicity as part of healthy identity formation:

62. Zaner, "Keeping One's Balance in the Face of Death."

63. Blaine-Wallace, "The Politics of Tears," 195.

64. Ibid., 184.

65. Nandy, *The Intimate Enemy*, 57.

66. Nandy, *The Intimate Enemy*, 98. Many affirm the strategic value of humor and irony. For example, Hermans argues from a social-constructionist perspective that laughter and irony serve as "great equalizers" (Hermans, "Ultimate Meaning as Silence," 133). From a pragmatic perspective, Richard Rorty also lifts up irony and poetry as strategies for living in a pluralistic world (Rorty, *Contingency, Irony, and Solidarity*).

> This century has shown that in every situation of organized op-
> pression the true antonyms are always the exclusive part versus
> the inclusive whole—not masculinity versus femininity but ei-
> ther of them versus androgyny, not the past versus the present
> but either of them versus the timelessness in which the past is
> the present and the present is the past, not the oppressor versus
> the oppressed, but both of them versus the rationality which
> turns them into co-victims.[67]

A more "fluid self-definition" with somewhat permeable boundaries embraces inherent human complexities and ambiguities. Psychologically,
resolution of identity crisis that recognizes legacies of colonialism af-
fecting present-day psychology resists a tight, mechanistic split between
self/not-self, me/not-me, self/other, we/they, us/them, etc.[68] Pastoral
theology has embraced resistance as a core function of good enough
care that supports liberation and empowerment in lived experiences.
Strategies of resistance are those practices oriented toward recognition:
"[Anyone] who sees every being [in his or her] own self and sees [him-
self or herself] in every other being, [he or she], because of this vision,
abhors nothing."[69] Rather than delivering a final conclusive interpretation, an integrated vision of human beings in encounter who navigate
both prior knowledge and an ethical imperative for continual learning
integrates academic rigor and practices of neighbor love.[70]

RECOGNITION BEGINS WITH ASSENT

Misunderstanding stories in MoiKonde evoked layers of personal and
communal identity crisis, including the best way to understand identity
crisis and how to address it in community. Developmental psychology
has been used by analogy as a strategy of dehumanization played out
in historical colonialism by limiting opportunities of success to those
in power at the expense of dehumanizing those whose power has been

67. Nandy, *The Intimate Enemy*, 99.

68. Ibid., 104–7.

69. Ibid., 108–9, 108n77, 109n78.

70. Ibid., 113. Again, Nandy has many interdisciplinary companions who come to
similar conclusions, such as H. Richard Niebuhr in *The Responsible Self*, or Derrida,
who argues that "history can be neither a decidable object nor a totality capable of
being mastered, precisely because it is tied to *responsibility*, to *faith*, and to the *gift*,"
which involve the undecidable, the absolutely risky, and the mysteriously transcen-
dent, respectively (Derrida, *The Gift of Death*, 5–6; italics original).

strategically minimized. While modern developmental psychology recognizes the centrality of identity crisis in experiences of normal growth over the lifespan, postcolonial theorists unearth ways in which developmental theory has instituted rather than resolved identity crises through colonizing languages, images, theories, and practices.

Both Erikson's modern developmental psychology and Nandy's postcolonial criticism of developmental psychology view recognition as essential for healthy development and endurance of identities. Erikson sees recognition as both a gift offered and capacity gained in the course of life through the major identity crisis in adolescence. Nandy interrogates how stage theories have served historically to impede recognition by opening pathways to development for some persons at the expense of others, which, he argues, diminishes the fullness of identity and increases a sense of constant identity crisis for all human beings.

This chapter has argued for the importance of turning and returning to narrative to be accountable for how and to what end identity crisis is storied. Any model has embedded norms and values that include and exclude by framing experience. Neither Erikson nor Nandy nor you nor I have the luxury of an Archimedean standpoint from which to examine the ebbs and flows of identity across the lifespan from outside of our postcolonial lived experience. Embodied narratives of lived experience testify to our essential embeddedness in the thick of our own and others' unfolding identities. In a world characterized by increasingly diverse intercultural networks of relationships, misunderstandings stories contribute to and are consequences of identities in crisis.

In this intercultural world shaped by the legacy of colonialism, is it such a bad thing to recognize multiplicity within a soul? Rather than worry about the inherent value of identifying more than one facet of any particular human being's experience of soul, healthy growth, change, movement, and shifts in identity are more about recognizing and navigating multiplicity within my sense of self, my sense of other human beings with whom I share the world, and my sense of constant becoming in relation to other human beings. Neurologist Oliver Sacks notes: "It is all too easy to take language, one's own language, for granted—one may need to encounter another language, or rather another *mode* of language, in order to be astonished, to be pushed into wonder, again."[71] Misunderstanding stories in intercultural relationships reveal just how

71. Sacks, *Seeing Voices*, xi.

challenging it is to identify oneself and others in the midst of the translation work required for cross-contextual fluency.

Recognition begins with assenting to the personhood of other human beings as neighbor. This also throws me back on myself, which I can expect to raise questions for me around my previously held assumptions grounded in problematic yet historically reified dehumanizing representations. Encountering an other around language, particularly language used to frame identity crises, can provoke "an unexpected perspective on the human condition"[72] in which I am at once neighbor and stranger. Resolving the identity crises we experience and share requires practices, social structures, and theologies that support recognition. Telling and retelling our misunderstanding stories in which we human beings suffer and perpetuate suffering through dehumanizing strategies dependent on theories of "development" invite reconstructing narratives to "[open] up the present and the future"[73] to questions of "who am I?" and "who are we?" in order to participate in more liberative and more mutual relationships of intercultural understanding. Recognition activates the challenging practice of thinking that opens pathways for cognitive love through telling and retelling stories graciously not at the expense of our neighbors, but in their presence as we learn what we share and celebrate where we differ.

72. Sacks, "Preface," xiii.
73. Nandy, "Themes of State, History, and Exile," 171.

4

Sharing in Vulnerability

TELLING AND RETELLING, HEARING and overhearing misunderstanding stories will help to open pathways for deeper and more mutual understanding. Receiving and offering misunderstanding stories requires courage and acknowledgement of being misguided in assumptions and conclusions. This kind of acknowledgement requires a disciplined desire for understanding. Theologians and philosophers have argued for centuries that human desire is distorted and requires discipline. Saying, thinking, or writing that I want to reach points of mutual understanding in relationships is one thing. Experiencing humility and acknowledging my contributions to misunderstanding are much more difficult to sustain because these practices require vulnerability. A willingness to be vulnerable to learning in direct relation to neighbors across cultural and other differences depends on the kind of recognition theorized in chapter 3. This chapter engages the sharing in vulnerability that accompanies recognition. Drawing on feminist insights from psychology and theology through Jessica Benjamin's psychological concept of intersubjectivity and Wendy Farley's theological notion of distorted desire, I argue for engaging a discipline of accountability that respects the complexity of embodied desire in relation to understanding oneself and other people, *particularly* in those moments when misunderstandings and violations wound bodies, relationships, and communities.

That desire is wounded in a postcolonial context is a guiding assumption and starting point of this chapter. We can imagine a spectrum of responses to the difficult task of attending to oppression and injustice in contemporary forms of pastoral and religious care, ranging from the desire not to know to the desire for idealistic change to the desire to recognize complicity and responsibility. Paradoxes of privilege make this task more complicated and difficult. The goal of this chapter is to invite religious reflection and moral imagination around cultivating a desire for learning that can activate movement toward new possibilities of sharing in vulnerability and subsequently more mutual understanding.

More mutual understanding is needed in relation to matters of justice that are (and are made to be) invisible right in our midst in churches, hospitals, other local institutions, and local communities, and far beyond the scope of our habitual gazing. Looking *at* others through dehumanizing representations rather than *recognizing* others as sharing in humanity is important with respect to our neighbors both close to home and often far beyond the purview of our daily life. We need courageous self-reflection to address our complicity in strategies of dehumanization that endure as a legacy of historical colonialism. When we consider practices of justice and practices of exclusion or injustice, we must account for the complex interaction of the personal, familial, communal, local, intercultural, national, and international relationships and structural systems.

In relation to attending suffering and facilitating healing, pastoral theology and care practices oriented toward expansive goals of liberation, empowerment, and resistance include, first, a sense of *shared vulnerability*. Overemphasis on an individualistic mindset has shielded us from being vulnerable to each other, particularly when we encounter interpersonal and intercultural differences. Second, justice-oriented theology and care practices also involve *responsibility*. We feel responsible to those with whom we are in relationship. With no perception of a relationship, or a relationship where one partner is devalued, comes the feeling that there is no claim on me or my commitments toward another human being. Without relationship, we lose a sense of responsibility to the other.[1] Third, justice-oriented care calls for *"authentic participation."*[2] I participate authentically when I recognize my participation in a breach in understanding *and* I recognize the need to participate in conditions for resolution. The following narrative fragment exemplifies that shared vulnerability, responsibility, and authentic participation are deeply interrelated.

1. Gill-Austern, "Engaging Diversity and Difference," 33.
2. Lartey, *In Living Color*, 32–34.

A NARRATIVE FRAGMENT

In our absence, my life partner and I learned through a New Year's Day phone call with a friend in the village that a break-in of our home in MoiKonde had occurred. We were disappointed but at the same time strangely and uncomfortably understanding. Simultaneously shocked and unsurprised. The reason we were not surprised was not because of any ill-formed opinion of the character of the children who broke the wooden window and explored our home while we were away, ironically leaving food storage containers opened but otherwise undisturbed and only stealing the holiday treats we left for them to be given by a neighbor who had a key to the house.

We respected and adored our neighbors and their children. In one sense, we were not surprised to hear of the break-in because our home was in many ways a communal space for being in community with children. Their artwork adorned the walls. They ate and drank and played in the space as much as we did. It was our home in a robust communal sense. At the same time, we were disappointed out of a strong sense of personal property; we locked the house while we left and assumed that our neighbors—these same children and their families—would watch over it for us.

Experiences of ambiguity and a range of emotions accompanied and followed that telephone call on New Year's morning. We desired communication and reconciliation. We were confident that we knew what a process for reconciliation could and should look like. We strategized about how to implement our plan in an interculturally sensitive and respectful way that honored our disappointment while also making space for healing.

We prepared to return to MoiKonde to resume and complete our service with a clear plan ready to offer to our neighbors. We resolved crisis of identity by appealing to this confident clarity with a renewed commitment to our roles as Peace Corps volunteers invested in the challenges and possibilities of intercultural understanding through friendship. This all quickly dissolved once we returned into the experience of living in (and not just thinking about) the challenges of intercultural partnering.

Only later after returning to the village did we learn that the break-in had already been addressed internally via communal beatings of the girls. We could only begin to piece together a picture of whatever had resulted in bruised faces of our closest young neighbors. We had never witnessed this kind of communal beating, though we were all too aware of the daily physical violence to children, animals, women, and occasionally men in our midst.

The larger insider community seemed to have placed shame on the families of the girls. As with most village houses, the front part of our house was a public space, especially, in our experience, to welcome children. Though our neighbors—the girls and their families—had been frequent visitors to our home throughout each and every day, all relationships between us and the girls' families (our neighbors and close friends) were severed in a way we experienced but did not understand. The girls and their siblings were now banned from entering our house.

We were initially unaware of the internal response of the village. Once we returned to MoiKonde, evidence of communally sanctioned physical violence toward children from visible scarring and verbal reporting prompted our return to crises-of-identity, questions about human nature and conflicting norms of human interaction. We realized that we held a robust vision of reconciliation: accountability and apology based on a model of restorative justice, which we envisioned would naturally provide a mechanism for recovering relationships by restoring a sense of health and vitality. Differing norms of communication thwarted our efforts toward restorative justice through face-to-face encounters with any of the girls or their families, sending us back to crises of identity and an extended experience of misunderstanding.

When I had unintentionally violated the sacred trust of MaLespeki some months earlier, we were able to resolve the breach by communicating with her daughter, another respected matriarch in MoiKonde. However, in this case of returning to severed relationships, no one conversation seemed to hold any reconciliatory potential. Rather, each conversation added layers of complexity to intercultural misunderstanding around a process of reconciliation.

Narrative fragments swirled around and within us in the long weeks of being suspended in crisis about how to restore meaningful intercultural relationships. We heard a story about children who simply entered the house through an open window, which is culturally acceptable, therefore restoring relationships. At the same time, we overheard a story about how children who steal will escalate in violence over time, so therefore there can be no restoration because of this inevitable slippery slope. We heard and overheard stories that we deserved the break-in for being white, for living well in the village, for being American, for leaving, for coming back. We heard that we were on the agenda for the annual yali kuutu, the New Year's community-wide meeting.

Captain began the yali kuutu by unearthing the narrative of MoiKonde from Africa to the colonies to the rainforest and most recently to forced relocation after the human-made lake had flooded their previous land. All items on the agenda were framed by their place in a much longer and much more *complex historical narrative in which this community endured oppression and broken promises from those in power. Even though we had previously met with village elders and Peace Corps administrators to voice our commitment to return to MoiKonde after the break-in, this time we were asked to make an account of our commitment and of our understanding of our role in relation to the cultural history of MoiKonde in front of the whole community.*

We reiterated our disappointment in the news of the break-in, along with our desire and commitment for restoring relationships with those in MoiKonde, who had welcomed us, and for whom we were grateful. We restated our desire to learn to live well even in the face of misunderstandings and cross-cultural mistakes and poor choices from all parties. We exchanged traditional forms of mutual recognition through phrases, applause, traditional handshakes, and embraces.

The yali kuutu *went on for another several hours, attending to the other important discussion items of the year. This formal event did not resolve the breach; however, it opened a pathway for possibilities of resolution. The journal entry where we first reflected on the experience of the* yali kuutu *is titled "the day life may have started turning around."*

VULNERABLE TO QUESTIONS?

Beginning to negotiate a vision of reconciliation within experiences of misunderstandings—what Victor Turner calls "redress"—is often a shared, communal, public event. At the same time, negotiations toward healing after a crisis event also necessarily occur, at least initially, in a limited and privileged space among persons who share particular understandings of social structures. Persons often begin to address conflict internally within communities of support. Eventually, reconciliatory activity can be hosted in institutions oriented toward response and resolution. However, the drive to address conflict in public is often in tension with the drive to hold conflict tightly within an inner circle with little public attention.[3] The predictable tension wears on relationships and communities.

Telling and retelling misunderstanding stories even and especially within moments of heightened stress and palpable tension requires sharing in vulnerability. This is complicated because experiences of splitting that are felt within relationships are part of an intercultural ritual process. Turner considered the *redress* phase a sometimes theatrical, public

---

3. This same tension often structures congregational and denominational conflict, as well as other contexts for interpersonal misunderstanding and disagreement.

forum that addresses social behavior.[4] While I find Turner's idea of redress helpful, the term "redress" is problematic. To redress assumes knowledge about how a particular transgression needs to be made right. In the aftermath of crises of understanding, part of the challenge is figuring out what happened, what is going on now, and how to reimagine the future. Rather than knowing the ins and outs of a crisis and how it needs to be addressed, these factors are unknowns and must be found in careful attention and learning. In the early aftermath of heightened crisis, sharing in vulnerability around questions of events and their meanings is to address in the spirit of restoration rather than to redress according to a particular pre-understanding.

Communal values, norms, and rules find expression through ritualized social responses. Remember the example of the formal courtroom ritual that promises to redress breaches in a United States context. In the above narrative fragment, the *yali kuutu* provided space for public attention to resolving the layers of intercultural breaches we were experiencing. Relational stress along cultural, subcultural, familial, gendered, racialized, and other seemingly distinct lines can also lead to exclusive or private ritualistic pathways to resolution. We must remember that one family often activates resolution such that persons outside of the family not only do not participate but also might not even be aware of the familial process. At the same time, this familial process affects and is deeply connected to social relationships that exist well beyond members of this particular family.

An initial communal response to any crisis of understanding is only a beginning. Both experiences of crisis and efforts toward resolution focus attention on various fault lines in relational matrixes. This phenomenon is amplified in relation to cultural differences. In the experience described above, my plan for reconciliation came into sharp conflict with a model of reconciliation that I did not understand. I can guess that cultural difference is a factor at play; however, the only thing I know with certainty in the face of conflict is that I don't know or understand all of the factors at play. Nor does anyone else. Therefore, in the face of tension and stress on relationships, persons must be intentionally focused and disciplined in listening and speaking. One must become vulnerable to questions: What am I missing? What am I misunderstanding? What is being shared? What am I sharing? What am I withholding? What do I need to learn? Where do I need to hear and overhear? Where do I need to tell and retell?

---

4. Turner, *From Ritual to Theatre*, 11.

If asking these kinds of self-reflective questions under pressure were *easy*, then there would be a lot less suffering in the world. Careful attention to oneself and to others is *more difficult* under pressure than when everything is or seems to be going well. We can all think of examples from our individualized experience. Phyllis Tickle also highlights this phenomenon on a systemic level: when the whole church in all its wonderful diversity is under pressure around declining membership in the midst of worldwide economic crisis, human beings tend to retreat into the simplest yet most extreme position regarding any particular issue.[5] Predictably, in times of stress, it is more difficult to speak clearly and more difficult to listen and to hear anything that anyone is saying. No wonder misunderstanding stories are so difficult to tell and retell, to hear and overhear!

Human beings simply do not desire vulnerability in the precise moments that they experience destabilization of a sense of self and communal identity. When what normally feels stable suddenly feels unstable, we tend to desire some stability rather than to identify the string of connected uncertainties now in our awareness. Shifting in identity always involves loss; we must engage practices of discipline in order to differentiate between, on the one hand, the loss that comes with participating in courageous change; and, on the other hand, forced experiences of loss that result from an abusive misuse of power. In the context of courageous change, intercultural sharing in uncertainties can lead to greater depth of understanding precisely when so much is at stake *if and when* we are willing to unmask power differentials and invite a multiplicity of voices and opinions. Recognition of human beings beyond habits of gazing structured by dehumanizing representations opens us to shared vulnerability. An other human being is seen no longer as representing a category or as less than, but rather as a potential partner fundamentally sharing in humanity. We recognize that sharing in questions means sharing in a *desire* to acknowledge misunderstanding in the service of a deeper, more mutual understanding.

POSSIBILITIES FOR HEALING THE WOUNDEDNESS OF POSTCOLONIAL DESIRE AND THE PARADOX OF PRIVILEGE

Embodied learning affects one's sense of self and sense of community and is therefore challenging and often disruptive. Learning to attend to oppression within practices and visions of pastoral care is particularly disruptive

5. Tickle, *The Great Emergence*.

and can evoke that tricky trio: fight, flight, or freeze. Fighting often takes the form of resistance to recognizing complicity in the privilege afforded through complicity in strategic dehumanization of other human beings. Defensive speech and body language can provoke others to join in the fight. Some show little emotion. Others rage. The *desire not to know* both facilitates and impedes openness to learning as movement toward new possibilities of understanding. Another common response is flight, which can happen by envisioning an idealistic beyond to white privilege, which we might actually reach in the near future. Some of us shed tears. Others ask, how long? as if realizing the gravity of this question for the first time. Recognizing the depth of suffering in local and global communities issues a call to wrestle with the theological concept of hope. The *desire for change* both facilitates and impedes openness to learning as movement toward new possibilities of understanding. Still other students freeze: they see their complicity in a new way and become stuck in despair. Eyes widen. The *desire to recognize* complicity, vulnerability, and responsibility both facilitates and impedes openness to learning as movement toward new possibilities of understanding. Each response contributes to important conversations in the pastoral theology classroom. Many experience all of these responses at one time or another. Whatever our response, all of us are entangled in sticky webs of privilege. What resources can help us understand and offer hospitality to these complex desires for the sake of justice in a world of inequality and systemic dehumanization?

Acknowledging this as a valid question for *my* consideration is being vulnerable to it. The question requires recognizing that strategic, systemic dehumanization supports a world of inequality and oppression—and our complicity in them. In addition, we must recognize the challenges of how this postcolonial legacy characterizes the context for contemporary pastoral theologies and care practices. Recent shifts in the field from individualistic, caregiver-centered care to a more expansive view of care as communal, intercultural, and participatory foster contextual understanding. The important work of theorizing this expansive move must, like the best of pastoral theologies, give an account of its embodiment in practices in lived experience. Honing practices of telling, retelling, hearing, and overhearing misunderstanding stories is a way of considering lived experience as the field moves in more liberative directions.

Misunderstanding stories underscore the need to understand that desire is wounded in our postcolonial context. Day after day in MoiKonde that January, we lived with failures of reconciliation found in intercultural misunderstanding that we embodied but did not understand. At our best, our openness to learning included both a willingness to understand and a willingness to recognize misunderstanding. Yet, we resisted the desire to learn during these weeks as well, even finding pleasure in the feeling of certainly being right. Desire for discerning *both* that I need to learn *and* what I have misunderstood is difficult to maintain, particularly in relation to the stress of intercultural breach in understanding. In the weeks after returning to MoiKonde, the experience of engaging in the long process oriented toward these dual goals of yearning for understanding required the difficult disciplined work of remaining vulnerable to recognizing misunderstanding. We resisted, we argued, we cried, we flew off into idealistic views of intercultural harmony, we disengaged, we got angry, we stared into space, we reengaged, we encountered our emotions, we journaled, we sat with neighbors in silence, we yearned to sit with neighbors. We experienced both the distortions of desire for resolution and a strong desire for sharing in the long process toward reconciliation. Lived experience, with all its emotional, moral, psychological, and other complexities reveals the importance of pastoral theologies and care practices that attend to suffering while desiring to limit harm as much as possible and staying open to recognizing unintentional violations through communal investment and interaction.

This work is even more complicated when we recognize connections between desire and domination that continue to fuel interpersonal and communal violence. In the next sections, I engage an interdisciplinary study of feminist psychoanalytic and theological perspectives on complex desires and subsequent complexity of vulnerability in our postcolonial contexts.

INTERSUBJECTIVE DESIRE AND MISUNDERSTANDING STORIES

Pastoral theologians appeal to depth psychology to help us understand the challenge of mutual understanding, particularly with respect to differences. *Tension* is important in many depth psychologies in relation to processes oriented toward understanding within and between human beings. Further, tension is central to Victor Turner's relational anthropology and to sociologist Kurt Wolff's conception of the serious play of vulnerabilities oriented toward practices of cognitive love reviewed in chapter 2. In chapter 3, I outlined the role of identity crises in opening space both for recognizing the personhood of other human beings and also for recognizing my complicity in practices of non-recognition. While I constantly negotiate this tension, it also creates space for mutual sharing in vulnerability.

Feminist psychoanalyst Jessica Benjamin also places tension at the core of healthy relational life. Her influential book *Bonds of Love: Psychoanalysis, Feminism, and the Problem of Domination* (1988) continues to be a significant resource in pastoral theology and gender studies classrooms. Benjamin's understanding of intersubjective desire is a way to better understand the vulnerability that can open to conditions for resolution within experiences of intercultural misunderstanding.

Like other psychoanalysts, Benjamin theorizes by first appealing to the analogy of the infant-mother relationship. However, Benjamin criticizes post-Freudians like Margaret Mahler who theorize separation and individuation as the ultimate and most desirable goals of child development.[6] This is significant because, according to Benjamin, two human beings exist as subjects any time a baby is born of a mother.[7] Rather than one-way development, Benjamin envisions a "continual, dynamic, evolving balance" to recognize subjectivity across all parties in relationships.[8] She theorizes about an *intersubjective relationality* in which human beings interact with parents and other authority figures in patterns of separation (establishing a sense of identity set apart from other human beings) *and* attachment (establishing a sense of identity connected to other human beings). For Benjamin, growing in relationship requires navigating this as one of many tensions. Coming to terms with interpersonal differences through mutual recognition is a much more adequate conception of relational life than what she considers to be the false premise of parental authority as that from which the infant must strive to separate.[9]

Recall that we also learn with Nandy's postcolonial psychology in chapter 3 how dangerous it is to use a parent-child model to hypothesize about international relations and social development on the level of communities. Nandy criticizes the analogy from personal development

6. Benjamin writes, "The problem with this formulation is the idea of separation from oneness; it contains the implicit assumption that we grow *out of* relationships rather than becoming more active and sovereign *within* them; that we start in a state of dual oneness and wind up in a state of singular oneness" (Benjamin, *The Bonds of Love*, 18). See also Mahler et al., *The Psychological Birth of the Human Infant*.

7. Benjamin, *The Bonds of Love*, 24.

8. Ibid., 25.

9. Ibid., 181, 112, 114.

to national development because he sees the risk of infantilizing and feminizing developing nations based on a so-called gold standard of the developed world. Nandy implores us to see how this flawed vision is operative in our own imaginations. It is flawed because it *prevents* mutual understanding by employing a colonizing gaze and therefore perpetuating dehumanizing representations rather than supporting opportunities for mutual recognition.

Both Nandy and Benjamin theorize that *gender* is a central factor in how relationships play out in social contexts. While *The Bonds of Love* tends to view gender in a United States context—for instance, Benjamin considers the inadequate resources for affordable daycare given United States laws and social norms[10]—examples of the weight of parenting responsibilities that structurally fall on women are certainly relevant beyond the internal contextual diversity of the United States. Benjamin criticizes the dualisms of Western culture particularly around *gender polarity* as *the* structure that supported traditional patterns of male domination and that continues to structure the present day. Like Nandy, Benjamin exposes the dangers of choosing to identify with one "pole" of identity by participating in strategies that dehumanize any part of oneself or other human beings who "choose" to identify with the opposite "pole" of identity. We see this dynamic in dualistic language, such as American and un-American, Christian and non-Christian, churched and un-churched, and so on. As outlined in chapter 3, this kind of bipolarity sets up false dichotomies around race, gender, and age, as well as nationality, religious affiliation, and other identity markers. Gender polarity now supports more subtle patterns of domination that work via the myth that identity is a matter of rigid choice rather than honoring the complex multiplicity of identity.[11]

A model of *intersubjective relationality* serves as an alternative to a flawed model of individuality supported by dualistic thinking that diminishes the humanity of anyone who identifies with the opposite or negation of *me*. In contrast, an intersubjective model considers that human beings play an active part struggling toward a more integrated process of creatively discovering and accepting the ambiguity of his or her context.[12] Intersubjectivity aims to unmask traditional patterns of *domination* that regulate relationships, particularly around gender differences but also around cultural differences, according to a model of a recognizable

10. Ibid., 211.
11. Ibid., 7, 184, 172–73.
12. Ibid., 45.

"master" who requires submission and non-recognition. *Submission* in this model becomes pleasurable for those who submit to the system as commanded by the one who embodies the so-called master role. Other theorists take up what Benjamin calls submission in terms of silence,[13] harmful adaptation,[14] tolerance of inauthentically received identity,[15] or conformity.[16] The myth that this "crushing objectification," maintained through these and other distorted adaptations is pleasurable has been and continues to be a key strategy of dehumanization. Images of submission cemented in narratives of domination must therefore be disrupted.

Disrupting narratives of domination is especially challenging because you and I (who, for example, have access to higher education) are invested in the structural problem of domination. We benefit from it. We often ignore the messy, fatal costs for our brothers and sisters, for the earth, and for our connectedness to all of God's good creation. In MoiKonde, it was especially challenging to discern that the most empowering practices regarding education for young women eventually require their separation from the village, family, and cultural context because of the lack of access to higher education in local contexts. Education is a human right according to the *United Nations Declaration on the Rights of the Child*;[17] how long until education is accessible to all children? Being vulnerable to the disruptions and difficult questions that accompany practices of telling and retelling misunderstanding stories can unearth counter-narratives of sharing in human dignity and creativity.

Challenging normalized patterns of relationships structured by domination and submission, Benjamin argues that we human beings can participate more intentionally and more actively in processes of recognition. Benjamin defines *recognition* as "that response from the other which makes meaningful the feelings, intentions, and actions of the self."[18] Recognizing another human being as *both* like *and* unlike me contributes to a deeper *mutuality*. Vulnerability to possibilities of mutual understanding demands openness to a constant play of resonance and

13. For example, Belenky et al., *Women's Ways of Knowing*.

14. For example, Neuger, *Counseling Women*.

15. For example, Marshall, *Counseling Lesbian Partners*.

16. For example, Tatum, *"Why Are All the Black Kids Sitting Together in the Cafeteria?"*; Van Beek, *Cross-Cultural Counseling*.

17. Office of the United Nations High Commissioner on Human Rights, *Convention on the Rights of the Child*. See Article 28; online: http://www2.ohchr.org/english/law/crc.htm/.

18. Benjamin, *The Bonds of Love*, 12.

difference.[19] Recognition is paradoxical in that *I* grow by recognizing *you* both as related to *me* and as existing in *your* own right without assuming that *you* exist for *me* in a posture of submission.

Recognition itself sparks identity crisis because of how difficult it is to sustain in practice. Benjamin considers that "the ideal 'resolution' of the paradox of recognition is for it to endure and be endured as a *constant tension*."[20] She disrupts ideals of wholeness as a singular matter of individual achievement by arguing that wholeness requires the difficult practice of "maintaining contradiction."[21] In a relational orientation toward mutual recognition, human beings live in paradoxical tension that acknowledges inevitable breakdowns and misunderstandings. Mutual love is the action of sharing in vulnerability rather than forcing vulnerability onto other human beings, which would be not vulnerability but violence. Mutual love embodied and enacted in community while acknowledging the tensions and ambiguities involved in so doing can disrupt normalized patterns that maintain, reinforce, justify, and ignore violence.

Patterns of gender polarity structure social relationships in subtle and powerful ways that continually threaten possibilities of recognition. Benjamin points to liberative ways in which *both* theorizing about disrupting power *and* attempting practices with the intention of disrupting power can begin to dismantle engrained structures of polarity.[22] However, she argues for a different kind of *destruction* in which human beings do not destroy others and themselves through "righteous revolution" that simply tries to reverse the violence of a particular polarity by redirecting violence the other way. Like Nandy, Benjamin contends that a violent response to violence threatens human dignity for all. Rather than reversing poles of a dualism, Benjamin advocates idealism in constant tension with destruction directed toward "challeng[ing] and criticiz[ing] authority, the very persons, ideas, and institutions that have been idealized."[23] Practices of successful destruction occur within the constant tension of recognition that restores visions and recovers practices of mutual human dignity and possibilities of sharing in experiences across a multiplicity of differences.[24]

19. Ibid., 30, 26.
20. Ibid., 36.
21. Ibid., 63.
22. Ibid., 223.
23. Ibid., 293n56.
24. Ibid.

Is intercultural mutuality possible even when recognizing pervasive long held intercultural misunderstandings? Benjamin suggests that the bonds of love frame recognition paradoxically. Questioning possibilities of understanding must accompany questioning its impossibilities: "The anchoring of [the structure of domination] so deep in the psyche is what gives domination its appearance of inevitability, makes it seem that a relationship in which both participants are subjects—both empowered and mutually respectful—is impossible."[25] Bonds of love catch human beings in a process of recognition in which each human being is considered a subject who "grow[s] in and through the relationships to other subjects."[26] If identity crisis opens space for recognizing human dignity across human beings, then subsequent sharing in vulnerability creates opportunities for the deeper recognition of empathy. Benjamin's psychoanalytic theory of recognition contributes to the central argument of this book: that sharing misunderstanding stories opens possibilities for deeper, more mutual understanding than previously imagined.

Healthy liberative intercultural relationships recognize and navigate tension. Benjamin characterizes *mutual love* as the willingness to live intentionally in tension oriented toward recognizing human beings—one's sense of personal identity and human dignity *and* the identity and human dignity of other human beings—without demanding or finding pleasure in submission. She writes, "The joy I take in your existence must include *both* my connection to you *and* your independent existence [which is unknown to me]—I recognize that you are real."[27] Recognition is a practice of acknowledging the limits of knowledge as well as reevaluating prior knowledge as a challenging path that invites the conditions for resolving intercultural breaches in understanding so that reconciliation becomes possible.

NONRECOGNITION, SUFFERING, AND THE HEALING OF DESIRE

I risk participating in violence even when *I* alone am envisioning and trying to embody possibilities of mutual recognition for the purposes of fostering a more peaceful and mutually loving human community. We can see this in my relationship with MaLespeki where in the very process of

25. Ibid., 8.

26. Ibid., 19–20.

27. Ibid., 15.

educating future Peace Corps volunteers to respect cultural norms and practices, I violated a cultural norm and practice. In an attempt to educate not to cross the threshold of sacred spaces, I was revealing markers of sacred space. Actions oriented toward mutual respect do not always embody mutual respect. In this case, MaLespeki let me know this and I could almost immediately recognize my unintentional complicity. In other cases such as in the narrative fragment above where I simply could not wrap my head around how to move toward an embodied and communal recovery, I am responsible to ask questions and to bear to hear the response. Learning of a breach in understanding intercultural norms and practices is the beginning of a movement toward more mutual understanding and not its conclusion. Intercultural understanding is a process of learning bound in the powers of love, creativity, mystery, and intimacy that both order and disorder our life together. Both pastoral and systematic theologians grapple with theological reasons for participating with care in speaking, hearing, overhearing, and otherwise sharing in the vulnerability required by living in community oriented toward mutual understanding across cultural, historical, and other differences.

Pastoral theologians have also turned to systematic theologians as partners in understanding human suffering and practices oriented toward healing. Theologians, particularly those who have engaged in the emerging field of theologies of religious pluralism, have begun to produce scholarship to help better understand intercultural misunderstanding. One such scholar is constructive theologian Wendy Farley. Like Fanon, Farley argues that we may become skilled in recognizing ourselves (though this takes a great deal of courage) but often fail each other with our lack of desire for mutual recognition. Farley invites us to consider *despair* as a form of suffering in which we all need to recognize our part. We cannot ask "how long?" without actively participating in suffering in solidarity with neighbors. Yet, recognizing our participation in suffering often threatens to immobilize us in despair. Acknowledging this is what promises to move us into new possibilities of understanding.

Pastoral theologians can find resources for attending to recognition through Farley's *The Wounding and Healing of Desire: Weaving Heaven and Earth* (2005). In her book, Farley argues that "there is a sense in which we hardly exist without recognition."[28] She warns of the damage that results without sufficient attention to recognition: "My instinctual knowledge that I am not one iota more important or real than anyone or anything

---

28. Farley, *The Wounding and Healing of Desire*, 5.

else does not translate into felt experience. In the absence of an immediate awareness of others as vivid as my awareness of myself, I will constantly act out of this root experience of the brilliance of my own experience and the comparatively pale, tepid, and inessential reality of everything else."[29] The human longing for fulfillment tempts us to find solace and comfort in finite things that cannot by definition endure through eternity. Like Benjamin, Farley argues that the human tendency to find fulfillment in *our idea* of what an other(ed) human being should be for our own benefit limits possibilities of mutuality.[30] Farley contends that we "inhabit" desire in ways that are deeply problematic to ourselves, the world, and one another.[31] She writes, "We want what we want and deplore the thought that we inhabit the webs that carry the consequences of our actions far beyond us."[32] The core of the problem is the human tendency to *possess* that which or whom we desire, which upsets the kind of negotiated tension Benjamin argues is a condition for the possibility of mutual understanding.

Farley's theological anthropology depicts human beings as highly skilled in what postcolonial theorists call *masking*. Postcolonial theorists across genres and academic disciplines point to the ways that physical distance from human beings deemed as "other" facilitates psychological distance and leads to what mistakenly appears to be the justified violence of dehumanization. Farley argues that the "most dangerous temptations"—the ways we deceive ourselves into believing that a neighbor's suffering is not like my suffering, and that a neighbor's healing is not like my healing—these "most dangerous temptations are present in the guise of something we think of as good."[33] What becomes good in my mind starts to resemble self-deception fueled by a perception that I am unlike all others, what Farley and others call egocentricism. The woundedness we embody is that we humans often disguise this as good.

As the delusion of totalizing self-sufficiency seeps into our heart's desire, Farley points out that we risk taking on "massive responsibility [that] maintains others in dependence."[34] If I am responsible for the whole world as a disembodied idea, then I don't need to listen to *you* and therefore can "legitimately" minimize you, continuing to fray the threads of our many

29. Ibid., 49.
30. Ibid.,16.
31. Ibid., 13.
32. Ibid., 66.
33. Ibid., 75.
34. Ibid., 91.

connections, including the paramount connection of all humans in the *imago dei*. In terms of recognition, if I inhabit the representation of myself as savior, then I simply work tirelessly to save the world without feeling the need to recognize anyone else as a partner in the process. As novelist and nonfiction writer Anne Lamott writes, "You can safely assume you've created God in your own image when it turns out that God hates all the same people you do."[35] Farley argues that the woundedness of our desires harms our image of ourselves, neighboring human beings, and of God. To resist colluding in this harm, development work must therefore be oriented by a model of mutual partnership rather than a morally hierarchical approach that appeals to a distorted analogy to developmental psychology.

Woundedness, by not being shared, endures. In other words, vulnerability unshared becomes not one-sided vulnerability but violence for both the one who claims invulnerability and the one violently ordered to submit. The woundedness of our desire cuts us off from ourselves, from our neighbors, and indeed from God. Farley outlines a vision of dressing these deep and divisive wounds:

> The vividness of [my egocentric self-awareness as a person isolated in my ego] produces the illusion that we exist alone, trapped with our ceaselessly nagging fears and hopes, sufferings and desires. In this way we are bereft of the consolations of companionship, sharing only faint shadows of the joy of intimacy or compassion in suffering. Our emotional and spiritual life denigrates into a struggle with passions that bind us ever more tightly to our sorry attempts to ease our pain. But as the ever-fresh rivers of the Divine Eros flow through us, this illusion and its debilitating consequences dissipate. Our natural powers for joy and compassion, the strength of our courage, and the light of wisdom trickle through the bars of our prison.[36]

Farley hopes that there is a hinge, a place to pivot from isolationism and individualism toward deeper connections to oneself, other human beings, the world, and God. Like identities, the intricacies of passionate, deeper connection in postcolonial contexts are complexly multiple.[37] When we become aware, really become aware of our complicity, we must receive the *rage* that flows as a consequence of the violence of embodying

35. Lamott, *Bird by Bird*, 22.

36. Farley, *The Wounding and Healing of Desire*, 34.

37. Gloria Wekker and Philomena Essed explore the intricacies of passionate, deeper connection in postcolonial Suriname (Wekker, *Politics of Passion*; Essed, *Everyday Racism*).

a dehumanizing gaze toward other human beings. An enormous amount of sharing in vulnerability, courage, responsibility, and work to maintain avenues for participation is required to resist the often overwhelming tendency to fight, flight, or freeze in relation to learning of *my* complicity.

Sharing in vulnerability includes recognizing a range of emotions in community. After viewing a recent documentary about a 1921 race riot with consequences for all of us, my class voiced their emotional responses ranging from despair, anger, rage, helplessness, and hopelessness to a sense of openness, possibility, courage, and hope. As pastoral theologian Lee Butler defines it in relation to the legacy of slavery in the United States, "Rage develops when my humanity is denied and my existence is controlled by a force that seeks to diminish my identity."[38] Both Butler and Farley find hope in the midst of rage. However, hope is *not* to shield ourselves from expressions and realities of rage. Hope stands in the midst of difficult conversations that acknowledge the rage that emerges when we *see* and *hear* the extent to which the beloved human community—the earth, the silenced millions of women, children, men—continues to be torn apart by violence masquerading as benevolent good deeds. Rage says "no" clearly. It is a dissonant ringing in our ears. Hopefully!

Hope in the midst of rage helps engineer the hinges as places of turning and reconnecting. When we can sustain vulnerability in the process of unearthing past suffering and attending present suffering, hope is "more secure" because it accounts for the not-yet-possible but never impossible: that healing is possible.[39] Acknowledging that healing is not yet fully present requires seeing and raging at the suffering that is and that *I* maintain by *my* investment in disconnections. Butler writes, "the task . . . is not to deny the rage, but to transform its energy into a creative force."[40] Farley adds that "rage becomes the divine energy of compassionate wrath."[41] Farley reminds Christians that divine creativity "entered into the world in a human body through the blood and pain and muck of childbirth"[42] without the sterility of a modern hospital delivery room. Divine and human creativity meet in the "anguish of suffering . . . in refugee camps, in hunger, in greed and violence, in self-hatred and paralysis, in illness that opens up only on more pain, in prisons and the terror of dangerous homes, in the emptiness

38. Butler, *Liberating Our Dignity*, 165.
39. Lester, *Hope in Pastoral Care and Counseling*, 64–65.
40. Butler, *Liberating Our Dignity*, 165.
41. Farley, *The Wounding and Healing of Desire*, 34
42. Ibid., 105.

of luxury and meaningless work."[43] Divine and human creativity meet in the suffering of non-recognition. Courage to tell, retell, hear, and overhear misunderstanding stories for the sake of deeper and more mutual recognition is messy, creative, empowering work. Neither the misunderstanding stories shared in this book nor your misunderstanding stories evoked by this book have clear resolutions. The work of our calling as leaders in participating in God's justice on earth through *tikkun olam*, participating as partners in the work of mending the woundedness of creation, invites this challenging and courageous work of vulnerability.

Participating in partnerships of mutuality involves neighbor love. Central to both Jewish and Christian ethics, love of neighbor flows from participating in love of God. Neighbor love has come to serve as a bridge of understanding across religious differences where Christians can embody this moral duty through joining in dialogue with other human beings, who represent both Christianity and other religious traditions, to love in the face of dehumanizing poverty, victimization, violence, patriarchy, and other colonizing strategies of non-recognition between human beings and within all of creation.[44] In the face of differences that often make mutuality tense and misunderstanding likely, neighbor love offers a model for moving toward the deeper recognition of mutual intercultural empathy:

> Love requires not just that we do "good" to others but that we respect them, affirm them, listen to them, and be ready to learn from them. To truly love others, we have to stand ready to receive from them, at least as much as we hope to give to them. If "doing good" is not accompanied by respect and mutuality, then love becomes patronizing kindness. Which means it is no longer love. Love calls for relationships of mutuality in which there is reciprocal giving and taking, teaching and learning, speaking and listening. And that's what dialogue is all about. "Love thy neighbor" means "Dialogue with thy neighbor."[45]

How better to resist the distancing gaze that lingers on as a legacy of colonialism than to be neighborly in our postcolonial context? Recognizing that we participate in the postcolonial world for good and for ill calls for a new honesty in relation to what neighbor love means. Postcolonial neighbor love involves owning up to *my* social location and the privileges afforded me at the expense of neighboring human beings. Desiring not

43. Farley, *Gathering Those Driven Away*, 155–56.

44. Knitter, *Introducing Theologies of Religions*, 137.

45. Ibid., 102

to know the suffering I perpetuate is a product of the woundedness of desire. The identity crises that raise questions for me about who *I* am and who *we* are prompt disciplined reflection and self-awareness that opens *me* to growing, changing, shifting, and moving. Participating in the surrender and catch of cognitive love not only opens questions about previously held assumptions but also reveals to me my complicity in suffering. But it doesn't have to end there in despair. When caught up in moments of distilled awareness, a new kind of neighbor love begins in vulnerability to learning and proceeds toward a deeper recognition of mutual understanding.

Recognition exists only within our past and present entanglements with harmful ways of life.[46] And dehumanizing practices of non-recognition remain: what is harmful is often disguised as good. What a challenge therefore to see clearly! What courage required to acknowledge misunderstanding harm for good! Farley imagines possibilities of recognition as "the loving delight that others exist"[47] not *for* or *because* of my benevolence but *with me and I with other human beings* as we navigate the ambivalence of our desires.

And so, I must ask myself, others, the world, and God to what extent I understand. I must probe the extent to which I am vulnerable to questions. When we can bear to listen to what is said, to that which necessarily exceeds my knowledge and awareness, recognition becomes more possible. Human stories of suffering and healing become *our* story unable to be *possessed* by any one of us to the detriment of all. The misunderstanding story represented in the narrative fragments of each chapter describes a multilayered breach in intercultural understanding, raises questions of identity, and yearns for resolution and reconciliation. This movement is facilitated in community. We become more mutual partners in healing when we can recognize shared stories as necessarily complex and ambiguous. Can we learn to be vulnerable to "bear the truths that few want to hear" where vulnerability is safely shared albeit risky?[48] How might we practice this deep and courageous co-participation?

Studying psychological and theological perspectives on the woundedness of desire is relevant today in a postcolonial context of systemic inequality and strategic dehumanization. This interdisciplinary study of desire merits attention in part because the authors participate in privilege

46. Farley, *The Wounding and Healing of Desire*, 93.

47. Ibid., 34.

48. Rambo, *Spirit and Trauma*, 150.

and seek to dismantle it from within their American contexts. Many seminary students and leaders in ministry aim to do the same in their religious vocations. Both Benjamin and Farley weave personal/individuated and social/systemic motivations for, embodiments of, and consequences of desire. Both theorize possibilities for healing the woundedness of desire in a postcolonial context. In a postcolonial context attentive to interdisciplinary conversation partners and partnering with accounts of lived experiences, pastoral theory is well poised to consider voice and vulnerability.

COAUTHORING VULNERABILITY

Given that desire is wounded by the polarities that structure myths of the legitimacy of dehumanization, desiring to co-author rather than author stories is a resistive strategy that requires vulnerability to partnering. A practice of *coauthoring* recognizes that no one person authors any story.[49] The concept of coauthoring helps us to understand ministry practices, and it also helps me reflect on the integrity of my academic contribution. Our disciplined practice of writing through journaling sustained over our two years living in MoiKonde enabled me to take ownership of my own assumptions, moments of intercultural understandings, and complex intercultural misunderstanding stories. My academic contribution as a pastoral theologian and Christian ethicist includes narrative fragments as the fruit of revisiting my own journal writing and revisiting partners in MoiKonde for subsequent conversation and communal reflection. It also evokes my own affective experiences, memories of what I hope are shared experiences, and contradictions I embody as a returned Peace Corps volunteer. Writing, both personal and academic, can facilitate opening to vulnerability that becomes a robust basis for hope. Writing creates room for shared vulnerability and negotiating silences, but *I* don't have the last word. As a pastoral theologian, I leave open the possibility that I didn't hear well, that I don't remember well, that there is more to learn through communal partnerships.

Pastoral theologian and ethnographer Mary Moschella defines coauthoring as participating in possibilities for an open future oriented toward mutual transformation:

> Understanding our historical, religious, and cultural particularity through ethnography strengthens our clarity and resolve

49. Moschella, *Ethnography as a Pastoral Practice*, 238.

> as we strive to co-author a more faithful, just, and life-giving future . . . we have at least some freedom to alter the scripts we speak and the actions we perform . . . With this power comes the responsibility to speak wisely and fairly, to exercise power *with* the people, helping people find voice, rather than speaking *for them*, or exercising power *over* them . . . And in any ethnography, even if research is conducted well, the narratives composed have the potential to inflict harm upon the participants. Ethnographic portraits, like mirrors, may startle or confuse as well as empower or liberate.[50]

Narratives enlist authors and readers in the participatory exercise of scripting future possibilities. Narrative structures can point to problems, grab attention, evoke affective experiences, and transform memories.[51] Encountering stories that matter in the midst of participating in the play of listening and hearing leads to academic obligations of telling and retelling misunderstanding stories.[52]

Coauthoring is a practice of navigating tensions around silence and voice through humility and care in academic writing. Telling, retelling, hearing, and overhearing misunderstanding stories recognize human finitude that *both* prevents complete understanding *and* recognize that narratives of complete understanding therefore necessarily dehumanize. In a variety of ways, pastoral theologians have long recognized that *I* cannot and should not always be the story-teller but must first and foremost be a story-listener. How do *I* then navigate the tensions between silence and speech? It is *we* who come to be in community and to behold community through writing.[53]

Reflecting on voice as a moral concern includes recognizing that choosing a voice is a privilege of both writing and textuality. When ought silence be considered a last resort, or an immoral option? On one hand, silence is associated with deep reverence and intimate experiences of awe, wonder, and stillness. Silence, or the pursuit of silence, accompanies many meditative and spiritual practices oriented toward calming or awakening. Silence can also be claimed as a tool of protest. For example, silence can

---

50. Moschella, *Ethnography as a Pastoral Practice*, 238–39, 253 (italics original).

51. Carroll, "Narrative and the Ethical Life," 44, 52.

52. Zaner, "On the Telling of Stories"; See also Zaner, *Conversations of the Edge.*

53. Holmes and Farley, *Women Writing Theology*; Greider et al., "Three Generations of Women Writing for Our Lives." Decentered writing in community opens one to being moved (see also Moody-Adams, *Fieldwork in Familiar Places;* Behar, *The Vulnerable Observer*).

serve to protect dignity and safety within vulnerable populations.[54] Many have recognized the importance of silence among women survivors of sexualized violence.[55] Silence can be a trust-gathering space for persons rightly not yet ready for a more intimate vulnerability. Pastoral theologians are deeply attentive to the value of silence, as the practice of listening is at the heart of pastoral presence.[56] Silence opens new ways of listening, discerning, hearing, and practicing. Silence invites mystery, spiritual formation, and unimagined possibilities.

Silence also indicts. Institutional silence, which is deeply engrained in and around us, justifies and normalizes the violence of both commission and omission. Institutional silences regarding sexism or racism or heterosexism or ableism render differences invisible and force normative declarations.[57] Yet, one must ask, is it even possible to speak or come to voice other than through colonizing means? I write as a returned Peace Corps volunteer and recognize the responsibilities and choices played out in lived experiences involved in embodying the role in a particular way. How can I write while being self-reflective, remaining open to being mistaken, realizing possibilities for both understanding and misunderstanding, participating in sustainability, and sustaining vulnerability to learning?

Responsible writing is deeply connected to social concerns of both local and global communities. For example, African theologian Musa Dube asks how anyone in any discipline can write without addressing HIV/AIDS as a global crisis.[58] Scholars who write on the Shoah ask how anyone in theology can write anything that could be used to justify burning children.[59] How can we write without mentioning that some governments are considering instituting the death penalty for homosexual acts?[60] At the time of completing this book, the United States is caught up in

---

54. See Annica Kronsell's example of military women who, when invited to participate in interviews, remained silent so as not to be singled out from their male counterparts more than they already were by the visible mark of gender (in Kronsell, "Methods for Studying Silences," 122).

55. See D'Costa, "Marginalized Identity"; Fortune, *Sexual Violence*; Leslie, *When Violence Is No Stranger*.

56. For example, see Dittes, *Pastoral Counseling*; Justes, *Hearing beyond the Words*.

57. See for example, Kronsell, "Methods for Studying Silences," 109.

58. Dube,"*Go tla Siama. O tla Fola.*"

59. Halivni, *The Book and the Sword.*

60. "Uganda: International Bar Association's Human Rights Institute (IBAHRI) Condemns Introduction of Death Penalty for 'Aggravated Homosexuality.'"

the systemic dehumanization unmasked by the recent killing of African America teen Trayvon Martin. Do you see the human rights violations in the world at this moment? Where is the *imago dei* being denied to some of God's children? Where am I participating in, condoning, ignoring violence at home and abroad? Writing is necessarily limited by authorial voice(s), context(s), and the limits of language(s); however, we must yet strive to represent suffering and healing in as much complexity as possible given the limitations. Moschella writes, "Be careful not to overgeneralize. Instead, offer some of the 'situated wisdom' of your setting. Hold your new wisdom lightly; offer it gently as a gift, not arrogantly as a rule."[61] Hopefully, writing itself as provisional understanding opens pathways to more mutual understanding.

Responsibly beholding misunderstanding stories includes retelling, reinterpreting, analyzing, writing with integrity, and engaging the disturbing realities of the day. Writing reveals my "assumptions, presumptions, and contradictions" in a way that silence cannot.[62] However, writing is also affected by the ways in which it is embodied.[63] Consider the following reflections on writing and voicing from diverse sources:

> It's because we can *reflect on and identify* what we do as well as just doing it that we *can* exercise moral judgement; it's because we can *choose* what we do, rather than being over-determined by instinct or destiny, that we *ought* to exercise that judgement. Language, which enables these capacities by providing the tools—a symbolic register—in which to process them, is often identified as a key to human identity. And the capacities for reflection and selection are so significant for the writing process they suggest we could think of writing as a form of *responsibility* to our material.[64]

> Gray Panthers founder Maggie Kuhn said: Speak your mind even if your voice shakes . . . It hits you, doesn't it? Right there. Suddenly, you have permission not to be perfect or polished or even particularly brave. It's not who hears you that matters. It's the speaking up that'll save you every time. And here's the thing about that shaky voice. People will listen anyway. I see it time and time again as I travel the state and meet women who just can't be silent any longer . . . "My voice is not real strong, and

61. Moschella, *Ethnography as a Pastoral Practice*, 211.
62. D'Costa, "Marginalized Identity," 149.
63. Hunt, 144
64. Hunt and Sampson, *Writing*, 153, italics in original.

it usually shakes," [one woman] said softly as she grabbed my hand before speaking. "But sometimes. Sometimes, I think if I don't speak out? Well, I'm afraid I will lose my mind." A few minutes later, she took the stage. Her voice shook that night, just as she feared, and she stumbled over her words a few times as she shifted from side to side. But for the entire time that she spoke, her soft, trembling voice was the only sound in the room.[65]

First they came for the Socialists, and I did not speak out—
Because I was not a Socialist.
Then they came for the Trade Unionists, and I did not speak out—
Because I was not a Trade Unionist.
Then they came for the Jews, and I did not speak out—
Because I was not a Jew.
Then they came for me—and there was no one left to speak for me.[66]

Silence is the real crime against humanity.[67]

Responsible writing as coauthoring negotiates tensions around silence and speech in part by being vulnerable to questions about my understanding and misunderstanding. On a regular basis, I can ask and then bear to hear or be asked and then bear to respond to questions: What is missing? Where are the silences? How are the silences oppressive and/or liberative?[68] Where are we silencing? How am I exercising my voice? How is this method of writing and speaking and ministering responsible? Stories of untold, unnamed memorials must be unearthed from the writing of those who have had privileged voices and access to the printed, published word. What may need to be unearthed from my storying? Writers like the above who probe silence and suffering remind us of responsibilities to voice embodied memories that live and breathe on against all odds.

Pastoral theologians have honed the craft of approaching the privilege of writing with an orientation toward rich description as "faithful and recognizable description of a setting or an experience."[69] Complex misunderstanding stories, especially when told in multiple ways, can handle

65. Schultz, Connie, "Fearless Politics: Speak Your Mind Even If Your Voice Shakes." Posted on www.huffingtonpost.com/ on September 4, 2006; online: http://www.huffingtonpost.com/connie-schultz/fearless-politics-speak-_b_28706.html/.

66. United States Holocaust Memorial Museum, *Holocaust Encyclopedia*, "Martin Niemöller."

67. Sarah Berkowitz, quoted in Mitchell, *Plantations and Death Camps*, 109.

68. We can point to recent examples of genocide, human trafficking, complex systems of economic disempowerment, and countless other examples.

69. Moschella, *Ethnography as a Pastoral Practice*, 198.

such tensions.[70] It is not my goal to resolve tensions but instead to lift them up as significant aspects of intercultural encounters. I am persuaded by Benjamin, Farley, Butler, and Moschella that living in and with tensions is a condition for resolving intercultural crises in understanding and the subsequent identity crises that threaten to activate resistance or despair and instead can activate a deeper and more mutual understanding.

A SPECTRUM OF SHARING IN VULNERABILITY

Sharing in vulnerability can empower bodies and embodied communities when it bridges the reflective work of identity crisis and the affective openness to neighbor love. The word *share* is related in Old English and Dutch to the word *shear*, "to cut or to divide." A contemporary definition of *share* reads, "to join with others or to receive in common with others."[71] Sharing as a receptive gesture leaves one vulnerable to a new experience. Openness to the provisional status of understanding shared experience is an experience of vulnerability because of its acknowledgement of partiality, limitations, capacity for change.

In MoiKonde, I yearned for reconciliation in the middle of the story, the same place of maximal disruption, confusion, identity crisis, and misunderstanding. Eventually, through disciplined effort in community and not without confronting the tense woundedness of desire for learning, formal pathways of conflict resolution opened. The misunderstanding story went public. Yet, the peace, relief, and neighbor love of reconciliation were not yet realized. Rather, sharing in the vulnerability required for mutual learning opened hope for future peace, relief, and neighbor love. Formal recognition of other human beings as partners in community opened potential space for transforming understanding. In these tense, in-between spaces of misunderstanding stories, practices of attention, when sustained, must resist the competing temptations of despair or self-righteousness non-recognition.

When sharing in vulnerability in the classroom, ministry students often ask for "the right answer" to any number of imaginable pastoral dilemmas. What is a healing response, and what creates more harm when another human being shares an experience of suffering? Hearing and telling of human suffering with these questions in mind can unmask connections and disconnections within and among human beings. The only

70. Ibid., 203.

71. Online: http://dictionary.reference.com/browse/share

certain answer to any dilemma is that we don't know ahead of the shared experience what will be healing and what will be harmful. Therefore, good enough pastoral practice includes being vulnerable to the questions: What are you going through? Am I helping or harming? The even more challenging next step is to bear to hear the response: the silences, the words that emerge from courageous encounter.

Attending to suffering is the starting point of pastoral theology. It is also the starting point of any act of pastoral care or pastoral counseling. My experiences living in a post-colony help me understand how difficult it is to attend to suffering.[72] The stakes are high: our embodied and historied limitations blind us to the suffering in our midst, particularly suffering we perpetuate without even consciously knowing. The theories reviewed in this chapter help us understand suffering as a complex phenomenon in which we all participate. Attending to suffering is facilitated by sharing in vulnerability, being open to receiving a share in new experiences. Being vulnerable to learning includes attending to precisely those places of deep misunderstanding in all aspects of life. Sharing in vulnerability is a resistive counterpoint to practices of gazing supported by dehumanizing representations of other people and resultant habits of non-recognition. Telling and retelling, hearing and overhearing misunderstanding stories can help train faculties of attention required for enduring the sustained presence of shared experiences.

Only after engaging this challenging work of attention can we leaders in ministry then begin to participate in healing that endures. I aim to advance a *participatory model of healing*. The basic idea is that caregivers do *not* transmit healing to a person in need. A participatory model of healing disrupts the whole idea of one person who merely gives care to another needy person who merely receives. What offers healing is a relational practice in which both the so-called caregiver and the so-called care receiver participate in the caring encounter: both are in need, both give, and both receive.

Students of religion continue to be moved by Martin Luther King Jr.'s conviction that the long arc of history bends toward justice. I desire that students be moved and I with them—but the desire to be moved issues a call to participate in movement, which is never easy and always involves ambiguity. Some students fight this task. Others seek to lead immediate concrete progress toward justice. Some freeze in exasperation. The task

<hr>

72. Weil, "Reflections on the Right Use of School Studies with a View to the Love of God," 64–65.

is so complex and unfinished. The very forces that motivate optimism toward realizing justice can also impede possibilities of recognition that mutual sharing in justice requires.

One of the many paradoxes of privilege is that the desire to heal the wounds made apparent by postcolonialism is itself entwined in systems of oppression that frustrate and impede desire leading to systemic change. We cannot just go in and bend the arc of history toward our own isolated and privileged visions of justice. Rather, we must work together to envision partnerships across differences wherein the arc that connects colonial histories with more liberative, open futures bends through relationships of mutual learning as movement toward new possibilities. When we returned to MoiKonde with a renewed commitment to intercultural partnership at the same time that its possibility was most severely challenged for us, the bridge into the village happened to be impassable and under repair. This physical impasse symbolized much more than heavy seasonal rains and issued an invitation into the challenging work of intercultural understanding. While formal processes reopened bridges to understanding, more work awaits.

5

Misunderstanding Empathy

MISUNDERSTANDING STORIES ABOUND IN and among us and can seem to issue no obvious intrinsic moral demand. Conflict can seem to hover indefinitely in superficial cycles of "I'm right" and "you're wrong" supported by dehumanizing representations of superiority based on culture, age, religion, gender, race, ethnicity, nationality, political affiliation, class, education, sexual orientation, marital status, fertility, and other identity markers that have been correlated with so-called advanced development. Participating in reconciliation, however, is a matter of sharing in a great responsibility. When breaches in understanding provoke me to raise questions around my assumptions, activated by identity markers such as those listed above, I glimpse what it might be like to see without the gaze. When these questions open me to the vulnerability required for shared learning, communal space is pregnant with possibilities for creative conversation. Ever cognizant of human finitude yet maximally open to being moved to participate in healing, maximally aware that I might be harming you and therefore be complicit in suffering, and maximally suspending my previously held assumptions, sharing in vulnerability opens up possibilities for profoundly mutual understanding. But there is yet work to be done in the process of sustaining hope when despair and apathy loom as quite reasonable-sounding responses. Reconciliation that sustains human beings in mutual recognition does not just happen, but it is possible.

In MoiKonde, I yearned for an embodied experience of reconciliation that would lead disrupted relationships into a more hopeful future.

I experienced disruption in understanding and layers of identity crisis even while working to be open to learning; formal sanctioning of reconciliation's possibility eased the irritation of misunderstanding embodied in communal life together. How long must we work to understand? How long until reconciliation will not be considered or declared or legislated but rather embodied and mutually shared in experience?

Experiences of breach in intercultural understanding raise questions of identity that, in a postcolonial context, reveal just how much deeply engrained dehumanizing representations block our ability to participate in recognition. With disciplined commitment to the possibility of reconciliation in the midst of divisive misunderstandings, shared vulnerability can open us to realizing that desires and relationships are fraught with dilemmas. Recognition then begins right in the midst of unsettling tensions as we assent to the personhood of other human beings, paving the way for reconciliation, which is only realized in a larger process of sharing in the basic human experience of empathy as deeper recognition.

What is the relationship between reconciliation and intercultural empathy? Empathy, as a deeper layer of recognition, is a process of being moved by another human being and also recognizing the imprint of other human beings in one's sense of self. It is the embodied hope that other human beings are understandable. Through our bodies, we realize the ability and necessity of connection with other human beings.[1] Empathy as connection flows from awareness and respect for interpersonal differences. Margaret Kornfeld writes, "To be empathic, we must acknowledge that, initially, we don't know the other."[2] Theological anthropology that considers empathy a necessity for human beings assumes the mutual possibility of my understanding you *and* your understanding me. Empathy is participating appropriately in the ideas, feelings, and experiences of other human beings,[3] embracing the truly other[4] through recognition. Empathy is crucial in a postcolonial pastoral theology oriented toward more mutual intercultural understanding.

While pastoral theologians envision and expect possibilities of empathy, we also recognize limits and obstacles to it. Empathy can be "confounded by its limitations" because good enough pastoral practice includes recognizing "an inability to understand fully the lived reality of

---

1. Paulsell, *Honoring the Body*, 11; Gaillardetz, *Transforming Our Days*, 37.

2. Kornfeld, *Cultivating Wholeness*, 52–53.

3. Glaz and Moessner, *Women in Travail and Transition*.

4. Graham, *Care of Persons, Care of Worlds*, 20.

the oppressions suffered by another."[5] Therefore, harmful pastoral care can result when caregivers, trained to embody a non-anxious presence, become too anxious around the difficulties of understanding another's stories, particularly in relation to culture, gender, sexuality, race, and other elements of identity.[6] Sociologist Patricia Hill Collins, who has helped pastoral theology appreciate how challenging empathy is across multiple differences in identities and experiences, reminds us that "people are not naturally good at empathy" because of its requirement for disciplined reflection on identities and contexts that are constantly shifting in response to living in the world.[7] If *my* understanding of *you* requires self-understanding and introspection, then understanding only becomes possible through responsible participation in empathy. In our postcolonial context, empathy includes recognizing pleasurable connections, painful disconnections, and our institutionalized ways of masking this crucial distinction that confuses disconnections as pleasurable and the discipline of connecting as pain.[8]

Postcolonial challenges lead pastoral theologians to rethink empathy around pastoral skills such as the attentive listening needed *both* to attend suffering by being present in the midst of shared woundedness *and* to facilitate hope and healing. As Emma Justes says, "The problem with listening is that it is so easy *not* to do," both generally and particularly across cultural differences.[9] Before assuming that more mutual understanding depends on improving already present practices of empathy that simply need fine tuning, we must also attend to the ways we are schooled to mask resistance to healing as misunderstanding. While I generally maintain that empathy can be learned within relationships of proximity, focusing on proper empathic technique can evade difficult questions around empathic limits.[10] Pastoral theology classrooms address this tension by cultivating

5. Miller-McLemore, "The Living Human Web," 21.

6. Glaz and Moessner, *Women in Travail and Transition*; Butler, *Liberating Our Dignity*; Ali, *Survival and Liberation*; Anderson and Miller-McLemore, "Gender and Pastoral Care," 110.

7. Furthermore, she reminds us that "our own position is never finished and we cannot understand our own position in isolation." Hill Collins, *Another Kind of Public Education*, 101–2.

8. Benjamin, *The Bonds of Love*; Gay, *Understanding the Occult*, 39, 85; Scarry, *The Body in Pain*.

9. Justes, *Hearing beyond the Words*, xi–xii.

10. Kohut, "Introspection, Empathy, and the Semi-Circle of Mental Health," 397; Miller-McLemore, "The Subject and Practice of Pastoral Theology"; Gay, *Understanding the Occult*.

pastoral imagination in practices like role plays in which students exercise and then reflect on self-aware listening.[11] Case studies in pastoral theology classrooms can lead to new understandings in hopes that practicing and subsequently reflecting on one's habits of attention in relation to subtle forms of power can translate into more liberative and empowering care practices in ministry. Self-reflective assessment of communal dynamics in reconstructed verbatims from on-campus role plays or transcripts of online role plays provides a context for identifying aspects of pastoral practice that facilitate good enough care and those practices and habits that impede it.[12] Reflective practice in communities of learning helps us recognize hearing and overhearing as equally important to speaking and acting in practicing the neighbor love that characterizes good enough care.

In the following section, I return to the misunderstanding story that has been woven throughout this book. As in previous chapters, the following narrative fragment describes only a small part of a longer unfolding process of reconciliation in one particular intercultural community. I have used Victor Turner's anthropological understanding of the structure of social dramas to attend to complex stories of intercultural misunderstanding from my experience as a Peace Corps volunteer living in MoiKonde. Recall from chapter 1 that Turner considers reconciliation to be a long process that requires sustained participation across community members. Narratives of intercultural reconciliation that begin with appreciation for the inevitability of intercultural misunderstanding raise questions about the possibilities of intercultural empathy. Chapter 3 proposed dilemmas with dominant models of personality development. Then, chapter 4 probed just why shifting or moving models is so challenging. Now, I attend to the process of reconciliation within an intercultural misunderstanding story by appealing to psychological theories of empathy that continue to be influential in pastoral theology. This chapter imagines change by revising these influential models to account for the challenges of postcolonial recognition.

A hopeful future becomes possible through liberating and empowering care practices oriented toward mutual understanding that resists harmful habits of forgetting and of non-recognition. Breaches in intercultural understanding, subsequent experiences of intensified identity crises, and participating in opening pathways for resolution raise challenging and

---

11. Justes, *Hearing Beyond the Words*; Doehring, *The Practice of Pastoral Care*; Couture, "Ritualized Play."

12. McGarrah Sharp and Morris, "Virtual Empathy?"

important questions. Yet, one cannot live one's whole life suspended in these questions, reaching toward a not yet, disembodied from the now.[13] Experiences of healing within misunderstanding stories include *both* asking and hearing challenging questions *and* being present to participate in the disciplined work of understanding responses that follow. Reconciliation in the face of misunderstanding stories is possible when understood as moving cognitive love deeper into embodied experience as an assent not only to personhood but indeed to one's—and one another's—whole being.

A NARRATIVE FRAGMENT OF RECONCILIATION IN MISUNDERSTANDING STORIES

Weeks after the initial event that precipitated intercultural crisis where young neighbors broke into our home while we were away and were then publicly beaten in our absence, money was presented to us by the girls' mothers and village elders. Eventually, the central event of reconciliation was our refusal of money offered to us as literal repayment for the stolen goods. After the initial breach, crises of self-understanding and dilemmas in intercultural understanding unfolded around property, norms of child discipline, and possibilities of reconciliation. Ironically, the damage to the prior relationship and subsequent possibility of reconciliation was due more to the hard plastic tops that were left off of salt meat buckets of rice and grains, which had then been ruined by rats. We had left a key with a neighbor to get the chocolate (which was stolen in advance) out of the house and give it to these same girls on Christmas morning. A child's curiosity in relation to impending surprises and gifts was also invasion of space and trust. And it resulted in layers of violation of and misunderstanding in space, bodies, and community life.

All involved seemed interested in reconciliation, although there appeared to be obstructions to its possibility in the form of a seemingly unending loop of crises of identity and understanding. We were only able to understand the reconciling act of monetary refusal after a series of intercultural conversations that spanned more than a month of delicate interactions. We knew that being "paid off" was not the kind of reconciliation that we sought. What kind of reconciliation did we seek?

One difficulty was that we were interculturally fluent enough and attentive to power dynamics in the village and in relation to our identity as United States citizens that we knew but could not yet name the specifics of

13. Levy, *Hope will Find You*; Winnicott, *Playing and Reality.*

deep intercultural misunderstandings in relation to this situation. We first attempted our version of redress in several ways and with the help of several people within the Peace Corps organization, village, and local school. The breaking point of this painful social drama appeared to be a last-resort effort from the village, inviting us to accept the monetary value of the stolen and damaged items. This event took place on our porch and was the first time since before the breach that the mothers (our closest neighbors) crossed the threshold of our home. Over several hours one evening, we attempted to understand the meaning of the invitation.

Our perceptual core was the experience of sitting at the table on our front porch with the girls' mothers and two village elders. The raw experience included a seemingly impassable disconnect within the very relationships that before the breach had become among our closest in the village. Unlike in most American neighborhoods, in Saakiki villages, neighbors live together in close and continual proximity. The metal-roofed houses in an equatorial climate are used mostly for sleeping and not for residing in under the heat of the day. Most of life, outside of night sleeping, happens in the communal outdoors under shared shade of mango, coconut, papaya and banana trees. What was the future of these treasured relationships that suddenly seemed so fragile?

We lived in invisible yet tangible disruptions in shared space and time. Visibly broken connections—among we who now carefully negotiated the sanctioning of shared spaces—made the future of the relationships precarious. Uncertainty about the future status of shared relationships propelled us back into crises regarding the very possibilities of intercultural understanding.

Who are we if we cannot be in relationship? What is relationship without understanding?

We remembered past reconciliations based on restorative models that predated our encounter with the village; we knew something of what reconciliation can look like in rural and urban southeast United States American contexts. We shared memories of more recent past experiences with our friends at the table. We distinctly remembered sharing the popular afternoon activity of Tiki-tiki (literally "stick, stick," our made-up version of the card game "Spoons"—spoons are not playthings in the village. In contrast, sticks serve as a common toy among their other many functions) around the same porch table with these same families every day leading up to our time away from the village. We remembered joining with these girls just before the holiday for an interculturally reimagined version of carol singing around the village, spending hours delivering popcorn and pumpkin cakes to our larger community of neighbors. Other than shared intercultural experiences, the seeming inaccessibility of our friends' culturally specific past images spun us back into crises of understanding and made communication around the shared table difficult.

After a year and a half, we had reached a depth of integration in the village that had already far surpassed our expectations. We were becoming more deeply fluent in the Saakiki language. We had learned the importance of speaking in metaphors, learning to tell and retell histories so that counterhistories could emerge, honoring religious practices that recognized the ancestral community of saints more deeply than anything we had ever imagined, and responding to invitations to share space even in the midst of tensions and misunderstandings.

We felt a growing sense of shared understanding with many villagers. It seemed as if we were finally being seen as somewhat differentiated from the volunteers who preceded us, whom we did not have much of a chance to get to know in the brief overlap of our respective service, yet we still navigated that in terms of representation, we were much the same. We had gained more confidence in lasting possibilities of intercultural relationships. We experienced a growing sense of participating in established friendships across what initially seemed to be impassable or incommensurable cultural boundaries. An additional aspect of our context included our recent travels to the United States, in which we had glimpsed future possibilities and difficulties that would accompany our eventual reentry into a United States cultural context. After this glimpse, we were looking forward to the final months of our service with a renewed intentionality and investment in our intercultural friendships.

In the midst of crisis, our feelings expressed both culturally specific and shared intercultural communal states. Past memories converged in the present, feeding crises of understanding. The value of experiences that linked the past to present included a communal willingness to sit at the table for hours, in community with villagers, yearning to achieve some form of mutual intercultural understanding. Formal pathways to resolution had been instituted, but experiences of reconciliation were still fleeting. Distinct moments of realization emerged where new embodied knowledge led to new understanding. For hours this night, we listened to the mothers' efforts to convince us that the only way to begin mending relationships was for us to accept money, which we did not want to do. We could sense but not yet name that something was awry in the disempowered tone of the pleading. Suddenly, we experienced a profound moment of new understanding.

Misunderstanding Stories

We realized through the efforts of the elders, who were also at the shared table that they had convened hours earlier, that the reverse of this request was more in line with possibilities of restoration and repair in relation to our understanding of reconciliation.

We reached an intercultural understanding—a moment of insight across cultural differences in the presence of unintended misunderstandings.

We learned: if we had accepted the money then, the event would have ended in complete severing of all relationships with all members of the girls' families. According to our own preconceived understandings, we felt that we needed to refuse the village's genuine and impassioned offer to us in order to maintain relationships that had become so important to us. Some understanding of multiple meanings of the offer opened a bridge, a momentarily steady or trustworthy connection in the presence of estrangement and splintered relationships. Realizations of new knowledge enabled us to rephrase and to retranslate our intentions for reconciliation. New words, metaphors, and images were created in the process of face-to-face struggle and yearning for understanding. To some extent, we were finally also able to share again in experiences with our friends sitting with us. In the midst of sustained effort to understand, every experience of missing each other created little opportunities for recommitment to participate communally in cycles of intercultural misunderstanding oriented toward understanding. We joined in the effort to understand: we kept missing each other and then recommitted to the long process of trying again and again.

Did we finally understand each other after two years of living interculturally in community, even in some small measure? Consequences of the breach extended into our last days in the village at the close of our Peace Corps service. We were not able to achieve the highest form of artistic expression that Turner so richly describes. However, we did experience initial expressions of reconciliation that began with the collective sigh of relief and with renewed if hesitant communal contact upon our final ritualized refusal of the monetary offer. Expressions of reconciliation extended into our final weeks when our neighbors—and eventually their children—returned to our home.

Months later, as our departure drew near, we exchanged gifts with each of our neighbors, receiving beautifully crafted wood and sewn materials. We gave away or sold everything we could. Did the material exchange of the American and the Saakiki symbolize tangible progress toward intercultural reconciliation? On our final morning in the village, we were invited to be blessed by the spiritual leaders of the village in one of the most sacred spaces

140

there, in a clearing adjacent to our house, but which we had never previously been invited to enter. Our embodied participation in and limited understanding of the blessing deeply expressed the experience of mutual reconciliation.

Throughout the different (albeit overlapping) phases of experiencing and then reflecting on the experience of intercultural misunderstanding around reconciliation, we experienced and reexperienced crisis of identity and understanding: Who are we? Can relationship with any other endure? Can I sustain my commitment to an other? What kind of risk is involved?

Long after the historical event of the breach, we continued to experience this splitting in the form of culturally specific histories and understanding. Finally, at the stage in which meaning united past and present, we were able to glimpse a future relationship where I am seen as someone with whom the other could again relate and vice versa. Together we came to share in a collective identity of mutual recognition without collapsing or ignoring our differences. Reconciliation is a structured, communally embodied process of response that requires the discipline of time, patience, self-examination, and continually renewed commitment to community. Communities are rife with risks for misunderstanding that wound alongside possibilities for a deeper understanding that heal. We live together in constant tension between wounding and healing.

YEARNING FOR A MORE HOPEFUL FUTURE

A key postcolonial question is whether any of us can ever see that which we ourselves render invisible. And when we do glimpse beyond the gaze, then what? As we begin to recognize cultural and religious pluralism more deeply, how do we face the risk that our own caring practices inadvertently harm the very human beings for whom we intend to care? Among the complex intercultural realities that characterize the present day is the sheer fact that we keep misunderstanding each other despite our best intentions. In popular culture as well as in faith communities, misunderstandings and lack of knowledge of people who appear unknown and different tend to perpetuate suspicion and mistrust. We only need look to governmental and societal reactivity to recognizing cultural and religious differences as a good. At our best, we commit to stay within uncomfortable spaces of misunderstanding long enough to learn, to translate, to discern body language, to give and receive in order to begin to understand—certainly with close family and friends, and even stretching to practicing neighbor love beyond the familiar. However, we are not always at our best, and rarely are our efforts to understand mutually participatory.

How might pastoral theology, as a discipline deeply invested in human experience with a rich history of theorizing about how empathy facilitates healing within human relationships, respond to realities and risks of intercultural and interreligious misunderstandings in our academic, ecclesial, and larger social settings? What does pastoral theology look like when it takes into account the abundant need for greater understanding within our plural contexts? On one hand, pastoral theology is uniquely poised to consider global realities, diversity, disagreement, varied forms of healing, and creative communities. Our robust conversations with psychologies help train attention to understanding *and* misunderstanding complexities and dynamics of conflict, which, when not too overwhelming, can facilitate growth. Can we imagine sustaining shared vulnerability to make room for learning, growth, and recognizing being wrong in ways that can lead to more mutual practices of relating interculturally?

On the other hand, pastoral theology has room for growth. We are situated within churches, hospitals, and educational institutions that have a long way to go to understand how to invite interreligious and intercultural dynamics as the context in which we must more intentionally and proactively participate. While hospitals and chaplaincies may be more adept at navigating these challenges,[14] there is no doubt that Christian denominations, church congregations, and even theological schools struggle in relation to theologies of religious pluralism and discerning just how to embody celebratory practices around cultural, religious, and other differences. We all have work to do to care well around differences within our local contexts while simultaneously considering our role in a complex global economy. Local and global contexts are inextricably intertwined. Disputing these connections is no excuse for dismissing our responsibilities both to reflect on our participation in local, intercultural, and international misunderstanding stories and to participate in dynamic practices of empathy that facilitate healing in the form of intercultural reconciliation.

A TRADITION OF UNDERSTANDING EMPATHY THROUGH DEPTH PSYCHOLOGY

Empathy forms a crucial part of any process of reconciliation. To understand empathy in relation to experiences of reconciliation such as in the

14. Greider, "Soul Care amid Religious Plurality."

narrative fragment above, depth psychology continues to provide critical tools for practicing pastoral care even in our contemporary postcolonial context. Without reducing care to a matter of psychological theory, pastoral theologians have long respected the ways that depth psychology helps us to acknowledge suffering and facilitate healing. It helps us understand just how intercultural empathy does and does not work to deepen mutual understanding. I devote this section to a review of some of this important theoretical work to better appreciate the basic human experience of empathy as a starting point for considering how these traditional models can be shifted in relation to postcolonial recognition.

Self-psychology can clarify empathy as the framing work for understanding some psychological dynamics of mutual recognition. Austrian born Heinz Kohut (1913–1981) established *self-psychology*, a psychological theory about the structural impact of relationships on the psychology of human beings that affirms the role of mature love directed both toward oneself and toward other human beings. Departing from Freud's conflictual model of the self, Kohut adopted a more positive and deeply relational model of human interactions. Self-psychology helps us understand the dynamics of mutual recognition because it assumes distinct *selves* with discernible interior psychological structure but who must recognize the constant presence of and relationship with other human beings in order to love.[15] It is not the case that one learns to love oneself in isolation and then starts relating well with other people through practices of neighbor love. Rather, one of Kohut's main contributions to psychology (and cultures) is the reclaiming of narcissism as a healthy human need. While Freud considered the development of narcissism to lead from archaic self love to mature self love, Kohut added a second line of development to this model where human beings learn to love others as well in the process.[16]

In this context, Kohut defines empathy as the "[aim] to understand what is going on in the other without major participation in the other's experience."[17] He outlined a specific method for how empathy works with-

---

15. In self psychology, other people are technically referred to as *objects*, as in the case of object-relations theory (ORT). In both theories, this is in part to signify that the category of object exceeds discrete individualized persons, as places, experiences, and even material reality also have an impact on individuated personality development (i.e., the classic recognition in ORT of the importance of the blanket in early human development in many cultures). For the purposes of this book, I use the less problematic term "other human beings" for purposes of clarity.

16. Siegel, *Heinz Kohut and the Psychology of the Self*, 59–61.

17. Wolf, *Treating the Self*, 37.

in relationships. Human beings understand other human beings through vicarious introspection; introspection in turn facilitates understanding. Introspection is the processes of incorporating thoughts, feelings, sensory perceptions, and fantasies from relationships with other people into a human being's internal world.[18] According to Kohut, "What I can introspect in myself, another person *with sufficient empathy* should be able to comprehend."[19] Empathy and its method of introspection are value neutral in this theory and can be used in the service of good or ill. Kohut claimed that any of us can use knowledge of other human beings gained in processes of vicarious introspection (best facilitated by the kind of shared vulnerability I discussed in chapter 4) for a variety of purposes, oriented toward kindness or toward "utter hostility."[20] Reflection on responsible empathy in the service of mutual recognition is crucial for practices of good enough pastoral care.

Like other twentieth-century theorists, Kohut viewed fragmentation as a primary contributing factor to suffering. Healthy empathic relationships oriented toward recognition facilitate hope often expressed as an experience of cohesion, whereas unhealthy relationships oriented toward harmful nonrecognition or toward avoiding empathy contribute to what Farley identifies as despair experienced as fragmentation, or a falling apart.[21] This gets tricky when we reflect on institutionalized social oppression. While twentieth-century thinkers assumed that fragmentation was necessarily bad, twenty-first-century theorists are starting to theorize at least a measure of fragmentation as necessary for healing. For example, fragmentation of stereotypes and oppressive systems that support habits of gazing and other strategies of dehumanization opens spaces for practices of confession, lamentation, and forgiveness that facilitate opportunities for mutual intercultural recognition.[22] In other words, empathy may sometimes demand a particular kind of fragmentation. In MoiKonde, feelings of fragmentation as despair in the midst of misunderstanding at

18. Gay, *Understanding the Occult*, 34–35.

19. Kohut, cited by Gay, *Understanding the Occult*, 38–39 (italics added).

20. Kohut, "Reflections on Empathy"; for a study of empathy directed toward harm, see Baron-Cohen, *The Science of Evil*.

21. "Self-selfobject experience" contributes to human flourishing: "Proper selfobject experiences favor the structural *cohesion* and energetic *vigor* of the self; *faulty* selfobject experiences facilitate the *fragmentation* and *emptiness* of the self" (Wolf, *Treating the Self*, 11; italics original).

22. Arms,"When Forgiveness is Not the Issue in Forgiveness;" Blaine-Wallace, "The Politics of Tears"; Brueggemann, *Disruptive Grace*, 179–205.

times signaled the need for fragmenting previously held assumptions now exposed. I hungered for the hope found within a co-authoring process of mutual telling, retelling, hearing, and understanding. Before this could be embodied and shared, I had to learn that co-authoring includes mutual challenge that can fragment dehumanizing representations or worldviews. Self-psychology has since helped me theorize co-authoring as an empathic process of mutual imprinting oriented toward recognition that flows from shared vulnerability.

Empathy is a process in which human beings resonate in the experiences of other human beings through vicarious introspection.[23] More commonly referred to with expressions like "walking in another's shoes," empathy is not psychic activity, compassion, or affection, nor is it necessarily positive, intuitive, or always accurate. Rather, empathy is a "mode of observation attuned to the inner life" that provokes wonder that I and others are understandable while acknowledging that *I* don't know the whole of *you* and *you* don't know the whole of *me*.[24] Respecting that your shoes are yours and that I could be wrong, I can imagine with you what the contours of your shoes might feel like in my embodied experience. In a partnership, this is mutual so that, eventually, we walk together. In self-psychology, healthy relationships of walking together, metaphorically speaking, unfold through a cyclical two-step process.

First, human beings *tune in* to other human beings or important places, events, or even material objects. Self-psychology argues that all life experiences unfold within overlapping relationships that deeply affect each of us. *I* am who *I* am because of relationships with *you*. Simply put, "You need other people in order to become yourself."[25] My participation in relationship(s) affects but does not determine who *you* are, just as *your* participation in relationship(s) affects but does not determine who *I* am. Here, the *I*'s and *you*'s indicate experiences of any and all of us. Empathy facilitates this process when *I* understand *myself* as in relationship with you and accept that this is never a guarantee that *I* understand *you*. In contrast, postcolonial theories like Fanon's, which I review below, help unmask that *I* often understand *myself* in relation to *you* in a way that denies *you* any say in who *you* are. This is the basis of dehumanization. Dehumanization is intensified by relationships of distance that rely solely on representations of

23. Kohut, *Self Psychology and the Humanities*, 222.

24. In Kohut's words, we must take care to "postpone our closures" (Kohut, "Introspection, Empathy, and the Semi-Circle of Mental Health," 396)

25. Kohut, *Self Psychology and the Humanities*, 238.

other people without any face-to-face contact with "othered" human beings. While proximity certainly does not guarantee understanding, more distance in relationships is more likely to contribute to misunderstanding stories. Consider how development work, church mission initiatives, and academic reflection are so often physically removed from on-the-ground experience of intercultural encounter. Kohut insists that empathy operates in what he calls an "experience-near" realm.[26] When *we* can resist this habitual non-recognition while negotiating relationships in relative proximity, then we glimpse that *we* are always in the process of understanding each other. Trying to achieve a static state of understanding both near and far is not only dangerous but impossible. By being "in tune" with you, empathic recognition is not *my* claiming to finally or fully understand *you* but rather an account of myself as fundamentally capable of being moved and moving in relationship.

Second, within relationships oriented toward this kind of understanding in depth, human beings experience and survive necessary and inevitable failures, or *optimal frustration*, from relationships with these same human beings, places, events, or material objects.[27] Here the word "failure" is not equivalent to abuse, neglect, or intentional harm, as these latter failures signify an unhealthy, dangerous relationship of non-recognition. Rather, optimal failure and frustration signify the reality that other human beings cannot finally fully understand *me* because *you* fail to anticipate *my* particular needs and vice versa.[28] Kohut described as a basic human need the recognition of other human beings as "like me" *and* "not like me." A sense of self forms from desiring to be in tune while also experiencing these discordant failures within communal life.

The most common optimal failure in MoiKonde came in my process of learning Saakiki, the local language. I did not experience as destructive making mistakes and being corrected for them in community, which was generally oriented toward mutual understanding and proper use of language; rather, these optimal failures, while certainly frustrating but also often humorous, facilitated my learning and therefore our ability to communicate. More complex breaches in understanding offer examples of optimal failures when there is mutual investment in the processual movement toward a more hopeful future.

26. See Kohut, "Introspection, Empathy, and the Semi-Circle of Mental Health," 396–99. In contrast, what Kohut calls "experience-distant" theorizing is removed from experience and corresponds not to understanding, but to theoretical explanation.

27. Kohut, *How Does Analysis Cure?*, 70.

28. Ibid., 102.

Self-psychology also theorizes that cultural dynamics contribute to the formation and continuity of a sense of self, practices of empathy, and experiences of optimal failure. Kohut advocates for experiences of cohesion not only within human beings but within discrete cultural identities that he calls "group selves." This conception of identifiable individual and group identities is problematic in light of our previous discussion of cultures as dynamic and selves as navigating multiplicity. In other words, Kohut's concept of group selves is helpful given that like human beings, groups are always moving and changing. Kohut theorizes that cultural practices contribute to the harmful and/or healing nature of community; however, like other modern theorists, he views "challenges" like the "horrors of colonization" as extreme deviations from the norm.[29] Feminists have challenged Kohut by underscoring just how embedded social oppression is within our sense of self, parenting practices, cultural contexts, and communal life.[30] Acknowledging the postcolonial context of all contemporary communities entails recognizing that identifying what contributes to suffering and what contributes to healing is a huge challenge that can only be approached communally because of our embeddedness in complex matrices of empowering and disempowering structures.

I appreciate Kohut's insistence that only after cultivating a deep sense of understanding over a long time can anyone discern explanation, the more theoretical interpretation of shared experience. In MoiKonde, time, patience, disciplined self-examination, and continually renewed commitment to community filled our extended intercultural immersion. We learned the importance of ongoing self-reflection through practices of journaling, intercultural conversations, and expressing a range of emotions in order to learn beyond what we imagined we needed to learn.[31] We participated in the misunderstanding stories represented in this text oriented toward partnership and understanding but often experienced and contributed to optimal frustrations. By the time we experienced the narrative fragment of moving toward reconciliation represented above, we only had four months of service remaining. Reconciliation began but could not yet be completed because intercultural empathy requires ongoing participation in community, processes of dialogue, and opening shared space to

29. Kohut, *Self Psychology and the Humanities*, 255–56.

30. Lang, "Notes toward a Psychology of the Feminine Self;" Hertzberg, "Feminist Psychotherapy and Diversity," 284.

31. We did not enter relationships with a research method or question; therefore, the multiple-case-study method here is retrospective analysis on experience rather than qualitative study (Stake, *Multiple Case Study Analysis*).

learning. In the next paragraphs, we turn to another depth psychology that pastoral theologians have long used to theorize human shared spaces.

Shared space is central to the depth psychology known as object relations theory (ORT) represented here in the work of British pediatrician and psychotherapist D. W. Winnicott (1896–1971). Even though it is based on the infant-mother relationship as the location of personality development, like many other psychological theories, the concept of shared space in ORT has helped pastoral theologians to theorize other kinds of relationships by analogy, including interpersonal relationships, intercultural relationships, and relationships between the human and the divine. I continue to find ORT a helpful conversation partner in reflecting on experiences around shared space in MoiKonde, although, as you will see at the end of the chapter, my experiences also shift the theory's model of shared space.

Basically, Winnicott theorized that (1) all human beings have internal worlds, including and especially infants; (2) other human beings, places, experiences, and even material objects affect internal worlds; and (3) shared space exists in an area of "experiencing" that involves participation in both the internal world and external life.[32] Winnicott theorized that while infants are born into relationality, the infant at first considers all others to be part of *me*. Therefore, key among the first achievements is an infant's recognition that there is a *not-me* quality that defines others. Recognition unfolds as a process in shared space where both other human beings and shared space are acknowledged in sharper relief than first imagined. The shared space is precisely what allows for acknowledging human dignity and integrity of others. Like Kohut's theory of empathy, shared space is value neutral; therefore, all of us, particularly when granted positional power (parents in this case, ministers in faith communities, teachers in the classroom) must attend to keeping good boundaries and safety for the space to host shared vulnerability.[33] Using infants as a model, Winnicott explained that eventually, the parent (the mother in Winnicott's theory) faces the existential inability to anticipate and immediately respond to every need. In turn, the infant becomes frustrated by not experiencing total control over external reality.[34] A *good enough parent* is "one who makes active adaptation that gradually lessens, according to the infant's growing ability to account for failure of adaptation and to

---

32. Winnicott, *Playing and Reality*, 3.
33. Herman, *Trauma and Recovery*.
34. Winnicott, *Playing and Reality*, 14–17.

tolerate the results of frustration."[35] This concept of "good enough" continues to be one of the most helpful metaphors that pastoral theology has adopted in conversation with the modern psychologies as offering tools for understanding responsible care practices.

The pastoral theology classroom models a safe shared space in which to experience such optimal frustrations as will play out in care practices and helps students learn to negotiate them. Translating Winnicott's concept of "good enough" to pastoral theology, it is more helpful to aspire to be a good enough participant in care practices than a perfect one. The complexities of life will continue to surprise even the most prepared among us. In other words, we can count on unexpected situations and challenges. We can also be sure that we won't always immediately know how to respond. Indeed, thinking that we *will* always know how to respond undermines genuine presence and may therefore block empathy. Therefore, learning pastoral theology is not and cannot be about learning "right answers" for all situations requiring us to participate responsibly in caring practices. Rather, a study of pastoral theology in preparation for ministry helps train attention for remaining present and responding empathically through liberative and empowering partnering in the midst of surprising moments. Good enough pastoral care brings together self-reflection, critical academic reflection, and shared vulnerability to cultivate responsible practices of responding to suffering that bear witness to God's love and hope in the lives of persons and communities. The classroom provides a safe shared space to hold this important work of learning.

Both inside and outside the simulated empathy lab of the classroom, relationships frame a *holding environment* where *my* experience and *your* experience meet. Relationships are more mutual when *I* understand *myself* as an *I* in relationship to *you* without needing to control or to be controlled by *you*. In ORT, the term *potential spaces* names the critical shared spaces in between me and not me. When we unintentionally fail each other, space opens up for renewed understanding of oneself as a participant in relationships. In contrast, intentional failing closes space for what postcolonial theorists like Fanon call *self-determination*, or the human right to define for *myself* and for *you* who *I* am. As a pediatrician, Winnicott noted the importance of opportunities for self-determination for the development of children's personalities and for healthy family life. Potential space is a way of understanding the space where play, creativity,

---

35. Ibid., 14.

and communication unfold in culture(s).[36] Play facilitates recognition of differences and connections between and among people. Winnicott argues that play is a basic form of living.[37] *Living* entails interacting with real people external to *me*. In contrast, *fantasying* is a dissociative activity that does not involve interaction with human beings.[38]

Potential space, as holding environment, invites the active participation that characterizes living in relationship with other human beings where *we* play, create, and communicate. In contrast, colonizing relationships represent "others" in intentionally non-recognizable ways and thus deny a mutual holding environment. While colonized human beings participate in living with colonizing human beings in order to survive and subvert (chapter 3), dominant colonizers historically denied participation in freedom, reciprocity, and recognition to colonized as a dehumanized other. Like Anton de Kom in Suriname regarding European colonialism in South America, Senegalese critic of African colonialism Ken Bugul articulates the difference: "I identified myself in them, they did not identify themselves in me."[39] In our contemporary postcolonial contexts, colonizing relationships persist in spaces and practices of exclusion.

Naming the present "postcolonial" signals that institutional dehumanization surfaces where intercultural woundedness has constricted possibilities for mutual understanding as a dimension of intercultural healing. How ought we now understand oppressive cultural practices of non-recognition in this context? Who determines what is oppressive? According to what set of principles or understanding of neighbor love is such a determination made? Questions like these highlight the need for pastoral theology itself to become vulnerable to potential spaces where our traditional reliance on Western models of depth psychology is challenged by explicit attention to postcoloniality as norm rather than exception. The following section reviews Frantz Fanon's postcolonial psychology in order to then propose a model of potential space that accounts for challenges of postcolonial recognition.

---

36. Ibid., 139, see also ibid., 73.

37. Ibid., 67.

38. Ibid., 36–37.

39. Bugul, *The Abandoned Baobab*, 53. It is significant that the pen name Ken Bugul translates into "unwanted one." See University of Iowa News Services, "Unwanted One Becomes One of the Most Influential Writers."

POSTCOLONIALISM AND NON-RECOGNITION

Where the normative claims of modern Western psychology fail to account for the lingering dehumanization of historical colonialism, postcolonial theories provide conceptual tools relevant to encounters between me as a white, female American academic and Surinamese friends descended from West African slaves of European colonists who live together in the complex legacies of postcolonialism. Psychiatrist and activist Frantz Fanon (1925–1961) describes his experiences as a "colonized other" in his significant text *Black Skin, White Masks*.[40] Like Kohut and Winnicott, Fanon also prioritizes proximity, but in his experience as the violence of non-recognition rather than potential space for recognition.

According to Fanon, a colonized human being needs physically to encounter the colonizer's homeland (in his case to travel from Martinique to France) on a quest to be recognized as a human being.[41] Fanon considers himself as "overdetermined from without," in which assumptions about his identity based on preconceived notions about what his appearance signifies prevent authentic encounters.[42] The "myth of the Negro" precedes him, preventing encounters by restricting possibilities of recognition.[43] Fanon found no opportunities to participate in potential space in France. Instead, "the environment that has shaped [the Martinican] (but that he has not shaped) has horribly drawn and quartered him; and he feeds this cultural environment with his blood and his essences."[44] Fanon attempted to imagine freedom apart from colonization, in which "authentic communication" and understanding might be possible. However, he contends that his reality is "fixed" in disastrous histories of enslavement. Fanon asks, "Was my freedom not given to me then in order to build the world of the *You*?"[45]

---

40. Fanon, *Black Skin, White Masks*.

41. Ibid., 153.

42. Ibid., 116.

43. Ibid., 204.

44. Ibid., 216.

45. Ibid., 231–32. Note similarities with the recent response to Pat Robertson by Ambassador Raymond Joseph (Haitian Ambassador to the United States): "So, what pact the Haitian made with the devil, has helped the United States become what it is." (Among the many sources to enter this conversation, see "Haitian Ambassador [Raymond Joseph, Haitian Ambassador to the United States] Shames Pat Robertson;" see also Diakité, "The Myth of 'Voodoo.'"

Like other theorists surveyed in previous chapters, Fanon employs the *gaze* and *recognition* as theoretical concepts to analyze oppressive raced, gendered, classed, aged, and otherwise representationally marked structural legacies of colonialism. He considers the gaze as "a look through the [other] person that calls into question the recognition of his or her own subjectivity."[46] Fanon situates the gaze in interpersonal interactions embedded in larger systemic political histories. Thus, while he refers to dynamics within and among groups of people, genders, races, and nationalities in important ways, he focuses on the politics of interpersonal and intrapersonal identities. The gaze makes its greatest dehumanizing impact at the level of face-to-face interaction between human beings because the immediacy of this embodied gaze masks identity, wounds through nonrecognition, and upsets possibilities for mutual recognition.

When Fanon left his homeland of Martinique for France as an official representative of the French military, he discovered in the experience of *seeing being seen* that he was not recognized to be the French man that he considered to be a significant dimension of his identity.[47] He encountered himself as other, "overdetermined ontologically from without."[48] Fanon was astonished to experience oppression in which "it is as an actual being that [the Black skin] is a threat."[49] Not only does the gaze prohibit recognition, but the very being who desires recognition is also perceived as a threat that reinforces the power of the ever conflictual gaze. The gaze incites conflict even before "any conflictual elements" appear, widening gaps in intercultural, interpersonal, and internal understanding and making empathy nearly impossible. Fanon recognizes that this conflictual gaze extends beyond his context to all who must daily live the drama of the gaze.[50]

While the gaze wounds most deeply at the unique human level of the face, Fanon argues that exploitation transcends particularity; in all places and between all peoples, exploitation leaves persons devoid of their

46. *Dictionary of the Social Sciences.*

47. Fanon, *Black Skin, White Masks,* 115.

48. Ibid., 14, 110, 116, 191–92. Fanon claims that overdetermination causes the ultimate worth of the black man to reside in the person and power of the white Other (154). The white man assumes and depends upon the accuracy of his projections of the black man onto his very being (165). See also Bugul, *The Abandoned Baobab,* 37–38. Discourse about blackness as an ontological category emphasizes these claims (for example, Anderson, *Beyond Ontological Blackness*).

49. Fanon, *Black Skin, White Masks,* 163.

50. Ibid., 145.

"proper place."[51] Fanon encourages resisting dominant-assigned proper places by protesting unjust social structures that support colonization of peoples, cause lasting fragmentation, and alienate individuals from their own self-recognition.[52] Fanon explains that "because it is a systematized negation of the other, a frenzied determination to deny the other any attribute of humanity, colonialism forces the colonized to constantly ask the question, 'Who am I in reality?'"[53] As we saw in previous chapters, colonial crises evoke identity crises. Despite tending toward reinforcing dualisms between concrete categories of oppressor and oppressed, Fanon's "theorization of the consciousness of the colonized *and* the colonizers, his placing of psychopathology within this context," and "his linking of racism and colonialism" are relevant to theorizing intercultural relationality today.[54]

EMBODYING A DEEPER RECOGNITION

Breaches within intercultural relationships disrupt relational bonds, intercultural understanding, personal and communal identities, and recognition of oneself and others. Histories of colonialism institute dehumanizing practices of gazing that linger on in representations that block mutual recognition. Inevitable failures can fragment such representations when glimpses of a deeper recognition break through to the horizon of possibility. The misunderstanding stories in which I am a participant move toward more mutual understanding with self-awareness, patience, commitment, and the discipline of sustained partnership cognizant of inherent tensions.

The term *postcolonialism* signals the need to attend to power dynamics in contemporary experiences of social suffering in both everyday and acute forms.[55] Recognizing that many of the resources for resisting

51. Fanon, *Black Skin, White Masks*, 88. Fanon focuses explicitly on the experience of colonized men and is exclusive in his gendered language, but is nonetheless an important resource for women as well. Feminists disagree on the extent to which Fanon advocates for women, but he clearly addresses women, especially in his later work (see Sharpley-Whiting, *Frantz Fanon: Conflicts and Feminisms*).

52. Fanon, *Black Skin White Masks*, 100.

53. Fanon, *The Wretched of the Earth*, 182.

54. Good, *et. al.*, "Postcolonial Disorders," 12. At the 2009 Practical Theology section of the American Academy of Religion annual meeting, pastoral theologian Lee Butler asked why theorists turn to Foucault instead of Fanon when theorizing about violence and postcoloniality. I hope that this chapter in part appeals to his call for pastoral theological work that engages Fanon.

55. Good et al., "Postcolonial Disorders," 9–10, 15–16.

in a postcolonial context are hidden, unspoken, repressed, and unburied, postcolonial scholarship aims to start rather than conclude conversations that are "more provocative than prescriptive, opening up issues rather than providing closure, hinting at the hidden, at times intentionally subversive."[56] It is in this spirit that I probe personality theories in order to recognize tensions that seem to prevent resistance and invite easy collusion with strategic dehumanization that persists long after historical colonialism.

Exploitation and oppression infuse our lives and prevent mutual recognition, leading to ambiguity in relation to just what it means to participate in co-authoring potential space for liberation, empowerment, and resistance as goals of intercultural and communally minded care practices. Systemic violence has perpetuated suffering and fragmentation and needs dismantling to make room for embodied experiences of empathy. Pastoral theologian Larry Graham considers that "on a larger scale, racism, colonialism, and various forms of oppression are extreme forms of discounting: those in the disadvantaged position are commonly blamed for their condition, while those in power are excused and justified."[57] Violence disrupts possibilities of relational recognition, masking individuated *I*'s from each other and severing potential spaces for solidarity.[58]

Recognition begins with assent to *you* as a human being sharing in humanity with me. A horizon of shared potential space arises from the depths of embodied experience; then we must communicate through telling, retelling, hearing, and overhearing our misunderstanding stories in order to move to a deeper recognition. Preparing to respond to violence as if violence does not already characterize an aspect of all contexts and all communities is dangerous. Postcolonial theorists debate whether violence can be met finally with nonviolent recognition.[59] Part of recognition is acknowledging that we all reside in the question of violence with no simple answers. A postcolonial pastoral theology recognizes violence as a component of suffering and misunderstanding both in concrete breaches of trust and also in more abstract but equally consequential forms of everyday hermeneutical violence or investment in perpetuating misunderstanding stories.

56. Ibid., 29. For an exploration of the discomforts that these kinds of questions provoke in an ecclesial setting, see Garces-Foley, *Crossing the Ethnic Divide*.

57. Graham, *Care of Persons, Care of Worlds*, 145.

58. Eiesland, "Things Not Seen."

59. Fanon, *Black Skin, White Masks*; Gines, "Fanon and Sartre 50 Years Later"; Gines, personal conversation.

We are all caught up in misunderstanding stories at home, abroad, and everywhere in between. In addition, leaders in faith communities are called upon in the event of misunderstanding and/or miscommunication in clinical settings. In everyday life, when we try to connect in meaningful and not so meaningful ways, we often miss each other. This is only intensified when we glimpse a deeper recognition and the implications of human loss around the realization of a normative gaze, of a habit of forgetting, of a well-worn giving in to despair or helplessness. In light of the risk of perpetuating dehumanization, it makes sense to try to activate our imagination expansively, not to stop at glimpsing but to desire to see from within my body and reaching out with tentatively opened hands. Grasping based on glimpses is a dangerous thing: the thing for which we grasp can elude us and/or we can cause harm in our pursuit of it. Rather than firmly clenched fists, I read the narrative theorists, poets, ethicists, theologians, and Wolff's call to surrender to suggest a posture of open hands ready for the work that (paradoxically) surrendering requires.

I have appealed to anthropologist Victor Turner to depict some of the complex dimensions in misunderstanding stories from a disruptive experience to identity crises to formal declarations of resolution toward shared embodied experiences of reconciliation. Across these chapters, I have also partnered narrative fragments with Kurt Wolff's concept of surrender-and-catch as a guide for moral reflection in reflecting on misunderstanding stories. A breach in intercultural understanding raises walls between human beings already invested in various relationships. Identity crises raise questions that lead me to consider suspending previously held assumptions based on dehumanizing representations that I realize block possibilities for a hopeful future. Once glimpsed, I open to learning more, to working in community, to being moved. Opening a situation or oneself to surprise—surrendering to this possibility—is to risk being personally caught up in it. All of this has positioned us at the beginning of reconciliation. We can move together in cognitive love. I can expect to be caught up in cognitive love in which in the immediacy of my wanting to share in mutual understanding, I can expect to be "thrown back" on what I really am, which is what I share with every other person.[60] Physical, psychological, and spiritual connection and disconnection have been depicted and theorized at great length by pastoral theologians. In the next sections, I will review one standard depiction and adapt it to illustrate postcolonial connections and disconnections, building on the effort within pastoral

---

60. Zaner, "The Disciplining of Reason's Cunning," 373–75.

theology to hold empathy as central to good enough care and (for me) to rely on empathy as a requirement for embodied experience of reconciliation as a hopeful future opens to this relationship so immediately fragmented.

REIMAGINING EMPATHY

One way to image the development of empathy is, appealing to Winnicott, to imagine progress from an intertwined pair of human beings to human beings who *both* recognize and respect their differences *and* experience overlapping and therefore shared potential space. This movement facilitates a process of recognition:[61]

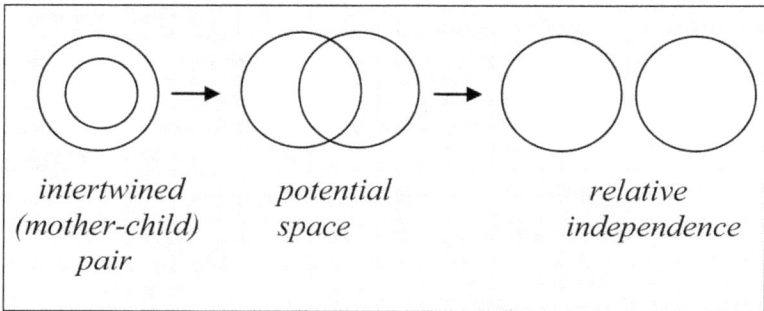

| *intertwined (mother-child) pair* | *potential space* | *relative independence* |

ORT lends itself to analogy since its theories about the infant-mother relationship are based on analogous reference to psychology and personality more generally.[62] ORT can model *good enough intercultural encounter* by differentiating encounter in terms of *mutuality* (human beings living in complex community with other human beings) and *colonization* (human beings fantasying about dehumanized others). In a good enough intercultural encounter, both parties participate in mutual living, become vulnerable and open to change, and negotiate the ever present tensions between stranger-ness and connection.

An intercultural pair gradually moves toward mutual recognition of "not me" through participating in play, communication, and creativity. Instead of starting with the image of an intertwined pair that suggests the illusion of control and participation based on a so-called "normal" form of dependency, I contend that intercultural encounter begins with relatively

61. A version of this image can be found in Gay, "Winnicott's Contribution to Religious Studies," 380. All subsequent images are original.

62. See Gay, "Winnicott's Contribution to Religious Studies," 388–90.

independent strangers. Before encounter, individuated selves, communities, or cultures could represent whole beings who hold particular expectations of others that are more or less closed off to revision. A more mutual encounter demands greater openness to surprise and expectation of revision. Before encounter, culturally discrete entities (granting that it is possible to imagine such a thing) occupy different and distinct physical, cultural, and metaphorical spaces. Encounter then means some sort of meeting in shared space and time—what Erikson characterizes as "a mutual sizing up."[63] What are the subsequent possibilities for intercultural understanding? We can imagine ways in which interpersonal encounter navigates cultural differences with the following divergent depictions of intercultural encounter:

Colonizing Intercultural Encounter Supported by Misunderstanding

strangers
strange land

colonized other
non-recognition

Intercultural Encounter Oriented toward Mutual Understanding

toward recognition

strangers
unknown

initial
contact

early
days

toward
mutuality

momentary
intimacy

we

I

you

63. Erikson, *Childhood and Society*, 49.

If intercultural encounter begins with separate strangers, then these depictions differ drastically depending on the experience of initial contact. Preconceived notions about other human beings affect habits of encountering. For example, some recognition of others as unknown and knowable contributes to an encounter more likely to follow a more mutual developmental trajectory. A colonizing encounter is an instance of fantasying where the internal colonizing world intentionally neglects to recognize the external reality of others. Instead, through non-recognition (depicted by the broken lines above), colonizers interact with colonized others only as constructed in the internal world of the colonizer. Colonizers presume foreknowledge of the colonized; this knowledge is not often open to positive revision. Histories record strategies of "proving" that the colonized is bad, overly sexual, and violent enough to make sense of and to justify colonization, all while simultaneously suppressing any acknowledgment of the insidious violence of exclusion that is colonization and even calling it good, normal, and nonviolent. There is no potential space for anyone involved because colonized intercultural relationships require and are supported by fantasying through misunderstanding stories, thus foreclosing any possibility of empathy.

In a colonizing encounter, one envelops the other, intending to fuse and confuse identities. Colonizing identities over-determine the identity of the colonized. It is well established that colonizers force the colonized to adopt the language and rules of the colonizer, leaving an enduring legacy from which humanity cannot easily recover. Even after national independence and legislated emancipation, once-colonized human beings and their children's children's children continue to be defined by terms set by colonizing powers. Legacies of colonization find expression in the prevalence of neocolonial forms present today.[64] Claims of heritage based in colonialism contribute to these legacies.[65]

In contrast, an encounter oriented toward mutual understanding occurs in the midst of living. Preconceived notions of others open to revision where human beings willingly become vulnerable to each other. In these diagrams, the uneven height of strangers is meant to depict the hierarchical ways in which we are schooled and habituated into gazing at strangers. However, frustration and misunderstanding can often break through. Both Kohut and Winnicott noted the importance of frustration. Fanon reminds us that some frustration must be unmasked as the dehumanization that it

---

64. See Wurgaft, Review of *The Intimate Enemy*, 434.

65. Lowenthal, "History Becomes 'Heritage' in Race Question," 17–18.

is. A good enough intercultural encounter might reframe mutual frustration upon reflection in terms of wonder, surprise, and learning. Empathy becomes possible. The potential space of intercultural encounter presumes a willingness of all parties, particularly the most privileged, to participate in learning other human beings' languages, to participate in co-creativity, and to participate in communal play. In the above diagram, an embodied recognition of "we" signals potential space for cross-contextual fluency and subsequent creativity with maximal healing potential. Language, here, becomes world creating.[66] Theological language characterizes this space by its hospitality to both lament and awe, characteristics of empathy as an embrace that does not flee from the body and its suffering but rather seeks a deeper embodied experience. In MoiKonde, the drumming and dancing of communal rituals helped to carve out this kind of potential space.[67] The *we* is both place and plea for the deeper recognition of neighbor love where other human beings are perpetual questions, but not to solve or to evoke suspicion, but rather as partners in the awesome mystery of humanity. We invite each other in this space of mutual recognition where empathy as mutual imprinting is the most possible and the most just.

In contrast to a colonizing imposition of preordained rules and languages that restrict access to participating in potential space, an encounter oriented toward mutual understanding invites diverse participation. Potential space rests on what Lartey calls the *principle of authentic participation* as "mutual concern for the integrity of the 'other'" that affirms human rights and appreciates multiple languages as a "theological imperative of creation" in which encounter flows from initial contact and subsequent desire to move toward mutual interaction.[68] A model of relationality oriented toward mutual understanding respects and acknowledges cultural differences.

Interculturality embodies ambiguity even in oppressive contexts. Recall that late-eighteenth-century Scotsman turned Dutch colonizer John Gabriel Stedman was employed to hunt escaped slaves, *and* he also tried to prevent or uncover actions toward slaves that he considered too harsh.[69]

---

66. Scarry, *The Body in Pain*.

67. Of note, drumming in MoiKonde is the most significant mode of cross-contextual fluency that has endured, to this day linking embodiment from Ghana to Suriname to such an extent that ethnomusicologists still wonder at this phenomenon. Music and dance continue to provide important metaphors for the embodied experience of empathy across interdisciplinary fields.

68. Lartey, *In Living Color*, 33–34.

69. Stedman, *Stedman's Surinam*.

While he romanticized "the black other" he met in Suriname, viewing "them" as "the sexualized savage,"[70] some hypothesize that he and his fifteen-year-old former-slave lover, Joanna, shared a mutual love relationship.[71] Editors of Stedman's journals point to paradoxes in his own psychology and familial history, connected to his ambivalence as both pro- and anti-slavery.[72] Further, Stedman's drawings depict his sexualized view of African slaves in Suriname. At the same time, he also named the sexualized violence of the masters and called them "murderers."[73] Consider Stedman's reflection on the purpose of his journal: "what gives me above all a peculiar satisfaction is that, by having so constantly employed my spare moments in drawing and writing, I have it now in my power to lay before my friends the history of a country so little explored and hitherto so very little known, particularly to the English nation, a nation which ever delights in new and useful discoveries."[74] Stedman perceived his power to describe and define "the other" exclusively in his own terms as a fantastic pleasure afforded by deliberate and sustained dehumanization.

In contrast to the colonizing encounters that Fanon and Stedman describe, in an encounter oriented toward mutual understanding, strangers move mutually toward understanding through sharing and conversation. Both may even participate in rare moments of intimate connection where the relationship emerges with a discernible and identifiable mutual "we" that expands potential space multidimensionally without diminishing differences or challenges of intercultural partnership. Intercultural friendships can exemplify this kind of mutual encounter. In his 1960 University of Michigan motivational graduation address, then-Senator John F. Kennedy challenged students to activate possibilities of world peace through intercultural friendship. Kennedy's address led to the development of the Peace Corps.[75] The philosophy of the Peace Corps, based on a model of partnership, provides a framework for possibilities of mutual encounter around the idea of intercultural friendship.[76] As an ideal, intercultural friendship respects as whole

70. Sharpley-Whiting, *Black Venus*.

71. Sharpe, *Ghosts of Slavery*, 73.

72. Stedman, *Stedman's Surinam*, xiv–xv.

73. See Stedman, *Stedman's Surinam*, 56. See also Sharpe, *Ghosts of Slavery*, 97.

74. Stedman, *Stedman's Surinam*, 315.

75. http://www.peacecorps.gov/index.cfm?shell=learn.whatispc.

76. The Peace Corps has the following three goals: (1) Helping people of interested countries in meeting their need for trained men and women, (2) Helping promote better understanding of Americans on the part of peoples served, and (3) Helping

persons both United States citizens and "host country nationals," along
with their respective heritage claims and individual and communal narratives. The Peace Corps outlines a framework that requires a certain
kind of participation, including "cultural curiosity, language facility, and
an unwavering commitment" to work well as partners in the face of significant challenges.[77] A hopeful framework of intercultural friendship
might facilitate movement of strangers toward rare moments of intimate
connection depending on embodying partnership oriented toward mutuality in a global economy that often glorifies and rewards hierarchies
instead.

In light of the complex histories of time and space in Suriname I develop in previous chapters, consider the following diagram:

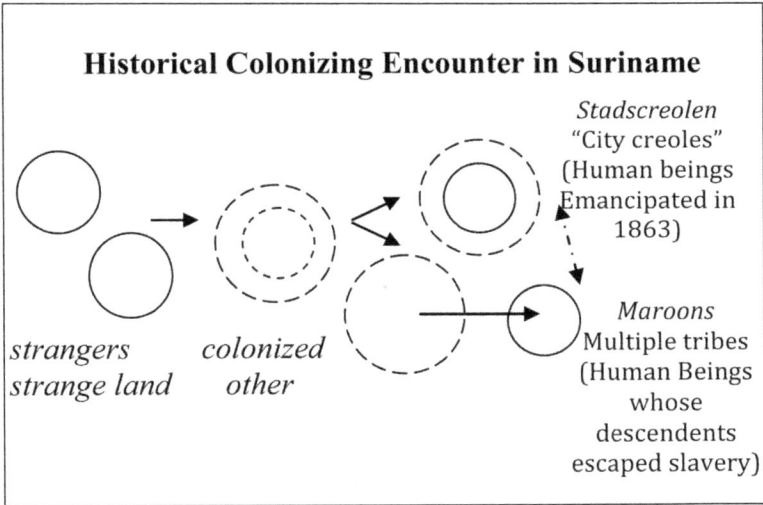

Historical Colonizing Encounter in Suriname

Stadscreolen "City creoles" (Human beings Emancipated in 1863)

Maroons Multiple tribes (Human Beings whose descendents escaped slavery)

strangers strange land *colonized other*

This depiction describes the current division of Afro-Surinamese
into *Stadscreolen* ("city creole") and multiple tribes of *Maroons*. Stadscreolen were emancipated from Dutch plantations in 1863. Maroons escaped
Dutch plantations and maintained tribal identities in the tropical rainforest of Suriname's interior. Stedman was among many soldiers sent to
hunt and kill Maroons; Joanna, his lover, was a Stadscreolen. The above
depicts a history that continues to divide Afro-Surinamese. While both
groups continue to experience global marginalization, Stadscreolen often

promote better understanding by Americans of other peoples (see online: http://www.
peacecorps.gov/index.cfm?shell=learn.whatispc.mission/).

77. Lucas and Lowther, *Keeping Kennedy's Promise*, vii.

seem to carry the so-called blessing, power, and privilege of an invisible Dutch occupation. In contrast, Maroons continue to be haunted by a more subtle colonial pursuit. With indigenous South American Amerindians, Maroons are often depicted as powerless, least represented, and most underserved peoples in Suriname. Surinamese Maroons often continue to serve as scapegoats for economic and political purposes through denial of their land rights and by shouldering much of the blame for Suriname's crime and economic distress. Psychologically and theologically, their identity continues to be diminished by persistent comparison with others. The dotted line is a reminder of the colonizing and dehumanizing strategy to pit marginalized groups against each other, while those most complicit in such violence strategically escape structural accountability. Can we—all of us—break out of this cycle of violent non-recognition?

In the narrative fragment earlier in this chapter, I experienced myself in self-psychological terms as a split self-object who participates in both kinds of encounter. In one instance, I identify with and am identified with the colonizer in colonizing encounter. In another instance, I experience and remember participating and being invited to participate in an encounter oriented toward mutual understanding. On one hand, active participation as a representative of the United States Peace Corps constantly risked invading Saakiki "me" space with "not me" in encounter. On the other hand, encounters oriented toward mutual understanding led to "we" experiences without diminishing concrete identities. Honoring invitations to participate in sacred space provided opportunities for moments of intimate connection. The juxtaposition of these two kinds of movements, even within a particular complex story and emerging from the same prolonged intercultural encounter, demonstrates complexities and possibilities of good enough moments alongside breaches in understanding within shared time and space. Tension and movement characterize the developmental trajectory of intercultural encounters. Recognizing and participating in reconciliatory processes around misunderstanding stories can serve as optimal failures to disrupt fused or distant colonizing relational structures in order to create the potential space required for co-participatory intercultural play, creativity, and communication.

While I find ORT relevant in a postcolonial context, my depiction is limited in that I have characterized intercultural relationality as split into two forms of encounter with inherent value claims—the *bad* colonizing encounter and the *good* encounter oriented toward mutual understanding. Interpersonal relationships are not so simple. Examining actual intercultural experiences illustrates complexities of intercultural encounter beyond simple dualisms. Winnicott relieves a drive toward perfection or goodness by recognizing that efforts need only be *good enough*. A good enough intercultural relationship navigates both understandings and misunderstandings.

We can respond to challenges of attending to our contemporary postcolonial context by reimagining intercultural empathy and participating in processes of reconciliation. Pastoral theology is a discipline deeply concerned with articulating and motivating more liberative practices of caring. Caring practices become distorted in light of human and institutional brokenness. Valuing persons as embedded in cultural contexts includes making visible our tendency to oversimplify culture(s) and insisting in our teaching, writing, and public speaking that cultures are dynamic, internally diverse, and internally contested. Points of contest where questions are safe and multiple voices are honored open maximal potential space for reconciliation. It is essential to acknowledge the fluid nature of culture, its complexities and ambiguities, and its complicated intersections with other changing cultures. Furthermore, *I* and *you* and *we* are caught up in the midst of it all. Paradoxically, if *you* and *I* feel distant, *we* are all the more at risk for complicity in colonizing relationships because of the dehumanizing tendency to dishonor "those people not like me identities" for the benefit of "these people like me." Deep intercultural disagreements can challenge and redefine empathy by breaking through this harmful dichotomy.

Rethinking intercultural empathy as oriented toward mutuality also leads to rethinking mutuality as a relational ideal. Postcolonial theorists outline tangible ways that cultural differences, especially surrounding privilege, constrain possibilities of mutuality. Psychological perspectives such as self-psychology and object-relations theory consider the limits of empathy that actually facilitate greater mutuality. Postcolonialism raises for *us* challenging moral questions, particularly around power and normative claims. To undertake a serious engagement with postcolonialism, pastoral theologians must consider mutuality both in the intercultural encounter and in academic methods of studying intercultural encounters.

AN ONGOING RECONCILIATION

What is the end point of a process of reconciliation? Are human beings finally limited in the ability to understand and to communicate?[78] How do we reconcile our finitude with ethical responsibilities within intercultural relationships as much as interculturality understood more broadly?[79] Kohut envisioned a "common denominator" within diverse groups.[80] Is this hope of empathy, of final experiential commonality, found in an experience of reconciliation within intercultural encounters?

In MoiKonde, we came back to the village with renewed commitment in the face of tension to complete our service. However, it was three and a half years later, when I returned to MoiKonde on my own accord, that partners in MoiKonde said to me: *"a now fosi wi o sabi yu o kon baka,"* or, "now we know that you are someone who will come back." Intercultural empathy, like the process of reconciliation, involves demonstrated returning and returning again to responsible participation in community.

If pastoral theology is committed to theorizing about healing and wholeness, and postcolonial theory stresses recognition of real obstacles to these ideals, then what might it mean to practice and cultivate empathy in more hopeful ways? I continue to experience wonder and amazement regarding capacities for understanding across linguistic, philosophical, theological, political, and other differences. Through committed engagement with Saakiki partners over time, I have experienced a depth of friendship and mutual understanding that surpasses any of my expectations. At the same time, I am constantly thrown back on myself by disruptions. My sources are primarily in English and Saakiki with limited access to Dutch scholarship from Suriname or the Netherlands. These and other factors shape cross-contextual fluency and also reveal room for learning. Misunderstanding stories immediately remind me of limitations in understanding Saakiki culture and being understood by Saakiki partners. This also always disrupts understanding and being understood.

Although this diagram represents an intercultural encounter oriented toward mutual understanding, the two-sided arrows indicate that relationships are always moving and always negotiating tensions and conflicts inherent to recognizing multiplicity as a good.[81] Sometimes this is a

---

78. Rizzuto, *The Birth of the Living God*, 11.

79. Browning, *Religious Ethics and Pastoral Care*, 110–15.

80. Kohut, *Self Psychology and the Humanities*, 227.

81. It is also crucial to remember the limits of the kind of two-dimensional depictions possible through type on a page. Intersecting trajectories of intercultural

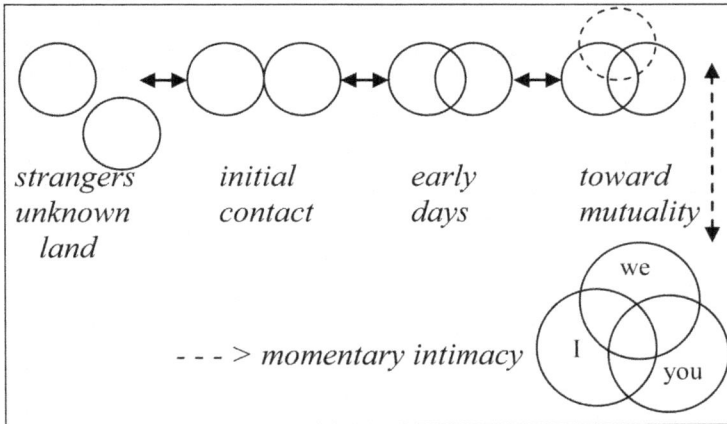

strangers   *initial*   *early*   *toward*
unknown   *contact*   *days*   *mutuality*
land

- - - > momentary intimacy

we / I / you

daily cycle of remembering again that we are in relationship. Movement builds with trust and experience ever so slowly toward mutuality over a long time. In MoiKonde, the breaches in understanding that had such impact between us and our neighbors occurred in a context oriented toward embodying a model of partnership. Our relationships were daily characterized by mutual play, creativity, and communication of stories upon stories even as we witnessed the unfolding of shared intercultural narratives. A breach in relationship moves all parties to the strangers/strange land end of the above continuum. Of course identity comes into question. Of course one wonders about the possibilities of moving again toward mutuality. In terms of the above depiction, I envision reconciliation as the relational understanding that movement toward mutuality is possible again in this context with these persons. When thrown back to a strange land with all the memories and shared stories of previous experiences of greater mutuality, we enter reconciliation in hopes that healthy connection is yet possible even in all the messiness of our broken and postcolonial internal and external worlds.

Narrative fragments in this text perform optimal failure and frustration to illustrate how narratives can work interculturally. Consider this book as structured to invite you the reader to reflect on misunderstanding in your complex experiences, including the experience of reading texts such as this one. Narrative fragments also serve as reminders that break into reading with moments of clarity that this topic matters. Focusing on tensions in intercultural relationships also helps us discern ways of

relationships are infinitely more complex. Intersecting mandalas or snowflakes would be more descriptive on paper.

understanding the potential space for both crises and possibilities for participating in reconciling misunderstanding stories. Probing inherent tensions and ambiguities of misunderstanding stories complexifies the model of intercultural crisis and repair I adapted from Turner. Understanding human beings as fundamentally relational includes recognizing tensions between ever present risks of intercultural misunderstanding and ever abundant possibilities of intercultural understanding.

Partnering with friends in MoiKonde challenges me to resist and transform my multiple roles. Do they have to represent the colonized other, and do I have to represent the colonizing white (male) American? Many who have reflected in depth on this question "from below" answer with a resounding yet sorrowful yes.[82] Must our encounter be controlled by the conflictual *gaze*? Fanon summarized colonialism's violent legacy: "His life is nothing but a long flight from others and from himself."[83] If "every ontology is made unattainable in a colonized and civilized society,"[84] then does colonization ultimately deprive us of our seeing *our* participation in mutual recognition? Is mutual encounter among selves who occupy roles circumscribed by colonizing structures of identity and national politics ultimately possible? Fanon asks, "Can the white man behave healthily toward the black man and can the black man behave healthily toward the white man?"[85] Can I, who by my skin and nationality represent the colonizer, choose to try not to avert my eyes but instead to be vulnerable to others? What is responsible embodiment of academic privilege? Can I participate in mutual loving friendship with my young neighbors and their families? Can my neighbors be my teachers? How can *we* invite encounters oriented toward mutual recognition? How can *we* be responsible givers and recipients of our embodied seeing knowing that habits of gazing have informed histories, social relationships, and self-understanding in both obvious and subtle ways? Can any of us ever "see" that which we ourselves inadvertently render invisible? Fanon laments, "Without Responsibility, straddling Nothingness and Infinity, I began to weep."[86] Yes,

---

82. See Tatum, *"Why Are All the Black Kids Sitting Together in the Cafeteria?"*

83. Fanon, *Black Skin, White Masks*, 181. Fanon observed, "The black Antillean is the slave of this cultural imposition. After having been the slave of the white man, he enslaves himself" (ibid., 192, see also 194).

84. Ibid., 109.

85. Ibid., 169. Rather than proposing negritude as the appropriate or possible response to anti-black racism, perhaps Fanon desires mutuality and "deep understanding." See also his statement, "I want to understand" (121).

86. Ibid., 140.

we are misunderstanding empathy. Yet participating in weeping and lamentation—around a table working to understand—opens new possibilities of reconciliation and empathy oriented toward mutual understanding in the midst of intercultural misunderstanding stories.

6

Toward a Postcolonial
Pastoral Theology

WHEN I RETURNED TO MoiKonde in the early stages of writing this book, I reconnected with a friend who had opened a new restaurant. A beautifully crafted wooden threshold, or limen, about a foot high, crossed the floors of the doorway. How could one not notice such a prominent barrier while walking through the door? The threshold, my friend said, reminds all who enter to do so intentionally. Those who try to run away without paying would likely trip on their way out. The foot-high wooden threshold is an apt image for the kind of liminal space in which creative spaces for understanding become more possible. Possibilities require intention, attention, and perseverance especially when craving retreat to the habitual practices of exclusion that keep us from understanding others and keep us from participating in the systemic change that supports liberative, empowering care practices and resists the strategic dehumanization that is a hallmark and legacy of historical colonialism.

This chapter proposes revised functions of pastoral theology and a revised guiding image of care that can better account for our contemporary context of postcoloniality in which intercultural misunderstandings are the norm and mutual intercultural understandings are rarely sustained. In so doing, this chapter begins the constructive theological work necessary to move toward a postcolonial pastoral theology. As mentioned in the introduction, a single-authored book cannot do this work alone. Therefore, this book also serves as an invitation both to pastoral theologians and to students of pastoral theology to carry the conversation further in connection with your experiences of misunderstanding stories.

My preliminary constructive work draws on the descriptive and methodological work of previous chapters. There I draw on the rich practice of ethnography as a responsible vehicle for a thick description of the postcolonial stories of misunderstanding that frame the book. These chapters recast and expand Victor Turner's anthropological description of cultural crisis to make sense of mutual intercultural understanding as a process that necessarily includes layers of misunderstandings. Previous chapters included representational narrative fragments of intercultural misunderstanding stories structured according to a revised model of intercultural experience based on Turner's work to depict just how complicated it can be to move from an initial awareness of misunderstanding toward a deeper and more mutual understanding. Pitfalls abound along the way. Desire not to understand meets desire for deeper understanding, both within myself and across persons and communities. Life together is complex.

Through a conversation between lived experiences and interdisciplinary theories, I expanded the first two steps of a strategic practical theological method where human experiences—in this case misunderstanding stories—come into dialogue with histories, psychologies, and theologies to pave the way for constructive pastoral theology and recommendations for practice, although these have been alluded to along the way.[1] Modern psychologies have not only been culture-forming,[2] but they also continue to undergird histories with implicit dehumanizing representations.

In previous chapters, I affirmed the nuanced tradition of interdisciplinary conversations as a site for theoretical innovation in relation to care practices because conversation among multiple voices facilitates possibilities of more mutual understanding in the face of cultural differences and histories of colonial violence. I evaluated identity crisis drawing on classical modern developmental psychology in conversation with postcolonial criticism of Western depictions of maturation. Through theoretical correlation between feminist psychology and feminist theology, I probed the exceedingly difficult challenge of sharing in mutual vulnerability, particularly in the midst of suffering, and given our human propensity

---

1. Browning, *A Fundamental Practical Theology*; Miller-McLemore, *Let the Children Come*, xxvii–xxxii.

2. Browning and Cooper, *Religious Thought and the Modern Psychologies*.

toward domination and non-recognition. Through conversation between the modern post-Freudian theories of self-psychology and object relations theory and postcolonial psychology, I raised intercultural empathy as a question and challenge for pastoral theologians. Together, these chapters recommend necessary elements for a postcolonial pastoral theology relevant to the situation of postcoloniality in which we all live and move in relation to complex power arrangements.

This book records stories in which I misunderstood and was misunderstood. Cultural differences played a tangible role in misunderstanding stories around norms of child discipline, private property, and communal conversation. International examples ought not diminish intercultural dynamics operating within seemingly more homogeneous communities right here at home. What misunderstanding stories have you experienced at home, abroad, and in the connections and disconnections between the local and global? We need to tell our misunderstanding stories as a pathway to expansive possibilities of mutual intercultural understanding. Misunderstanding stories challenge identity, complicate empathy, and blind us to appropriate vulnerability. They also invite deeper investment in practices of courageous self-awareness and sharing in vulnerability to mutual learning. Possibilities for intercultural understanding require openness to change: cultures are dynamic, always changing; through my participation and lack of participation in community, I am dynamic, always changing.

How do we understand the role of tradition in paradigm shifts? Is appealing to modern theories relevant or even responsible in the face of postcolonial and postmodern concerns? I have framed the flow of chapters according to Turner's anthropology of cultural ritual in which human beings move from a breach in intercultural understanding toward reconciliation by way of a process that includes identity crises and requires attention to communal practices of resolution. The process is not simply a linear progression; rather, it is dynamic, spiraling back and forth toward and away from recognition through the discipline of patience, self-awareness, and commitment to multiplicity in community. Liminality continues to be a crucial concept for understanding possibilities of change. Liminal space facilitates possibilities for second-order change,[3] or systemic change supported by sustaining courageous questions like: "Why are things broken the way that they are?" and "How am I complicit in the suffering that results from this systemic brokenness?"

---

3. Kornfeld, *Cultivating Wholeness*, 7.

Change does not mean abandoning tradition for new possibilities emerging within and around us. Narrative theory and narrative theology remind us that the desire to do so, while perhaps at times having noble intentions, is impossible to realize. There simply does not exist an entirely new liberative narrative totally disconnected from histories. Yet, unearthing, reimagining, and reframing describe narrative strategies for co-authoring change—always and everywhere in relation to the threads of our identities that have both knit us and unraveled us to this point. The histories of connections and disconnections complexly embedded in each narrative contribute to the awareness of just how courageous it is to claim our participation in facilitating and resisting the change going on in and around all of us all the time. For this reason, the proposals in this chapter draw on the rich history of pastoral theology with appreciation for the risky, courageous, and landmark nature of previous theoretical claims in previous times. Recognition of our contemporary context as postcolonial becomes a hermeneutical lens for critically engaging tradition.

REVISED FUNCTIONS OF POSTCOLONIAL PASTORAL THEOLOGY

Instead of fixed goals, I have argued for understanding the emerging functions of pastoral theology—empowerment, resistance, and liberation—as participatory processes that include understanding and misunderstanding in the form of empowering/disempowering, resisting/recognizing complicity, and liberating/being liberated. A participatory model of healing incorporates ambiguity, uncertainty, and misunderstanding as aspects of all relationships. Here Milton Mayeroff, a pragmatist in the tradition of John Dewey, can be a helpful conversation partner. In *On Caring*,[4] Mayeroff claims *basic certainty* as an orientation toward caring that "requires outgrowing the need to feel certain, to have absolute guarantees as to what is or what will be . . . it also includes being vulnerable and giving up the preoccupation with trying to be secure."[5] We may think of basic certainty as a form of intercultural trust or vulnerability that require putting into question whether or not our care practices are in fact empowering, liberating, or resisting dehumanization. Possibilities of mutual intercultural understanding that resist colonizing explanation are participatory. Participation, in turn, requires sharing in vulnerability and trust, which as Nandy

4. Mayeroff, *On Caring*.
5. Ibid., 49.

and Fanon so poignantly describe, have been abused as sites of violence. Participating in embodied empathic recognition unfolds in shared space claimed as liberative and empowering, but these goals must be enacted intentionally and with regard to histories and misunderstanding stories filled with dehumanizing representations.

A postcolonial pastoral theology will employ tools of history, theology, psychology, literature, and cultural criticism to portray a complex colonizer–colonized dynamic that continues to play out in we who live with this legacy. As part of this, we need to seriously consider the interlocking features of political and economic colonial consequences, including complex psychological, historical, theological, and literary dimensions of a less bounded, less definable, still comprehensively devastating colonialism. It is especially challenging to correlate and communicate best forms of caring and best ways of conceptualizing understanding across cultural differences because Western academics, theologians, ministers, community leaders, development organizations, and others of us passionate about healing have often adopted a top-down, salvation-oriented mindset lodged in colonialist structures that can frustrate rather than facilitate mutual intercultural interactions.[6] Practices oriented toward intercultural understanding become harmful when they limit access to participation in healing: it is not adequate to consider best practices of intercultural care as being directed solely by the caregiver. Our traditional patterns of giving and of theorizing care as giving are part of the problem. Theorists and practitioners of care alike need to face our vulnerability and tendency to misunderstand. A correlational analysis of intercultural misunderstanding invites diverse perspectives through co-authoring and co-participating that fosters mutual learning.[7]

How do we participate in care while evaluating the consequences of our care habits? How do we resist harm when we do not know how to recognize harm? How do we come to terms with recognizing that familiar ways of caring may actually harm when we intend for them to heal? Reflecting on disruptive experiences highlights the significance of intercultural co-participation. Essentially, I am arguing for living into processes that intercultural misunderstandings provoke. Living into understanding as a process includes facing uncertainties, reflecting on questions of

6. We see examples of this critique in sharp relief in the controversies over just what empowering international aid looks like. Interaction with the debate over the Invisible Children organization around their KONY 2012 video would be interesting in future work (see http://www.invisiblechildren.com/).

7. For example, see Pandolfo, "The Knot of the Soul."

meaning, and consciously inviting disruptive experiences to affect both one's interior life and spirituality, as well as to disrupt and expand relational networks. This is difficult to teach and difficult to learn (and keep learning). However, to patch up misunderstanding stories prematurely for the sake of securing a false sense of comfort restricts possibilities and thus colludes with colonizing orientations over and against other human beings.

The strong desire for answers, normative conclusions, and prescriptive suggestions to put into practice contributes to misunderstanding stories. Moving toward postcolonial pastoral theology is, fortunately, more complicated than that and resides in a thickly textured tradition that often resists this idea of caring by attending suffering and facilitating healing as easy. Postcolonial pastoral theology invites diverse participation in processes in which I empower and I disempower. I am empowered and I am disempowered. I resist and I recognize my own complicity in the problem. I liberate and I realize that I am being liberated. As pastoral theologians and as practitioners of pastoral care, we must rethink our goals and methods around empowerment, resistance, and liberation.

Misunderstanding stories evoke questions around the pastoral function of *empowerment*:

- How do experiences of intercultural misunderstanding embody power and resistance in historically sanctioned roles, memories, and sacred spaces?

- How do I hear and tell stories in a postcolonial context?

- Whose history explains the embrace of the Dutch and fear of United States Americans by Mia and Ella? Whose history is behind MaLespeki's protection of sacred space against the white man? What is the function of gender here?

- How do power and position affect representations that then come to define what we think of as the actual past?

- How does the power of the *gaze* influence identity construction over time, from colonial pasts to hoped-for decolonized futures? How does our disruptive, transformative exchange reveal kinds of imaginative poverty that result from the legacy of the colonial *gaze*?

- How do I live in relationships interculturally by recognizing and lamenting limits to understanding?

- Whose cultural values trump in examining situations of conflicting norms? On what grounds? Who negotiates values across cultures and how? How do intercultural misunderstandings encompass and cross spheres of private and public—guarded and open—spaces, property, and sense of belonging?

Misunderstanding stories also evoke questions around the pastoral function of *resistance*:

- Do I recognize experiences of violent and more subtle forms of oppression?

- How do power and ownership of stories enter my representations of experience?

- In what ways are my representations and writing colonizing?

- How do I participate in a postcolonial struggle to recognize oppressive structures in order to resist them in pursuit of liberation?

- How does the contemporary context of postcoloniality affect me? What does the contemporary context of postcoloniality afford me?

- Where is liminal space found for active, authentic participation within subtle neocolonial structures?

Misunderstanding stories evoke questions around the pastoral function of *liberation* in connection to a postcolonial resistance to absolute certainty:

- Do I question how and what I know by attending to "the irritation of doubt" in the midst of personal and professional practices of care?

- How do I trace concrete consequences of how knowledge is used in practice for liberatory and/or oppressive ends? Am I being self-reflective enough in my considerations about knowledge?

- Who are we? Can relationship with the other endure? Can I sustain my commitment to an other human being? What kind of risk is involved?

- How do I participate in moral imagination to envision possibilities of expansive intercultural understanding?

- Is it possible to view surrender-and-catch as an orientation toward the play of empowering/being empowered and disempowering/being disempowered, resisting/recognizing complicities, and liberating/being liberated?

Empowerment, resistance, and liberation are not achievable goals or ends of pastoral theology but rather processes of questioning, probing, and inviting diverse participation in mutual learning. Reframing functions as processes invites co-participating in "being on the way" toward mysteries of God and transforming (cognitive) love.[8] A model of good enough intercultural relationality adopts an in-process provisional understanding that recognizes the web of tensions in which we live. Good enough intercultural care includes asking good questions *and* bearing to hear and overhear responses to these questions and then to tell and retell narrative accounts of ensuing reflections and face-to-face conversations. Listening responsibly means living with provisional answers and misunderstandings without masking this as certainty. Misunderstanding stories can ground constructive theology in which good enough pastoral theologians hold disruptive experiences in tension with correlative experiences that glimpse intercultural mutuality.[9]

WEB OF TENSIONS

A postcolonial pastoral theology recognizes the many tensions that structure intercultural relationality. Discerning how to live well with others into tensions between risks and possibilities available in a postcolonial context becomes a central task. Any pastoral theological response to the difficult questions that arise in inevitable moments of intercultural misunderstanding must facilitate rather than squelch participation from diverse voices, both within and between cultural contexts. Previous chapters explored how networks of tension structure ways of both

8. Lester, *Hope in Pastoral Care and Counseling*, Especially chapter 4, in which Lester references Gabriel Marcel's journey metaphor of "being on the way" toward a more authentic expression of human existence as participation in God.

9. We read bits and pieces of the news of the recent devastation in Haiti that is almost too much to bear, and yet a reality I cannot ignore: "Convening with the dead is what allows Haitians to link themselves, directly by bloodline, to a pre-slave past," said Ira Lowenthal, an anthropologist who has lived in Haiti for thirty-eight years. He added that with so many bodies denied rest in family burial plots, where many rituals take place, countless spiritual connections would be severed. "It is a violation of everything these people hold dear," Mr. Lowenthal said. "On the other hand, people know they have no choice" (Cave, "As Haitians Flee, the Dead Go Uncounted"). An unthinkable natural disaster is one factor, of course. Underlying histories of colonization, poverty, and the strategic play of forgetting and remembering Haiti contributes to lack of infrastructure contextualize invitations for hosting spaces and places for repair (see Farmer, *Pathologies of Power*).

inviting and limiting diverse participation. Living into tensions holds open possibilities of new understanding *and* risks continual misunderstanding. Consider some of the pairings that hold us in tension and that I have probed in this project:

> *human beings—other human beings*
> *subject—other subjects*
> *sense of self—other selves*
> *me—not me*
> *embodied individuated self—selves embedded in networks*
> *disconnections—connections*
> *crisis—repair*
> *stuck in identity crisis—moving to/from reconciliation*
> *colonial histories—unearthed narratives*
> *habits of forgetting—vulnerability to learning*
> *surrender—catch*
> *understanding—explanation*
> *understanding as possibility—misunderstanding as risk*
> *colonizing orientation— mutuality orientation*
> *colonizer—colonized*
> *empowering—disempowering*
> *being empowered—being disempowered*
> *resisting—recognizing complicity*
> *liberating—being liberated*
> *possibilities of empathy—empathic failures*
> *call—response*
> *listening—speaking*
> *resisting silence—complicit silence*
> *telling and hearing—retelling and overhearing*
> *dialogue—textuality*
> *voice—acknowledging the "as yet unrecognized"*
> *loving—being loved*
> *violence—nonviolence*
> *recognition—nonrecognition*

We live somewhere in the liminal space of potentiality, represented above by the dashes in between. Psychoanalytic postcolonial theories stress ways in which both extremes in any of the above (particularly the colonizer—colonized) play out less dualistically and more multidimensionally within and among us. We need to live into these and other tensions without reifying the above descriptive categories into simple dualisms by embodying an responsible orientation toward recognition that contributes to multiple, deep, diverse, conflicting yet abundant life for all people. We must carefully navigate a sense of integrated selves within and across human beings oriented toward more mutual understandings without collapsing into colonizing, ideological, singular truth claims.

In the middle of a river in Australia, salt water and fresh water meet according to the tides and seasons. The place where and time when one water flows into and receives flow from another marks a sacred site for a particular aboriginal community.[10] Religious rituals tend to appear in sites of thirdness where entities come together in ways full of both risks and possibilities. Previous chapters have explored thirdness in terms of tensions, the potential spaces between, paradox, play, liminality, touch, the dash, co-presence, co-authoring, and co-participating. How do we continue to move toward and be moved by more inclusive third ways that respect diversity and particularity?

In-between spaces are opportunities for expansive horizons of understanding.[11] According to Maurice Merleau-Ponty, to think by participating in a kind of thirdness is "not to possess the objects of thought; it is to use them to mark out a realm to think about which we therefore are not yet thinking about."[12] We can envision thirdness as the space of insight and learning facilitated both by new connections and by experiences of disruption. The moment of encounter when my hand touches an other hand or when our eyes meet in a complicit and/or resistive *gaze*, we are already connected in ways that require ethical response. In the words of French philosopher Jean-Luc Nancy, "It is by touching the other that the body is a body, absolutely separated and absolutely shared."[13] Responsibility to widen horizons of understanding encourages dynamism in all kinds of interconnecting relationships.

Face-to-face encounters of proximity open possibilities of intercultural empathy that recognizes inevitable risks of empathic failures. Not only does this situate any generalizable understanding, but it also creates the necessity of interpersonal responsibility: "I cannot escape my responsibility for the other, because in a face to face encounter, I am related to

---

10. Whiting, "Multifaith Education and the Parliament of the World's Religions."

11. Gerkin, *The Living Human Document*; Gerkin, *Widening the Horizons*; Scarry, *The Body in Pain*; Merleau-Ponty, "The Philosopher and His Shadow," 159–60.

12. Merleau-Ponty, "The Philosopher and His Shadow," 160.

13. Quoted in Rivera, *The Touch of Transcendence*, 135.

the other before I can make the choice not to be related. This connection makes me responsible for the other. I have to respond to the other."[14] Can we reimagine care practices residing in the dash between ethical call of attention to suffering and responding through participating in healing?

REVISED METAPHOR OF CARE IN PARTICIPATORY POSTCOLONIAL PASTORAL THEOLOGY

Pastoral theology continues to rely on insights from various schools of psychology to understand the individuated human person and surrounding group dynamics. While this has tended to direct pastoral theologians toward the project of understanding individual persons, our field affirms that individuals can only be understood in context. After all, founding parent of pastoral theology, Anton Boisen, was influenced by George Herbert Mead's theory of the social nature of all selves.[15] Since the mid-1990s, the field has turned toward a guiding metaphor of the "living human web"[16] to further expand Boisen's classical metaphor and Charles Gerkin's adoption of this metaphor that views human persons as "living human documents" to be read, interpreted, and respected.[17] While we cannot underestimate the radical nature of considering human experience to hold the same authoritative weight as academic scholarship in projects of constructive pastoral theology, the shift from document to web suggests that human beings cannot understand one another without attending to our multiple contextual connections and disconnections in relation to families, institutions, and cultural identities.

Care practices necessarily involve conceptualizing individuated human beings and social networks in creative tension. Postcolonial theories claim that relationships in many dimensions are impeded by inadequate care and an inadequate sense of relationality based in structures that heal some at the expense of harming others. The basic tenet in ethics still holds: first, do no harm. But, there is a second step: first, do no harm; then, reflect

14. Hermans and DuPont, "Social Construction of Moral Identity," 252.

15. Mead, *Mind, Self & Society*; Burkitt, *Social Selves*; Hunter, *Dictionary of Pastoral Care and Counseling*.

16. Miller-McLemore, "The Living Human Web;" Dykstra, *Images of Pastoral Care*; Gill-Austern and Miller-McLemore, *Feminist and Womanist Pastoral Theology*; Miller-McLemore, "Revisiting the Living Human Web."

17. Boisen, *The Exploration of the Inner World*; Gerkin, *The Living Human Document*.

courageously on and lament unintentional harm done. While foundational pastoral practices of attentive listening and embodiment of empathy are just as important in liberationist and communal models as in traditional modalities,[18] pastoral theologians need postcolonial insights to better hear voices most affected by structural suffering and unmask complicity. We can deepen theoretical reflection on listening practices by attending more intentionally to ways in which histories record narratives of privilege over and against narratives "from below." In other words, as we know, the suffering of many tends to afford privileges for the few.

The field of pastoral theology has embraced the metaphor of *"living human web"* to account for the lively social, political, and cultural networks that hold human beings in relation to each other.[19] Considering intercultural empathy as a participatory orientation toward mutuality that is difficult to attain points to a *web of tensions* in which we are caught for better and for worse. Webs of complex networks support various relationships of health and well-being. At the same time, webs structure networks of oppression that trap us in relationships that contribute to suffering.[20] I recently heard a description of this metaphor in a different disciplinary context: in physics, "the more tangled the web, the harder it is to move one piece without bringing along all the rest . . . [because] a kind of cosmic molasses . . . pervades what we think of as 'empty' space'" between and around us.[21] In a 2008 update to the living human web metaphor, Bonnie Miller-McLemore revises the living human web metaphor to a more integrated *"living human document situated within the living human web."*[22] Moving beyond the earlier shift from self to context, this revision suggests tensions between selves and contexts. It also emphasizes that what the field typically thinks of as guiding metaphors are more than metaphorical. Guiding metaphors do just that—guide and structure pastoral responses. The shift from an individualistic to contextual to now more dynamic metaphor accounts for more complex understanding of human experience. However, in light of postcolonial challenges and recognition of greater pluralism, the guiding metaphor still needs additional revision.

The metaphor of the living human document suggests the thickly textured nature of each complex human being. However, that the image

18. Lartey, *In Living Color*, 116–123, 130.

19. Miller-McLemore, "The Living Human Web"; Dykstra, *Images of Pastoral Care.*

20. Keller, *From a Broken Web.*

21. Cole, "When Change is Hard, Blame Inertia."

22. Miller-McLemore, "Revisiting the Living Human Web," 3–18.

of selves as documents maintains such a prominent place within pastoral theology raises postcolonial concerns about *textuality* that restricts participation of most people in the world.[23] Is the intent behind the metaphor of *human document*—the shift from reliance on written books or articles as authoritative texts to diverse lived experiences as equally, if not more, authoritative texts—really that far removed from lifting up written texts as our ideal? And if written texts are not the gold standard, then how ought we think about the standard of measuring academic excellence by production of single-authored texts? Just who is authorized to write, to read, and to interpret these texts? While I rely heavily on lived experience as an authoritative source, I also recognize that my footnotes include, for the most part, published texts. There is a reason for this: namely, I assume that pastoral theologians are responsible for recognizing, studying, and teaching some of the most important shared histories and texts in the field. Yet, studying postcolonial theories encourages me to think critically about texts, particularly texts written in English published by the best presses and written by people highly educated in Western universities. We cannot escape the troubling reality that textuality is a mandatory avenue for success in the academic life that provides access for participating in education that is more empowering, liberative, and resists dehumanization.[24]

We can imagine other metaphors or descriptors that invite more diverse participation and a more complex recognition of the authoritative sources contributing to pastoral care practices as responses to suffering. Intercultural co-participation leads to a more accessible guiding metaphor or image of care. The powerful gaze that constructed socially and politically violent hierarchies in the past continues to wield power in contemporary globalized contexts. Fanon warned, "When one approaches a problem as important as that of taking inventory of the possibilities for understanding between two different peoples, one should be doubly careful."[25] Fanon argued that we all live with fragmentation as a result of the violence of historical colonialism. Fanon's call for de-occupation of breath still longs

23. A potential exception would be considering selves as texts in a Talmudic sense, where the living Torah is not only written as text, but also regularly spoken, heard, and enacted. However, pastoral theology has tended to be more of a Protestant Christian movement than a tradition that recognizes connections to or the importance of maintaining lively connections with Judaism (Browning recognized this problem early in his writing; see *The Moral Context of Pastoral Care*).

24. hook, *Teaching to Transgress*; Lorde, "The Master's Tools Will Never Dismantle the Master's House."

25. Fanon, *Black Skin, White Masks*, 84.

for response. Urgent global needs suggest the human longing for liberation *and* bread, freedom *and* breath. Participating in resistance includes lamentation and mourning through rituals of lived experience. What is at stake is somehow living together into a world of open, undetermined futures, even as pasts are unearthed, lamented, and globally contextualized. Resisting includes learning about liberation, bread, freedom, and breath by joining efforts oriented toward what one writer considers moving with "the breathing, sentient testament of the living world."[26] Academic concepts must be grounded in meaningful intercultural experiences and reality-tested in relation to participation in perpetuating suffering and facilitating healing by and through misunderstanding stories.

Participatory processes of resisting/frustrating resistance, liberating/frustrating liberation, and empowering/disempowering connect liberation, bread, freedom, and breath. The dynamic processes meet the woundedness of desires with practices of recognition as embodied awareness of suffering across cultural differences. Let us then consider the complex image of *breathing embodied selves within living human webs* in order to respect the tensions within and between human beings and communal contexts without restricting the metaphor as belonging to or able to be interpreted solely by the literate few.

TOWARD POSTCOLONIAL PASTORAL THEOLOGY

Constructive pastoral theology comes only after a layered process of both descriptive and methodological work. This project arose out of my lived human experience as a participant in intercultural misunderstandings in a context of stark cultural differences. The readily identifiable cultural differences help identify the sheer challenge of intercultural understanding. However, international examples where we might anticipate cultural differences from the outset are merely one instance of the kinds of cultural differences around and within all of us in our contemporary world of globalism characterized by postcoloniality.

The culture shock of returning to the United States from a two-year Peace Corps volunteer commitment was infinitely more difficult than the culture shock of moving overseas. Outside of the United States, we

26. Hawken, "To Remake the World." It is important to remember that there are plenty of opportunities for learning resistance and recognizing complicity in the United States, which is not immune to internal oppression and participation in oppression abroad, if these boundaries are even perceptible. Nor do I claim to be free from internal fragmentation.

expected cultural differences would be present and would feed a font of challenges living in a country and culture rendered as other from the application process to national and international "fact sheet" representations and on into our internal worlds. Returning, being known (or having been known), and the illusion of knowing what to expect compounded the shock of what the Peace Corps calls "reentry." I had changed and had to incorporate that change into what used to be the predictable contours of mundane life. Seemingly, everything had changed under the surface of what appeared as though nothing had changed. Overwhelming grocery stores, so many restaurants, abundantly accessible clean running water in public places all served as sites for recognizing the sheer number of misunderstandings. French philosopher and spiritual thinker Simone Weil invites us to consider just how hard it is to give one's attention to another person around the question: "What are you going through?"[27] Misunderstanding stories often begin when we think we already know the answer and pass right on by such a paradoxically basic and profound question.

Postcolonial stories of intercultural misunderstandings challenge pastoral theology from the ground up. Pastoral theology is a field that prioritizes and authorizes human experience as a legitimate and important source for theological reflection. Experiences of disjuncture translating between action and reflection, theory and experience, can challenge theological doctrine by calling into question the norms, values, and assumptions undergirding theological commitments. A postcolonial pastoral theology invites constructive theology around God's will, "natural" faith and human development, differently distributed blessing or grace, or one-directional missions that justify neocolonial violence rooted in historical colonialism and masked by an interpretation of "postcolonialism" that the world has moved beyond colonizing hierarchies. My intercultural misunderstandings call into question the optimism and privileged access to interpreting suffering and offering healing that are implied in our guiding metaphors of text and guiding functions of liberating, empowering, and resisting in the field of pastoral theology.

Practicing care in such a way that recognizes misunderstanding stories draws on psychology and theology. Good enough pastoral care practices are not reducible to psychology;[28] yet psychology continues to be an important resource for understanding human experience, for

---

27. Weil, "Reflections on the Right Use of School Studies with a View to the Love of God."

28. Gay, "Mapping Religion Psychologically."

affirming a positive role for emotions and other affective experience, and for theorizing interpersonal dynamics of mutual imprinting between human beings. Practicing good enough care includes sharing in mystery, learning the cross-contextual fluency required in this interdisciplinary field, and sustaining courageous presence in the face of acknowledged disruption. In response to crisis, good enough care practices bear witness to mystery while also drawing from the deep well of theology regarding human dignity even in suffering. In pastoral theology, psychological theory helps us prioritize the role of experience and self-awareness in care, while theological reflection helps us draw on the witness of experience in order to challenge habits of forgetting and histories, languages, and representations that continue to dehumanize and prevent mutuality in recognition. Good care is embodied to the end of mutual understanding, which is a perpetual becoming and not an end to be grasped or claimed as a victory. Care can be oriented toward good or ill because of the requirement for sharing in vulnerability, so we must ever hold open conversations about good boundaries in the midst of more participatory leadership. Good enough care is liberating, empowering, and resisting to the extent that we who participate in care practices are ones who will come back. Writing, teaching, telling misunderstanding stories, hearing and overhearing misunderstanding stories serve as avenues of return and invitations for our unfolding witness of experience not of absolute truth claims, but as a process of courageous unearthing in community.

I hope to contribute to a process of postcolonial constructive pastoral theology with this text. Paulo Friere once commented that we make the road through walking.[29] Misunderstanding stories pave a way for intercultural understanding by voicing the violence of systems that bind rather than facilitate creative possibilities of more mutual understanding across differences. Telling and retelling shared misunderstanding stories and hearing and overhearing misunderstanding stories of countless neighboring human beings so long rendered invisible will continue to pave dynamic roads full of possibilities.

A postcolonial pastoral theology functions to empower while being aware of disempowerment, to liberate while being aware of collusion in preventing liberation, to resist injustice while being aware of how I benefit from distorted visions of justice. Therefore, a postcolonial pastoral theology moves toward a revised theological anthropology. A postcolonial pastoral theology imagines breathing embodied human beings suffering

---

29. Bell et al., *We Make the Road by Walking*.

and healing through pathways and sticking points in which we are caught up in living human webs full of opportunities for participating in the constant mending required in this messy, complicated world. Therefore, a postcolonial pastoral theology will involve a revised and robust pneumatology. I look forward to participating in this scholarship that will correlate human fallibility and responsibility with the work of the spirit who breathes life into possibility.

Intercultural understanding is a process that deepens pastoral theological theories of mutuality by widening our sense of possibilities regarding occasions in which we can better participate in and call for mutuality as essential to interpersonal and intercultural justice and embodiment of God's love for all people and all of creation. A deep pastoral theological engagement with postcolonialism involves nurturing practices of living communally and interculturally in difficult questions. May *we* nurture practices that hold together an optimistic hope for a realized mutuality while expressing a realistic grief that reminds us of the sheer difficulty of experiencing mutual intercultural understanding. Remember, pastoral theologians know something about holding together hoping and grieving, celebration and lamentation, human fulfillment and human brokenness in a way that draws diverse participants together in a community that strives toward healing and wholeness while taking care not to minimize real challenges and differences in our midst.

In MoiKonde, in local United States contexts, in academic institutions, in faith communities, the local is inextricably bound to the global. Histories are inextricably bound to strategic dehumanization in which we are complicit and whose habits of forgetting we must resist. Wary of the lure of prescriptive remedies for the world's problems, we can recognize the ever present tensions that play out within and between us, as human beings who live together in complexly webbed connections and disconnections.

When recognized as such, ordinary moments of misunderstanding paradoxically form the shared space of mutually healing intercultural understanding. Intrapersonal, interpersonal, familial, intergenerational, and certainly intercultural relationships work in and through inherent failures and frustrations. Questions around assigning value to such conflicts must be worked out through embodied experience, rather than by appealing to universal norms and rules assumed from the outset. Within experience, recognition begins in assenting to the breathing human being embodied in my neighbor, both local and global. This initial recognition can lead to movements of liberation that can proclaim, declare, legislate, and otherwise formally institute emancipation. As a world community of humanity, we need emancipation. However, we must remember the deepest recognition at stake in which humanity shares in liberation as an embodied experience of memory and openness to the learning that accompanies moving and being moved in human partnerships. A deeper recognition beholds the mystery of human dignity and assents in wonder not only to personhood but indeed to embodied humanity itself. In MoiKonde, moving through a complex process of reconciliation freed possibilities for this kind of recognition: in the narrative fragment, initial recognition sanctioned mutual understanding, but only this deeper recognition opened embodied mutual understanding where we ate together, cooked together, played together, engaged strategic community planning together, and learned together in liberative, empowering community. Open to misunderstanding, we can move into embodied experiences oriented toward mutually understanding our shared stories.

Appendix

Journal Prompts and Discussion Questions

THEOLOGIANS AND MINISTERS AND ethicists are question bearers, invitation issuers, first responders in crisis, wonder beholders, and we can therefore embody steadfastness in our openness to questions, while at the same time recognizing the possibility for questions to destabilize the kinds of moral certainties often requested of us. The following list of questions in relation to each of the chapters could structure journal writing, online or classroom discussions, free writing exercises, or serve as bridges between personal reflection and public conversation.

INTRODUCTION

- What "big questions" have opened for you in theological education and life experience?

- How do you invest in ethnographic work in your present community? How might you attend to ethnography more intentionally in your present and future communities?

- As you critically reflect on your unique intercultural experiences, what understanding and misunderstanding stories come to mind?

- Where do you find your soul clapping for others? Where are the silences within your soul?

- How can your local faith community begin to confront its own participation in colonialism?

- When has your world both come together and apart all at the same time?

- Before engaging the thoughts found in this book, did you think it was possible to arrive in the land of "understanding" in relationship before first hiking through the thick complexity of misunderstanding?

- What one sentence or question from this section of the book do you find most moving, challenging, disturbing, thought provoking, agitating, or otherwise engaging? Why?

CHAPTER 1

- What is your first response to the questions: Who am I? Who are we?

- How do you understand yourself as one who participates in relationships with other people?

- What kinds of relationships do you participate in simultaneously?

- What is your cultural identity? How does culture(s) affect your relationships? Was this included in your first response to naming your identity? How does(/do) culture(s) both separate and enrich cross-generational relationships within your family(ies)?

- How do your relationships fit into your experiences and beliefs about the larger world in which we live?

- Can you name some things that have prohibited your process of meaning-making?

- How do you understand a "good enough" relationship? What makes for a relationship that is not good enough?

- What one sentence or question from this section of the book do you find most moving, challenging, disturbing, thought provoking, agitating, or otherwise engaging? Why?

CHAPTER 2

- When have you recovered a healthy relationship after a breach in understanding? What strategies of understanding seemed to work? What intensified the misunderstanding?

- What spaces do you find to be the most creative? What spaces do you find to be the most destructive? How have experiences of conflict related in each case?

- Suppose you were to tell the story of a momentous life occasion. Outline how you might narrate this story from multiple perspectives within and outside of yourself. Repeat this exercise by narrating a momentous story from the life of your church or faith community. What multiple voices emerge? What or who is missing? What is post-colonial about these stories?

- Where do you experience conflicting moral commitments or values? What strategies have you found to encourage conversation across multiple competing perspectives? Can you imagine additional strategies?

- What was stressed and what was missing from your history lessons as a child? What do you see emphasized and missing in learning histories today in contexts of school, faith communities, family, and other contexts?

- Who have you been guilty of gazing beyond?

- Why are we so resistant to "overhearing voices so long unheard"?

- Have you ever been faced with an experience of "surrender"? What was the "catch" for you?

- Consider this quotation from Paulo Freire: "to wash our hands of the struggle between the powerful and the powerless is not to be neutral but to side with the powerful." How has your faith community sided with the powerful? How have you personally done so?

- What stories do you have a hunch need unearthing in your life and local context? What informs this hunch? How do you understand an unearthing process that respects multiple voices and perspectives? What kind of risks do you associate with processes of unearthing?

- What one sentence or question from this section of the book do you find most moving, challenging, disturbing, thought provoking, agitating, or otherwise engaging? Why?

CHAPTER 3

- How would you begin to describe the story of your soul? What do you think of the idea of having more than one soul or of considering multiplicity within your soul?

- How would you characterize the trajectory of your identity formation? What significant times of transition can you identify? What experiences, rituals, struggles, or emotions do you associate with your life transitions? What norms and values undergird these rites of passage?

- Can you name some Biblical characters that seemed to be struggling with crises of identity?

- How do you prepare yourself and the communities in which you participate to recognize complicity in misunderstanding? Can you imagine locating this conversation around themes, such as food, economics, hospitality, education, mission? Can you imagine expanding rites of confession as sites for naming complicity? What other spaces can spark conversations about complicity?

- How can you and your faith community confront complicity while simultaneously maintain a spirit of hope?

- How would you define "successful" development? Can you think of counter examples to this model of success? Where does this model dehumanize and where does it invite possibilities for diverse ways of being successful? Is success the right word here? What other words can you imagine? How are your ideas about human development shaped by gender, race, age, religious experience, and nationality?

- How are children and elders welcomed into robust community in your school, faith community, family, and community?

- Do you recognize *Imago Dei* (the image of God) in all human beings in your midst? Where are you caught by surprise?

- How can you participate in leadership (in faith communities, in the academy, in other public contexts) responsibly? What risks can you take in writing? Where do you need courage in speaking your voice?

- How can we claim universal models of human experience or, by extension, universal human rights without dehumanizing or silencing other human beings?

- What comes to mind when you imagine participating in a mutual relationship? What are the characteristics of that relationship? Why are some of those characteristics absent in other relationships?

- Do you think of your relationship with God as mutual? Why or why not?

- Walk around the building, website, and printed materials in your school, home, and faith community. What kinds of images signify mission or service opportunities? How are human beings represented? Where are images dehumanizing? What images are affirming of human dignity?

- What one sentence or question from this section of the book do you find most moving, challenging, disturbing, thought provoking, agitating, or otherwise engaging? Why?

CHAPTER 4

- If you were to imagine your gaze as a pair of glasses, what do yours look like? Where are your blind spots? Where is your vision sharpest? Have you ever considered yourself as "caught in a sticky web of privilege"?

- Vulnerability can open us to harm and disconnection as well as to healing and connection. How do you understand the ethics of vulnerability? How do you participate in creating space for sharing in vulnerability? When is it more difficult and when is it more likely for you to be vulnerable?

- In the midst of crisis or in response to another's crisis, what kind of questions do you find yourself asking? What questions get in the way of and what questions help you be present?

- How do you identify your privilege in terms of the social power you have that you can attribute to identity markers such as gender, race, sexuality, age, nationality, etc.? In your life experiences, what is the role of privilege in places where you could name your desire for understanding as wounded? What kinds of emotions does this reflection raise for you?

- How are you accountable for your privilege?

- How is woundedness shared in your school, faith community, family? Where do you see healing and relief of suffering taking place? Do you feel connected to a global process of healing and relief of suffering in these places?

- Where are you most comfortable with silence? Where are you least comfortable with silence? When is your silence complicity and when does it make room for other voices? When have you found silence to be wounding? When have you experienced silence as "opening new ways of listening, discerning, hearing, and practicing"?

- When life calls you into a vulnerable space that is difficult to endure, are you most likely to default to despair or self-righteousness?

- Where in your life are you a single author and where are you a coauthor? Where do you see new opportunities for coauthoring? Engage this question theologically through concepts such as call, divine presence, steadfast love, or others that occur to you.

- Who is your neighbor? Is anyone not your neighbor? Why or why not?

- When have you experienced assent to your person? When have you shared most fully in mutuality with others? What has facilitated and sustained this experience? What has disrupted or prevented it?

- What practices in your school, faith community, family, and local community facilitate assenting to the person of your neighbor? Can you imagine new practices or prayers of assent?

- What one sentence or question from this section of the book do you find most moving, challenging, disturbing, thought provoking, agitating, or otherwise engaging? Why?

CHAPTER 5

- Where do you yearn for a more hopeful future? Where do you see needs for reconciliation in your person, school, faith community, family, community, world? What signals this need? What kind of interpersonal affirmation do you think could work toward reconciliation? Can you point to ways in which these hopes and needs are embodied?

- Where have you seen hopeful reconciliation? Do you think that reconciliation is ever finished? Why or why not?

- What misunderstanding stories are you caught up in at home, abroad, and all in between? Can you identity optimal failures and frustrations? How might these facilitate potential space for creativity and movement toward understanding?

- In what ways are you currently living in "a state of tension between wounding and healing"?

- Where are you overconfident in your claim of understanding in your own experiences, experiences of other human beings, or larger communities? Where are you too timid? How do you find potential space, strategies, and support for being good enough?

- Do the diagrams in this chapter open new understanding to you? Can you imagine mapping Scripture or other sacred texts, community dynamics, religious rituals and sacraments onto the diagrams? Can you image other ways of depicting movement from disconnection to connection?

- Where do you need to risk more proximal relationships with neighbors we claim not to understand but with whom we have no face-to-face experience?

- Where do you see God working in connected processes of recognition, empathy, and reconciliation?

- Is pastoral theology in particular and Christianity in general oriented toward an optimistic stance that aims to reduce disruptions and discomforts of suffering?

- Can you name a time when your faith community was forced to navigate an experience of "optimal frustration"? How did you grow through the experience? In what ways did the experience create greater understanding because of attending to the original misunderstanding?

- When have you experienced assent to your whole being? When have you shared most fully in mutuality with others? What has facilitated and sustained this experience? What has disrupted or prevented it?

- What one sentence or question from this section of the book do you find most moving, challenging, disturbing, thought provoking, agitating, or otherwise engaging? Why?

CHAPTER 6

- What misunderstanding stories have you experienced at home, abroad, and in the connections and disconnections between the local and global? How do you tell, retell, hear, and overhear narrative fragments of these stories?

- Which questions listed in the chapter stand out to you and grab your attention? What is your response? Which questions feel less relevant to you? Why?

- As you read through the web of tensions, what dynamics do you experience to be most prominent in your lived experiences? Do you feel a nudge to unearth any new attention to tensions? Which tensions are you resisting in this list or desire to collapse into a dualism? What other tensions can you imagine?

- How do your care practices affirm recognition and help facilitate mutual understanding? Where are your growing edges?

- Craft a prayer or fragment of a prayer for mutual understanding.

- What one sentence or question from this section of the book do you find most moving, challenging, disturbing, thought provoking, agitating, or otherwise engaging? Why?

Bibliography

Ackerly, Brooke. *Universal Human Rights in a World of Difference.* Cambridge: Cambridge University Press, 2008.

———. Personal conversations, Vanderbilt University, 2007–2010.

Ackerly, Brooke A., Maria Stern, and Jacqui True, editors. *Feminist Methodologies for International Relations.* Cambridge: Cambridge University Press, 2006.

Ackermann, Denise M., and Riet Bons-Storm. *Liberating Faith Practices: Feminist Practical Theologies in Context.* Leuven: Peeters, 1998.

Agathangelou, Anna M., and L. H. M. Ling. *Transforming World Politics: From Empire to Multiple Worlds.* The New International Relations Series. London: Routledge, 2009.

Aleshire, Daniel O. *Earthen Vessels: Hopeful Reflections on the Work and Future of Theological Schools.* Grand Rapids: Eerdmans, 2008.

Alexander, Bobby C. "Correcting Misinterpretations of Turner's Theory: An African American Pentecostal Illustration." *Journal for the Scientific Study of Religion* 30/1 (1991) 26–44.

———. *Victor Turner Revisited: Ritual as Social Change.* American Academy of Religion Academy Series 74. Atlanta: Scholars, 1991.

Ali, Carroll A. Watkins. *Survival and Liberation: Pastoral Theology in African American Context.* St. Louis: Chalice, 1999.

Anderson, Herbert, and Bonnie J. Miller-McLemore. "Gender and Pastoral Care." In *Pastoral Care and Social Conflict*, edited by Pamela D. Couture and Rodney J. Hunter, 99–113. Nashville: Abingdon, 1995.

Anderson, Victor. *Beyond Ontological Blackness: An Essay on African American Religious and Cultural Criticism.* New York: Continuum, 1995.

———. "Peirce Again: The Fixation of Belief." Vanderbilt University, and personal conversation, Fall 2006.

Anzaldúa, Gloria. *Borderlands/La Frontera: The New Mestiza.* 3rd ed. San Francisco: Aunt Lute Books, 2007.

Arms, Margaret F. "When Forgiveness is Not the Issue in Forgiveness: Religious Complicity in Abuse and Privatized Forgiveness." In *Forgiveness and Abuse: Jewish and Christian Reflections*, edited by Marie M. Fortune and Joretta L. Marshall, 107–28. New York: Haworth Pastoral Press, 2002.

Ashcroft, Bill, Gareth Griffiths, and Helen Tiffin. *The Empire Writes Back: Theory and Practice in Post-Colonial Literatures.* 2nd ed. New Accents. London: Routledge, 2002.

Bibliography

Associated Press. "Dutch MPs Want to Give Anne Frank Posthumous Citizenship." *Ha Aretz*, October 4, 2004.

———. "LeBron James' 'Vogue' Cover Called Racially Insensitive." *USA Today*, March 24, 2008. Online: http://usatoday30.usatoday.com/life/people/2008–03-24-vogue-controversy_N.htm/.

Barbour, Ian. *Religion and Science: Historical and Contemporary Issues.* San Francisco: HarperSanFrancisco, 1997.

Barnes, M. Craig. *The Pastor as Minor Poet: Texts and Subtexts in the Ministerial Life.* Grand Rapids: Eerdmans, 2009.

Baron-Cohen, Simon. *The Science of Evil: On Empathy and the Origins of Cruelty.* New York: BasicBooks, 2011.

Behar, Ruth. *The Vulnerable Observer: Anthropology That Breaks Your Heart.* Boston: Beacon, 1996.

Belenky, Mary Field et al. *Women's Ways of Knowing: The Development of Self, Voice, and Mind.* 10th anniversary ed. New York: BasicBooks, 1997.

Benjamin, Jessica. *The Bonds of Love: Psychoanalysis, Feminism, and The Problem of Domination.* New York: Pantheon, 1988.

Bettie, Julie. *Women without Class: Girls, Race, and Identity.* Berkeley: University of California Press, 2003.

Bhabha, Homi K. "Foreword: Framing Fanon." In *The Wretched of the Earth*, by Frantz Fanon, vii–xli. New York: Grove, 2004.

Blaine-Wallace, William. "The Politics of Tears: Lamentation as Justice Making." In *Injustice and the Care of Souls: Taking Oppression Seriously in Pastoral Care*, edited by Sheryl A. Kujawa-Holbrook and Karen B. Montagno, 183–97. Minneapolis: Fortress, 2009.

Blakely, Allison. *Blacks in the Dutch World: The Evolution of Racial Imagery in a Modern Society.* Blacks in the Diaspora. Bloomington: Indiana University Press, 1993.

Blue, Ellen. "Spiritual Mothers and Midwives: Reflections on Conversations with Women Rebirthing the United Methodist Church in Post-Katrina New Orleans." Paper prepared as Visiting Scholar for 2008–2009 at the Newcomb College Center for Research on Women, Tulane University. Online: http://tulane.edu/nccrow/upload/NCCROW_White_Papers_Blue.pdf/.

Boisen, Anton T. *The Exploration of the Inner World: A Study of Mental Disorder and Religious Experience.* Chicago: Willett, Clark, 1936.

———. *Out of the Depths: An Autobiographical Study of Mental Disorder and Religious Experience.* New York: Harper & Brothers, 1960.

Bourdieu, Pierre. *The Logic of Practice.* Stanford: Stanford University Press, 1990.

Brana-Shute, Gary. "Love among the Ruins: The United States and Suriname." In *The Dutch Caribbean: Prospects for Democracy*, edited by Betty Sedoc-Dahlberg, 191–202. Caribbean Studies. Amsterdam: Gordon & Breach, 1990.

Brennan, Patrick McKinley, editor. *The Vocation of the Child.* Grand Rapids: Eerdmans, 2008.

Brown, Laura S., and Maria P. P. Root, editors. *Diversity and Complexity in Feminist Therapy.* New York: Haworth, 1990.

Browning, Don S. *A Fundamental Practical Theology: Descriptive and Strategic Proposals.* Minneapolis: Fortress, 1991.

———. *The Moral Context of Pastoral Care.* Philadelphia: Westminster, 1976.

———. *Religious Ethics and Pastoral Care.* Philadelphia: Fortress, 1983.

Browning, Don S., and Terry D. Cooper. *Religious Thought and the Modern Psychologies.* 2nd ed. Minneapolis: Fortress, 2004.

Brueggemann, Walter. *Disruptive Grace: Reflections on God, Scripture, and the Church.* Minneapolis: Fortress, 2011.

Bugul, Ken. *The Abandoned Baobab: The Autobiography of a Senegalese Woman.* Translated by Marjolijn de Jager. New York: Lawrence Hill, 1991.

Burkitt, Ian. *Social Selves: Theories of the Social Formation of Personality.* London: Sage, 1991.

Butler, Judith. "Foreword." In *The Erotic Bird: Phenomenology in Literature*, by Maurice Natanson, ix–xvi. Princeton: Princeton University Press, 1998.

Butler, Lee H., Jr. *Liberating Our Dignity, Saving Our Souls.* St. Louis: Chalice, 2006.

Cannon, Katie Geneva. "Emancipatory Historiography." In *Dictionary of Feminist Theologies*, edited by Letty Russell and J. Shannon Clarkston, 81. Louisville: Westminster John Knox, 1996.

Carrette, Jeremy. "The Return to James: Psychology, Religion and the Amnesia of Neuroscience." In *The Varieties of Religious Experience: A Study in Human Nature*, by William James, xxxix–1. Centenary ed. London: Routledge, 2002.

Carroll, Noël. "Narrative and the Ethical Life." In *Art and Ethical Criticism*, edited by Garry L. Hagberg, 35–62. New Directions in Aesthetics 7. Malden, MA: Blackwell, 2008.

Cave, Damien. "As Haitians Flee, the Dead Go Uncounted." *New York Times*, January 18, 2010. Online: http://www.nytimes.com/2010/01/19/world/americas/19grave.html?pagewanted=all.

Chambers, Robert. *Whose Reality Counts?: Putting the First Last.* London: Intermediate Technology Publications, 1997.

Charon, Rita. *Narrative Medicine: Honoring the Stories of Illness.* Oxford: Oxford University Press, 2006.

The Circle of Concerned African Women Theologians. Website. Online: http://www.thecirclecawt.org/.

Cole, K. C. "When Change Is Hard, Blame Inertia." *Marketplace.* American Public Media, January 21, 2010. Online: http://www.marketplace.org/topics/when-change-hard-blame-inertia/.

Cole, Teju. "The White Savior Industrial Complex." *The Atlantic*, March 21, 2012. Online: http://www.theatlantic.com/international/archive/2012/03/the-white-savior-industrial-complex/254843/1/.

Connolly, William E. *Pluralism.* Durham: Duke University Press, 2005.

Cooper-White, Pamela, editor. "Conference Proceedings from 2009 Annual Study Conference: Engaging Difference in Pastoral Theology; Race/Ethnicity, Sexuality and Theology." *Journal of Pastoral Theology* 19/2 (Winter 2009).

———. *Many Voices: Pastoral Psychotherapy in Relational and Theological Perspective.* Minneapolis: Fortress, 2007.

———. *Shared Wisdom: Use of the Self in Pastoral Care and Counseling.* Minneapolis: Fortress, 2004.

Cooper-White, Pamela, and Karen Scheib, editors. "Conference Proceedings from 2007 Annual Study Conference: Doing Pastoral Theology in a Post-Colonial Context; Intercultural Models of Pastoral Care and Theology." *Journal of Pastoral Theology* 17/2 (Fall 2007).

Bibliography

Copeland, M. Shawn. *Enfleshing Freedom: Body, Race, and Being.* Innovations. Minneapolis: Fortress, 2010.

Couture, Pamela D. "Ritualized Play: Using Role Play to Teach Pastoral Care and Counseling." *Teaching Theology and Religion* 2/2 (1999) 96–102.

"Crisis." In *The Oxford Dictionary of English.* Vol. 4. Edited by J. A., Simpson and E. S. C. Weiner. 2nd ed. New York: Oxford University Press, 1991

Crossley, James G. "Defining History," In *Writing History, Constructing Religion*, edited by James G Crossley and Christian Karner, 9–30. Aldershot, UK: Ashgate, 2005.

D'Costa, Bina. "Marginalized Identity: New Frontiers of Research for IR." In *Feminist Methodologies for International Relations*, edited by Brooke A. Ackerly et al., 129–52. Cambridge: Cambridge University Press, 2006.

"Deliver." In *A Dictionary of Education*, edited by Susan Wallace. Oxford: Oxford University Press, 2009.

Derrida, Jacques. *The Gift of Death.* Translated by David Wills. Religion and Postmodernism. Chicago: University of Chicago Press, 1995.

Dewey, John. *Quest for Certainty: A Study of the Relation of Knowledge and Action.* Gifford Lectures 1929. New York: Putnam, 1960.

Diakité, Dianne. "The Myth of 'Voodoo': A Caribbean American Response to Representations of Haiti." *Religion Dispatches*, 20 January 2010. Online: http://www.religiondispatches.org/archive/ international/2204/the_myth_of_ "voodoo":_a_caribbean_american_response_to_representations_of_haiti/.

Dirlik, Arif. "Reading Ashis Nandy: The Return of the Past; Or Modernity with a Vengeance." In *Dissenting Knowledges, Open Futures: The Multiple Selves and Strange Destinations of Ashis Nandy*, edited by Vinay Lal, 260–86. New Delhi: Oxford University Press, 2000.

Dittes, James E. *Pastoral Counseling: The Basics.* Louisville: Westminster John Knox, 1999.

Doehring, Carrie. *The Practice of Pastoral Care: A Postmodern Approach.* Louisville: Westminster John Knox, 2006.

Dube, Musa. "'Go tla Siama. O tla Fola' Doing Biblical Studies in an HIV and AIDS Context." The Carpenter Program Lecture. Vanderbilt University Divinity School, November 19, 2009.

————. Personal conversation, November 19, 2009.

Dube, Saurabh. *Stitches on Time: Colonial Textures and Postcolonial Tangles.* Durham: Duke University Press, 2004.

Dykstra, Robert C., editor. *Images of Pastoral Care: Classic Readings.* St. Louis: Chalice, 2005.

Edwards, Jay. "Structural Analysis of the Afro-American Trickster Tale." In "Black Textual Strategies." Vol. 1, "Theory." *Black American Literature Forum* 15/4 (Winter 1981) 155–64.

Eiseland, Nancy, "Things Not Seen: Women with Physical Disabilities, Oppression and Practical Theology." In *Liberating Faith Practices: Feminist Practical Theologies in Context*, edited by Denise M. Ackermann and Riet Bons-Storm, 103–27. Leuven: Peeters, 1998.

Elshot, Kitty. Personal conversation, September 24, 2007.

Engelke, Matthew. "The Problem of Belief: Evans-Pritchard and Victor Turner on 'The Inner Life.'" *Anthropology Today* 18/6 (December 2002) 3–8.

————. "An Interview with Edith Turner." *Current Anthropology* 41 (2000) 843–52.

Erikson, Erik H. *The Life Cycle Completed*. New York: Norton, 1997.

————. *Childhood and Society*. New York: Norton, 1993.

Essed, Philomena. *Everyday Racism: Reports of Women of Two Cultures*. Translated by Cynthia Jaffé. Claremont, CA: Hunter, 1990.

Fanon, Frantz. *The Wretched of the Earth*. Translated by Richard Philcox. New York: Grove, 2004.

————. *A Dying Colonialism*. Translated by Haakon Chevalier. 1965. New York: Grove, 1994.

————. *Black Skin, White Masks*. Translated by Charles Lam Markmann. New York: Grove, 1967.

Farley, Edward. *Deep Symbols: Their Postmodern Effacement and Reclamation*. Valley Forge, PA: Trinity, 1996.

Farley, Wendy. *Gathering Those Driven Away: A Theology of Incarnation*. Louisville: Westminster John Knox, 2011.

————. *The Wounding and Healing of Desire: Weaving Heaven and Earth*. Louisville: Westminster John Knox, 2005.

Farmer, Paul. *Pathologies of Power: Health, Human Rights, and the New War on the Poor*. California Series in Public Anthropology 4. Berkeley: University of California Press, 2003.

Firmat, Gustavo Pérez. *Literature and Liminality: Festive Readings in the Hispanic Tradition*. Durham: Duke University Press, 1985.

Fortune, Marie. *Sexual Violence: The Sin Revisited*. Cleveland: Pilgrim, 2005.

Fowler, James W. *Stages of Faith: The Psychology of Human Development and the Quest for Meaning*. San Francisco: Harper & Row, 1981.

Frazier, Lessie Jo. *Salt in the Sand: Memory, Violence, and the Nation-State in Chile, 1890 to the Present*. Politics, History, and Culture. Durham: Duke University Press, 2007.

Freire, Paulo. *Pedagogy of the Oppressed*. Translated by Myra Bergman Ramos. New York: Herder & Herder, 1970.

Friedman, Edwin. *Friedman's Fables: Discussion Questions*. New York: Guilford, 1990.

Fuchs-Kreimer, Nancy. *Parenting as a Spiritual Journey: Deepening Ordinary and Extraordinary Events into Sacred Occasions*. 1998. 2nd printing. Woodstock, VT: Jewish Lights, 2002.

Fung, Katherine. "Geraldo Rivera: Trayvon Martin's'Hoodie Is as Much Responsible For [His] Death as George Zimmerman." Online: http://www.huffingtonpost.com/2012/03/23/geraldo-rivera-trayvon-martin-hoodie_n_1375080.html?ref=topbar.

Gaillardetz, Richard R. *Transforming Our Days: Spirituality, Community, and Liturgy in a Technological Culture*. New York: Crossroad, 2000.

Garces-Foley, Kathleen. *Crossing the Ethnic Divide: The Multiethnic Church on a Mission*. American Academy of Religion Academy Series. Oxford: Oxford University Press, 2007.

Gaskell, Ivan. "Ethical Judgments in Museums." In *Art and Ethical Criticism*, edited by Gerry L. Hagberg, 229–42. Oxford: Blackwell, 2008.

Gay, Volney P. *Joy and the Objects of Psychoanalysis: Literature, Belief, and Neurosis*. SUNY Series in Psychoanalysis and Culture. Albany: State University of New York Press, 2001.

————. "Mapping Religion Psychologically: Information Theory as a Corrective to Modernism." In *Religion and Psychology: Mapping the Terrain*, edited by Diane Jonte-Pace and William B. Parsons, 94–109. London: Routledge, 2001.

————. *Understanding the Occult: Fragmentation and Repair of the Self.* Philadelphia: Fortress, 1989.

————. "Winnicott's Contribution to Religious Studies: The Resurrection of the Culture Hero." *Journal of the American Academy of Religion* 51 (1983) 371–95.

————. "Syllabus on Methods," "Methods and Evaluation" course. Graduate Department of Religion, Vanderbilt University, Spring 2005.

"Gaze." In *The Dictionary of the Social Sciences.* Edited by Craig Calhoun. Oxford: Oxford University Press 2002.

Geertz, Clifford. "Deep Play: Notes on the Balinese Cockfight." *Daedalus* 101/1 (1972) 1–37.

Gerkin, Charles V. *The Living Human Document: Re-Visioning Pastoral Counseling in a Hermeneutical Mode.* Nashville: Abingdon, 1984.

————. *Widening the Horizons: Pastoral Responses to a Fragmented Society.* Philadelphia: Westminster, 1986.

Gibellini, Rosino, editor. *Paths of African Theology.* Maryknoll, NY: Orbis, 1994.

Gill-Austern, Brita L. "Engaging Diversity and Difference: From Practices of Exclusion to Practices of Practical Solidarity." In *Injustice and the Care of Souls: Taking Oppression Seriously in Pastoral Care*, edited by Sheryl A. Kujawa-Holbrook and Karen B. Montagno, 29–44. Minneapolis: Fortress, 2009.

Gill-Austern, Brita L., and Bonnie J. Miller-McLemore, editors. *Feminist and Womanist Pastoral Theology.* Nashville: Abingdon, 1999.

Gilligan, Carol. *In a Different Voice: Psychological Theory and Women's Development.* Cambridge: Harvard University Press, 1982.

Gines, Kathryn T. "Fanon and Sartre 50 Years Later: To Retain or Reject the Concept of Race." *Sartre Studies International* 9/2 (2003) 55–88.

————. Personal conversations, Vanderbilt University, 2006–2009.

Glaz, Maxine, and Jeanne Stevenson-Moessner, editors. *Women in Travail and Transition: A New Pastoral Care.* Minneapolis: Fortress, 1991.

"Global Gender Inequality and the Empowerment of Women: Discussion of *Half the Sky: Turning Oppression into Opportunity for Women Worldwide.*" Review Symposium. *Perspective on Politics* 8/1 (2010) 279–86.

Good, Byron J. et al. "Postcolonial Disorders: Reflections on Subjectivity in the Contemporary World." In *Postcolonial Disorders*, edited by Mary-Jo DelVecchio Good et al., 1–42. Berkeley: University of California Press, 2008.

Graham, Elaine L. *Transforming Practice: Pastoral Theology in an Age of Uncertainty.* London: Mowbray, 1996.

Graham, Larry K. *Care of Persons, Care of Worlds: A Psychosystems Approach to Pastoral Care and Counseling.* Nashville: Abingdon, 1992.

Grau, Marion. *Rethinking Mission in the Postcolony: Salvation, Society, and Subversion.* London: T. & T. Clark, 2011.

Greider, Kathleen J. "Soul Care amid Religious Plurality: Excavating an Emerging Dimension of Multicultural Challenge and Competence." In *Women Out of Order: Risking Change and Creating Care in a Multicultural World*, edited by Jeanne Stevenson-Moessner and Teresa Snorton, 293–313. Minneapolis: Fortress, 2010.

Greider, Kathleen J. et al., editors. *Healing Wisdom: Depth Psychology and the Pastoral Ministry.* Grand Rapids: Eerdmans, 2010.

Greider, Kathleen J. et al. "Three Generations of Women Writing for Our Lives." In *Feminist and Womanist Pastoral Theology,* edited by Bonnie J. Miller-McLemore and Brita L. Gill-Austern, 21–50. Nashville: Abingdon, 1999.

Hagberg, Garry L., editor. *Art and Ethical Criticism.* New Directions in Aesthetics 7. Oxford: Blackwell, 2008.

Halivni, Davis Weiss. *The Book and the Sword: A Life of Learning in the Shadow of Destruction.* New York: Farrar, Straus & Giroux, 1996.

Hawken, Paul. "To Remake the World." *Orion Magazine.* May/June 2007. Online: http://www.orionmagazine.org/index.php/articles/article/265/.

Herman, Judith. *Trauma and Recovery: The Aftermath of Violence—from Domestic Abuse to Political Terror.* New York: BasicBooks, 1997.

Hermans, Chris A. M., editor. *Social Constructionism and Theology.* Empirical Studies in Theology 7. Leiden: Brill, 2002.

———. "Ultimate Meaning as Silence: The Monologic and Polyphonic Author-God in Religious Communication." In *Social Constructionism and Theology,* edited by Chris A. M. Hermans, 113–46. Empirical Studies in Theology 7. Leiden: Brill, 2002.

Hermans, Chris A. M., and Joost Dupont. "Social Construction of Moral Identity in View of a Concrete Ethics." In *Social Constructionism and Theology,* edited by Chris A. M. Hermans, 239–72. Empirical Studies in Theology 7. Leiden: Brill, 2002.

Hertzberg, Joan F. "Feminist Psychotherapy and Diversity: Treatment Considerations from a Self Psychology Perspective." In *Diversity and Complexity in Feminist Therapy,* edited by Laura S. Brown and Maria P. P. Root, 275–97. New York: Haworth, 1990.

Hill Collins, Patricia. *Another Kind of Public Education: Race, Schools, The Media, and Democratic Possibilities.* Simmons College/Beacon Press Race, Education, and Democracy Series. Boston: Beacon, 2009.

———. *Black Feminist Thought: Knowledge, Consciousness, and the Politics of Empowerment.* 2nd ed. New York: Routledge, 2000.

Holmes, Emily A., and Wendy Farley, editors. *Women, Writing, Theology: Transforming a Tradition of Exclusion.* Waco, TX: Baylor University Press, 2011.

hooks, bell. *Teaching to Transgress: Education as the Practice of Freedom.* New York: Routledge, 1994.

Horton, Myles, and Paulo Freire. *We Make the Road by Walking: Conversations on Education and Social Change.* Edited by Brenda Bell et al. Philadelphia: Temple University Press, 1990.

Hunt, Celia, and Fiona Sampson. *Writing: Self and Reflexivity.* 3rd ed. Hampshire, UK: Palgrave Macmillan, 2006.

Hunter, Rodney J., general editor. *Dictionary of Pastoral Care and Counseling.* Nashville: Abingdon, 1990.

———. "Ministry in Depth: Three Critical Questions." In *Healing Wisdom: Depth Psychology and the Pastoral Ministry,* edited by Kathleen J. Greider et al., 3–15. Grand Rapids: Eerdmans, 2010.

Isasi-Díaz, Ada María. *En La Lucha = In the Struggle: Elaborating a Mujerista Theology.* 10th anniversary ed. Minneapolis: Fortress, 2004.

Jackson, Richard. "Remembering the 'Disremembered': Modern Black Writers and Slavery in Latin America." In *Callaloo* 13/1 (1990) 131–44..

James, William. *The Varieties of Religious Experience: A Study in Human Nature.* Centenary ed. London: Routledge, 2002.

———. *Pragmatism: A New Name for Some Old Ways of Thinking. The Meaning of Truth: A Sequel to Pragmatism.* Cambridge: Harvard University Press, 1978.

Joiner, Bill, and Stephen Josephs. *Leadership Agility: Five Levels of Mastery for Anticipating and Initiating Change.* San Francisco: Jossey-Bass, 2007.

Jonte-Pace, Diane E., and William B. Parsons, editors. *Religion and Psychology: Mapping the Terrain: Contemporary Dialogues, Future Prospects.* London: Routledge, 2001.

Jules-Rosette, Bennetta. "Decentering Ethnography: Victor Turner's Vision of Anthropology." In *Journal of Religion in Africa* 24/2 (1994) 160–81.

Justes, Emma J. *Hearing beyond the Words: How to Become a Listening Pastor.* Nashville: Abingdon, 2006.

Kalilombe, Patrick A. "Spirituality in the African Perspective." In *Paths of African Theology*, edited by Rosino Gibellini, 115–35. Maryknoll, NY: Orbis, 1994.

Keller, Catherine. *From a Broken Web: Separation, Sexism, and Self.* Boston: Beacon, 1986.

———. *On the Mystery: Discerning Divinity in Process.* Minneapolis: Fortress, 2008.

Kierkegaard, Søren. *Fear and Trembling.* Edited and translated by Howard Hong and Edna Hong. Kierkegaard's Writings 6. Princeton: Princeton University Press, 1983.

Kiernan, V. G. *The Lords of Human Kind: European Attitudes to the Outside World in the Imperial Age.* Harmondsworth, UK: Penguin, 1972.

King, Richard. *Orientalism and Religion: Post-colonial Theory, India and "the Mystic East."* London: Routledge, 1999.

Klarer, Mario. "Humanitarian Pornography: John Gabriel Stedman's *Narrative of a Five Years Expedition against the Revolted Negros of Surinam* (1796)." *New Literary History* 36 (Autumn 2005) 559–87.

Knitter, Paul F. *Introducing Theologies of Religions.* Maryknoll, NY: Orbis, 2002.

———, editor. *The Myth of Religious Superiority: Multifaith Explorations of Religious Pluralism.* Faith Meets Faith. Maryknoll, NY: Orbis, 2005.

Kohut, Heinz. *How Does Analysis Cure?* Edited by Arnold Goldberg, with the collaboration of Paul Stepansky. Chicago: University of Chicago Press, 1984.

———. "Introspection, Empathy, and the Semi-Circle of Mental Health." *International Journal of Psychoanalysis* 63 (1982) 395–407.

———. *Self Psychology and the Humanities: Reflections on a New Psychoanalytic Approach.* Edited by Charles B. Strozier. New York: Norton, 1985.

Kohut, Heinz. *Reflections on Empathy.* DVD recorded in 1981, copyrighted by Life Span Learning Institute. Online: www.lifespanlearning.com/.

Kornfeld, Margaret Zipse. *Cultivating Wholeness: A Guide to Care and Counseling in Faith Communities.* New York: Continuum, 2009.

Kristof, Nicholas D., and Sheryl WuDunn. *Half the Sky: Turning Oppression into Opportunity for Women Worldwide.* New York: Vintage, 2009.

Kronsell, Annica. "Methods for Studying Silences: Gender Analysis in Institutions of Hegemonic Masculinity." In *Feminist Methodologies for International Relations*, edited by Brooke A. Ackerly et al., 108–28. Cambridge: Cambridge University Press, 2006.

Kujawa-Holbrook, Sheryl A. and Karen B. Montagno. *Injustice and the Care of Souls: Taking Oppression Seriously in Pastoral Care*. Minneapolis: Fortress, 2009.

Lal, Vinay, editor. *Dissenting Knowledges, Open Futures: The Multiple Selves and Strange Destinations of Ashis Nandy*. Oxford: Oxford University Press, 2000.

Lamott, Anne. *Bird by Bird: Some Instructions on Writing and Life*. New York: Anchor, 1995.

Lang, Joan A. "Notes toward a Psychology of the Feminine Self." In *Kohut's Legacy: Contributions to Self Psychology*, edited by Paul E. Stepansky and Arnold Goldberg, 51–70. Hillsdale, NJ: Erlbaum, 1984.

Lartey, Emmanuel. *In Living Color: An Intercultural Approach to Pastoral Care and Counseling*. 2nd ed. London: Kingsley, 2003.

———. *Pastoral Theology in an Intercultural World*. Cleveland: Pilgrim, 2006.

———. "Practical Theology as a Theological Form." In *The Blackwell Reader in Pastoral and*

Lee, K. Samuel. "Engaging Difference in Pastoral Theology: Race and Ethnicity." *Journal of Pastoral Theology* 19/2 (December 2009) 1–20.

Lee, Nick. *Childhood and Society: Growing Up in an Age of Uncertainty*. Issues in Society. Buckingham, UK: Open University Press, 2001.

Leslie, Kristen. *When Violence Is No Stranger: Pastoral Counseling with Survivors of Acquaintance Rape*. Minneapolis: Fortress, 2003.

Lester, Andrew. *Hope in Pastoral Care and Counseling*. Louisville: Westminster John Knox, 1995.

Levy, Naomi. *Hope Will Find You: My Search for the Wisdom to Stop Waiting and Start Living*. New York: Random House, 2010

Liebert, Elizabeth, SNJM. "Seasons and Stages: Models and Metaphors of Human Development." In *In Her Own Time: Women and Developmental Issues in Pastoral Care*, edited by Jeanne Stevenson-Moessner, 19–44. Minneapolis: Fortress, 2000.

Lomax, Tamura A. "Who's Going to Sing a Black Boy's Song?" March 17, 2012. *The Feminist Wire Blog*. Online: http://thefeministwire.com/2012/03/whos-going-to-sing-a-black-boys-song/

Loomba, Ania. *Colonialism/Postcolonialism*. 2nd ed. The New Critical Idiom. London: Routledge, 2005.

Lorde, Audre. "The Master's Tools Will Never Dismantle the Master's House." In *This Bridge Called My Back*, edited by Cherríe Moraga and Gloria Anzaldúa, 25–28. New York: Third Woman Press, 1983.

———. "The Master's Tools Will Never Dismantle the Master's House." In *Feminist Postcolonial Theory: A Reader*, edited by Reina Lewis and Sara Mills, 25–28. New York: Routledge, 2003.

Lovin, Robin W. *Christian Ethics: An Essential Guide*. Abingdon Essential Guides. Nashville: Abingdon, 2000.

Lowenthal, David. "History Becomes 'Heritage' in Race Question." Letter to the Editor, *Perspectives: Newsletter of the American Historical Association* 32 (January 1994) 17–18.

Lowther, Kevin, and C. Payne Lucas. *Keeping Kennedy's Promise: The Peace Corps' Moment of Truth*. Special expanded ed. Baltimore: Peace Corps Online, 2002.

Mahler, Margaret S. et al., editors. *The Psychological Birth of the Human Infant: Symbiosis and Individuation*. New York: BasicBooks, 1975.

Marshall, Joretta L. "Models of Understanding Differences, Dialogues, and Discourses." *Journal of Pastoral Theology* 19/2 (2009) 29–47.

―――. *Counseling Lesbian Partners*. Counseling and Pastoral Theology. Louisville: Westminster John Knox, 1997.

Mayeroff, Milton. *On Caring*. New York: Harper & Row, 1971.

McGarrah Sharp, Melinda. "Globalization, Colonialism, and Postcolonialism." In *The Wiley-Blackwell Companion to Practical Theology*, edited by Bonnie J. Miller-McLemore, 422–31. Wiley-Blackwell Companions to Religion. Oxford: Wiley-Blackwell, 2012.

McGarrah Sharp, Melinda, and Mary Ann Morris. "Virtual Empathy?" Paper presented to the Person, Culture and Religion, American Academy of Religion Annual Meeting, San Francisco, CA, November 19, 2011.

McGarrah Sharp, Melinda, and Bonnie Miller-McLemore. "Are There Limits to Multicultural Inclusion? Difficult Questions for Feminist Pastoral Theology." In *Women Out of Order: Risking Change and Creating Care in a Multicultural World*, edited by Jeanne Stevenson-Moessner and Teresa Snorton, 314–30. Minneapolis: Fortress, 2010.

McGoldrick, Monica et al., editors. *Ethnicity & Family Therapy*. 3rd ed. New York: Guilford, 2005.

McGoldrick, Monica. *You Can Go Home Again: Reconnecting with Your Family*. New York: Norton, 1995.

McLeod, Cynthia. *The Cost of Sugar*. Paramaribo, Suriname: Waterfront Press, 2010.

McWilliams, Nancy. "Freud's Contemporary Relevance." In *Freud at 150: 21st-Century Essays on a Man of Genius*, edited by Joseph P. Merlino et al., 143–46. Lanham, MD: Rowan & Littlefield, 2008.

―――. *Psychoanalytic Case Formulation*. New York: Guilford, 1999.

Mead, George Herbert. *Mind, Self & Society: From the Standpoint of a Social Behaviorist*, edited by Charles W. Morris. Chicago: University of Chicago Press, 1934.

Meeks, Wayne A. "Assisting the World by Making (Up) History: Luke's Project and Ours." *Interpretation* 57/2 (2003) 151–62.

Merleau-Ponty, Maurice. "The Philosopher and His Shadow." In *Signs*, 159–81. Translated by Richard C. McCleary. Evanston: Northwestern University Press, 1964.

Merlino, Joseph P. et al., editors. *Freud at 150: 21st-Century Essays on a Man of Genius*. Lanham, MD: Rowan & Littlefield, 2008.

Miller-McLemore, Bonnie J. *Also a Mother: Work and Family as Theological Dilemma*. Nashville: Abingdon, 1994.

―――. *In the Midst of Chaos: Caring for Children as Spiritual Practice*. The Practices of Faith Series. San Francisco: Jossey-Bass, 2007.

―――. *Let the Children Come: Reimagining Childhood from a Christian Perspective*. Families and Faith Series. San Francisco: Jossey-Bass, 2003.

―――. "The Living Human Web: Pastoral Theology at the Turn of the Century." In *Through the Eyes of Women: Insights for Pastoral Care*, edited by Jeanne Stevenson-Moessner, 9–26. Minneapolis: Fortress, 1996.

―――. "Practicing What We Preach: The Case of Women in Ministry." *Practical Theology* 2/1 (2009) 45–62.

————. "Revisiting the Living Human Web: Theological Education and the Role of Clinical Pastoral Education." *Journal of Pastoral Care and Counseling* 62/1–2 (2008) 3–18.

————. "The Subject and Practice of Pastoral Theology as a Practical Theological Discipline." In *Liberating Faith Practices: Feminist Practical Theology in Context*, edited Denise M. Ackermann and Riet Bons-Storm, 175–98. Leuven: Peeters, 1998.

————, editor. *The Wiley-Blackwell Companion to Practical Theology*. Wiley-Blackwell Companions to Religion. Oxford: Wiley-Blackwell, 2012.

————. "Women Who Work and Love: Caught between Cultures." In *Women in Travail and Transition: A New Pastoral Care*, edited by Maxine Glaz and Jeanne Stevenson-Moessner, 63–85. Minneapolis: Fortress, 1991.

Mitchell, Beverly Eileen. *Plantations and Death Camps*. Minneapolis: Fortress, 2009.

Moody-Adams, Michele M. *Fieldwork in Familiar Places: Morality, Culture, and Philosophy*. Cambridge: Harvard University Press, 1997.

Montello, Martha. "Narrative Matters: What Stories Do for Medical Ethics." The Richard M. Zaner Lecture in Medical Ethics. Vanderbilt University, September 16, 2008.

Moraga, Cherríe, and Gloria Anzaldúa, editors. *This Bridge Called My Back*. New York: Third Woman Press, 1983.

Moschella, Mary Clark. *Ethnography as a Pastoral Practice: An Introduction*. Cleveland: Pilgrim, 2008.

Mucherera, Tapiwa N. *Meet Me at the Palaver: Narrative Pastoral Counseling in Postcolonial Contexts*. Eugene, OR: Cascade Books, 2009.

Nandy, Ashis. "Themes of State, History, and Exile in South Asian Politics: Modernity and the Landscape of Clandestine and Incommunicable Selves." In *Dissenting Knowledges, Open Futures: The Multiple Selves and Strange Destinations of Ashis Nandy*, edited by Vinay Lal, 151–75. Oxford: Oxford University Press, 2000.

————. *The Intimate Enemy: Loss and Recovery of Self under Colonialism*. New Delhi: Oxford University Press, 1983.

Narayan, Uma. *Dislocating Cultures: Identities, Traditions, and Third World Feminism*. London: Routledge, 1997.

Natanson, Maurice. *The Erotic Bird: Phenomenology in Literature*. Princeton: Princeton University Press, 1998.

National Public Radio. "For Bilingual Writer, 'No One True Language.'" October 17, 2011. Online: http://www.npr.org/2011/10/17/141368408/for-a-bilingual-writer-no-one-true-language/.

Neuger, Christie Cozad. *Counseling Women: A Narrative, Pastoral Approach*. Minneapolis: Fortress, 2001.

Niebuhr, H Richard. *The Responsible Self: An Essay in Christian Moral Philosophy*. Library of Theological Ethics. Louisville: Westminster John Knox, 1999.

Norton, Anastasia. "*U Da Sembe Fa Aki* (We Are People of This Place): Place-Attachment and Belonging: A Saramaka Response to Globalization." PhD diss., Brandeis University, 2005. UMI Dissertation Services (UMI No. 3179266).

Nussbaum, Martha C. *Women and Human Development: The Capabilities Approach*. The John Robert Seeley Lectures. Cambridge: Cambridge University Press, 2000.

Oliver, Mary. "What Is the Greatest Gift?" In *Red Bird: Poems by Mary Oliver*. Boston: Beacon, 2008.

Bibliography

Oostindie, Gert. *Postcolonial Netherlands: Sixty-five Years of Forgetting, Commemorating, Silencing.* Amsterdam: Amsterdam University Press, 2010.

Pandolfo, Stefania. "The Knot of the Soul: Postcolonial Conundrums, Madness, and the Imagination." In *Postcolonial Disorders,* edited by Mary-Jo DelVecchio Good et al., 329–58. Berkeley: University of California Press, 2008.

Panetta, Roger, editor. *Dutch New York: The Roots of Hudson Valley Culture.* Yonkers, NY: Hudson River Museum, 2009.

Parsons, William B., Diane Jonte-Pace, and Susan E. Henking, editors. *Mourning Religion.* Studies in Religion and Culture. Charlottesville: University Press of Virginia, 2008.

Pattison, Stephen. *The Challenge of Practical Theology: Selected Essays.* London: Kingsley, 2007.

———. *Pastoral Care and Liberation Theology.* Cambridge Studies in Ideology and Religion 5. Cambridge: Cambridge University Press, 1994.

Paulsell, Stephanie. *Honoring the Body: Meditations on a Christian Practice.* San Francisco: Jossey-Bass, 2002.

Peace Corps. "About Us." Online: http://www.peacecorps.gov/about/.

———. "Mission." Online: http://www.peacecorps.gov/mission/.

Peirce, Charles Sanders. *The Collected Papers of Charles Sanders Peirce.* Vol. 5, *Pragmatism and Pragmaticism.* Edited by Charles Hartschorne and Paul Weiss. Cambridge: Harvard University Press, 1965.

Penard, T. E. et al. "Surinam Folk-Tales." *Journal of American Folklore* 30/116 (Apr–Jun 1917) 239–50.

Price, Sally. *Co-wives and Calabashes.* Women and Culture Series. Ann Arbor: University of Michigan Press, 1984.

Price, Sally, and Richard Price. "Introduction." In *Stedman's Surinam: Life in an Eighteenth-Century Slave Society. An Abridged, Modernized Edition of Narrative of a Five Years Expedition against the Revolted Negroes of Surinam,* by John Gabriel Stedman. Edited by Sally Price and Richard Price, xi–lxxv. Baltimore: Johns Hopkins University Press, 1992.

Rambo, Shelly. *Spirit and Trauma: A Theology of Remaining.* Louisville: Westminster John Knox, 2010.

Ramsay, Nancy J., editor. *Pastoral Care and Counseling: Redefining the Paradigms.* Nashville: Abingdon, 2004.

Resch, Marc. *Only in Holland, Only the Dutch: An In-Depth Look into the Culture of Holland and its People.* Amsterdam: Rozenberg, 2004.

Rivera, Mayra. *The Touch of Transcendence: A Postcolonial Theology of God.* Louisville: Westminster John Knox, 2007.

Rizzuto, Ana-Maria. *The Birth of the Living God.* Chicago: University of Chicago Press, 1979.

Roland, Alan. *In Search of Self in India and Japan: Toward a Cross-Cultural Psychology.* Princeton: Princeton University Press, 1988.

Rorty, Richard. *Contingency, Irony, and Solidarity.* Cambridge: Cambridge University Press, 1989.

Russell, Letty M., and J. Shannon Clarkston, editors. *Dictionary of Feminist Theologies.* Louisville: Westminster John Knox, 1996.

Sacks, Oliver. *Seeing Voices: A Journey into the World of the Deaf.* New York: HarperCollins, 1990.

Said, Edward W. *Orientalism*. New York: Vintage, 1979.

Scarry, Elaine. *The Body in Pain: The Making and Unmaking of the World*. Oxford: Oxford University Press, 1987.

Schultz, Connie. "Fearless Politics: Speak Your Mind Even If Your Voice Shakes." September 4, 2006. Blog post on *Huffington Post*. Online: http://www .huffingtonpost.com/ connie-schultz/fearless-politics-speak-_b_28706.html/.

Shanks, Louis, editor. *A Buku fu Okanisi anga Ingiisi Wowtu: Aukan-English Dictionary and English-Aukan Index*. 2nd ed. Paramaribo, Suriname: SIL Suriname, 2000.

Sharpe, Jenny. *Ghosts of Slavery: A Literary Archeology of Black Women's Lives*. Minneapolis: University of Minnesota Press, 2003.

Sharpley-Whiting, T. Denean. *Pimps Up, Ho's Down: Hip Hop's Hold on Young Black Women*. New York: New York University Press, 2007.

———. *Black Venus: Sexualized Savages, Primal Fears, and Primitive Narratives in French*. Durham: Duke University Press, 1999.

———. *Frantz Fanon: Conflicts and Feminisms*. Lanham, MD: Rowman & Littlefield, 1998.

Shea, Danny. "Pat Robertson: Haiti 'Cursed' by 'Pact to the Devil'" *Huffington Post*, March 18, 2010; updated May 25, 2011. Online: http://www.huffingtonpost .com/2010/01/13/pat-robertson-haiti-curse_n_422099.html/.

Siegel, Allen M. *Heinz Kohut and the Psychology of the Self*. Makers of Modern Psychotherapy. New York: Brunner-Routledge, 2004.

Simpson, J. A., and E. S. C. Weiner, editors. *The Oxford Dictionary of English*. Volume 4. 2nd ed. New York: Oxford University Press, 1991

Singleton, Esther. *Dutch New York*. New York: Dodd, Mead, 1909.

Smith, Archie. *The Relational Self: Ethics & Therapy from a Black Church Perspective*. Nashville: Abingdon, 1982.

Smith, Roberta. "One Nation, in Broad Strokes." *New York Times*, October 15, 2009. Online: http://www.nytimes.com/2009/10/16/arts/design/16stories.html?_r=1&8dpc/.

Song, Sarah. *Justice, Gender, and the Politics of Multiculturalism*. Contemporary Political Theory. Cambridge: Cambridge University Press, 2007.

Spivak, Gayatri Chakravorty. *Thinking Academic Freedom in Gendered Post-Coloniality*. Capetown: University of Capetown, 1992.

Stake, Robert. *Multiple Case Study Analysis*. New York: Guilford, 2006.

Stedman, John Gabriel. *Stedman's Surinam: Life in an Eighteenth-Century Slave Society. An Abridged, Modernized Edition of Narrative of a Five Years Expedition against the Revolted Negroes of Surinam*. Edited by Richard Price and Sally Price. Baltimore: Johns Hopkins University Press, 1992.

Stevenson-Moessner, Jeanne. "A New Pastoral Paradigm and Practice." In *Women in Travail and Transition: A New Pastoral Care*, edited by Maxine Glaz and Jeanne Stevenson-Moessner, 198–225. Minneapolis: Fortress, 1991.

———, editor. *In Her Own Time: Women and Developmental Issues in Pastoral Care*. Minneapolis: Fortress, 2000.

———, editor. *Through the Eyes of Women: Insights for Pastoral Care*. Minneapolis: Fortress, 1996.

Stevenson-Moessner, Jeanne, and Teresa Snorton, editors. *Women Out of Order: Risking Change and Creating Care in a Multicultural World*. Minneapolis: Fortress, 2010.

Stone, Howard W. *Crisis Counseling*. 3rd ed. Creative Pastoral Care and Counseling Series. Minneapolis: Fortress, 2009.

Sullivan, Henry Stack. *The Interpersonal Theory of Psychiatry: A Systematic Presentation of the Later Thinking of One of the Great Leaders in Modern Psychiatry.* Edited by Helen Swick Perry and Mary Ladd Gawal. New York: Norton, 1953.

Sullivan, Lawrence E. "Victor W. Turner (1920–1983)." *History of Religions* 24 (1984) 160–63.

Swain, Storm. *Trauma and Transformation at Ground Zero: A Pastoral Theology.* Minneapolis: Fortress, 2011.

Switzer, David K. *The Minister as Crisis Counselor.* 2nd ed. Nashville: Abingdon, 1986.

Talburt, Susan. "Ethnographic Responsibility Without the 'Real.'" Special issue: Questions of Research and Methodology *Journal of Higher Education* 75/1 (Jan–Feb 2004) 80–103.

Tatum, Beverly Daniel. *"Why Are All the Black Kids Sitting Together in the Cafeteria?": And Other Conversations About Race.* 2nd ed. New York: BasicBooks, 1999.

Thatamanil, John. *The Immanent Divine: God, Creation, and the Human Predicament.* Minneapolis: Fortress, 2006.

Thoden van Velzen, H. U. E., and W. van Wetering. *In the Shadow of the Oracle: Religion as Politics in a Suriname Maroon Society.* Long Grove, IL: Waveland, 2004.

Tickle, Phyllis. *The Great Emergence: How Christianity Is Changing and Why.* Grand Rapids: Baker, 2008.

Tracy, David. *The Analogical Imagination: Christian Theology and the Culture of Pluralism.* New York: Crossroad, 1981.

Turner, Victor. *From Ritual to Theatre: The Human Seriousness of Play.* Performance Studies Series 1. New York: Performing Arts Journal Publications, 1982.

———. "Social Dramas and Stories about Them." *Critical Inquiry* 7/1 (1980) 141–68.

———. *The Ritual Process: Structure and Anti-Structure.* Piscataway, NJ: Aldine Transaction, 2009.

"Uganda: International Bar Association's Human Rights Institute (IBAHRI) Condemns Introduction of Death Penalty for 'Aggravated Homosexuality.'" International Bar Association Press Release, November 4, 2009. Online: http://allafrica.com/stories/200911041149.html/.

United Nations. Office of the United Nations High Commissioner on Human Rights, *Convention on the Rights of the Child.* November 1989. Online: http://www2.ohchr.org/english/law/crc.htm/.

United States Holocaust Memorial Museum. "Martin Niemöller." In *Holocaust Encyclopedia.* Online: http://www.ushmm.org/wlc/article.php?lang=en&ModuleId=10007392/.

University of Iowa News Services. "'Unwanted One Became One of Africa's Most Influential Writers." November 13, 2006. Online: http://news-releases.uiowa.edu/2006/november/111306ken-bugul.html

Van Beek, Aart. *Cross-Cultural Counseling.* Creative Pastoral Care and Counseling Series. Minneapolis: Fortress, 1996.

Van Eys, Jan. "Who Then is Normal?" *Church and Society* 73 (Sept–Oct 1982) 8–16.

Walsh, John, and Robert Gannon. *Time Is Short and the Water Rises: Operation Gwamba; The Story of the Rescue of 10,000 Animals from Certain Death in a South American Rain Forest.* New York: Dutton, 1967.

Weber, Donald. "From Limen to Border: A Meditation on the Legacy of Victor Turner for American Cultural Studies." *American Quarterly* 47 (1995) 525–36.

Weil, Simone. "Reflections on the Right Use of School Studies with a View to the Love of God." In *Waiting for God*, 57–65. Harper Perennial Modern Classics. New York: Harper, 2009.

Wekker, Gloria. *The Politics of Passion: Women's Sexual Culture in the Afro-Surinamese Diaspora*. Between Men—Between Women. New York: Columbia University Press, 2006.

Wekker, Gloria. Personal conversation, May 2011; April 12, 2012.

Whitehead, Alfred North, *Process and Reality: An Essay in Cosmology*, Ed. David Ray Griffin and Donald W. Sherburne, NY: Free Press, 1978, c. 1929.

Whiting, Elizabeth. "Multifaith Education and the Parliament of the World's Religions." Lecture presented at the Vanderbilt Divinity School Community Breakfast, January 21, 2010.

Wimberly, Edward P. *African American Pastoral Care*, Rev. ed. Nashville: Abingdon, 2008.

———. *African American Pastoral Care and Counseling: The Politics of Oppression and Empowerment*. Cleveland: Pilgrim, 2006.

Winnicott, D. W. *Playing and Reality*. Routledge Classics ed. New York: Routledge, 2005.

Witte, John Jr., et al., editors. *The Equal-Regard Family and Its Friendly Critics: Don Browning and the Practical Theological Ethics of the Family*. Grand Rapids: Eerdmans, 2007.

Wolf, Ernest S. *Treating the Self: Elements of Clinical Self Psychology*. New York: Guilford, 1988.

Wolff, Kurt. "Surrender-and-Catch and Phenomenology." *Human Studies* 7 (1984) 191–210.

———. *Surrender and Catch: Experience and Inquiry Today*. Dordrecht: Reidel, 1976.

Woodward, James, et al., editors. *The Blackwell Reader in Pastoral and Practical Theology*. Blackwell Readings in Modern Theology. Oxford: Blackwell, 2000.

"The World Fact Book: Suriname." Online: https://www.cia.gov/library/publications/the-world-factbook/geos/ns.html/.

Wurgaft, Lewis D. Review of *The Intimate Enemy: Loss and Recovery of Self under Colonialism* by Ashis Nandy. *Journal of Asian Studies* 44 (1985) 434–36.

Yee, Cheryl. Personal conversation, September 24, 2007.

Yoder, Christine Roy. "Two Associate Professors Reflect on Their Journeys." ATS Roundtable Conference, Pittsburgh, October 22, 2011.

Young, Iris Marion. "Lived Body versus Gender: Reflections on Social Structure and Subjectivity." In *Recognition, Responsibility, and Rights: Feminist Ethics and Social Theory*, edited by Robin N. Fiore and Hilde Lindemann Nelson, 3–18. Feminist Constructions. Lanham, MD: Rowman & Littlefield, 2003.

Young, Robert J. C. *Colonial Desire: Hybridity in Theory, Culture, and Race*. London: Routledge, 1995.

———. *Postcolonialism: An Historical Introduction*. Oxford: Blackwell, 2001.

Zaner, Richard M. *The Context of Self: A Phenomenological Inquiry Using Medicine as a Clue*. Athens: Ohio University Press, 1981.

———. *Conversations on the Edge: Narratives of Ethics and Illness*. Washington DC: Georgetown University Press, 2004.

———. "The Disciplining of Reason's Cunning: Kurt Wolff's *Surrender and Catch*." *Human Studies* 4 (1981) 365–89.

Bibliography

————. "Keeping One's Balance in the Face of Death: Moments along the Moral Edges of Life." Inaugural Richard M. Zaner Lecture in Ethics and Medicine. Vanderbilt University Medical Center. November 5, 2004.

————. "Keeping Balance in the Face of Death." In *Clinical Ethics and the Necessity of Stories*, edited by Osborne P. Wiggins and Annette C. Allen, 15–26. Philosophy and Medicine 109. Dordrecht: Springer, 2011.

———— "On the Telling of Stories." Unpublished paper.

Index

Index

Index